THE LOGIC OF ARCHITECTURE

DESIGN, COMPUTATION, AND COGNITION

THE LOGIC OF ARCHITECTURE

DESIGN, COMPUTATION, AND COGNITION

WILLIAM J. MITCHELL

The MIT Press
Cambridge, Massachusetts
London, England

Third printing, 1992
© 1990 Massachusetts Institute of Technology

This book was set in Trump Medieval and printed and bound by Halliday Lithograph in the United States of America

Library of Congress Cataloging-in-Publication Data

Mitchell, William J. (William John), 1944-
    The logic of architecture.

    Bibliography: p.
    Includes index.
    1. Architectural design.   2. Computer-aided design.   3. Visual perception.   I. Title.

NA2750.M58   1989   720'.1   88-27201
ISBN 0-262-13238-9
ISBN 0-262-63116-4 (pbk.)

I fell into these thoughts; of which, there were two ways to be delivered; the one historical, by description of the principal works...the other logical, by casting the rules and cautions of this art into some comportable method: whereof I have made choice; not only as the shortest and most elemental, but indeed as the soundest

Sir Henry Wotton, The Elements of Architecture, *1624*

CONTENTS

PREFACE

Architects concern themselves professionally with the forms of buildings, with the functions of buildings, and with how to relate the two. Louis Sullivan alliteratively proposed that form follows function, but this provides little practical guidance since he failed to specify precisely what he meant by "form" or "function" or (for that matter) "follows." In this book I attempt to give more precise definition to these terms, and on that foundation to elucidate the structure of design reasoning.

The argument that is developed here may be taken as a response to a crucial problem posed by John Summerson some three decades ago. In his essay "The Case for a Theory of Modern Architecture" (1957), Summerson wrote:

The conceptions which arise from a preoccupation with the programme have got, at some point, to crystallise into a final form and by the time the architect reaches that point he has to bring to his conception a weight of judgement, a sense of authority and conviction which clinches the whole design, causes the impending relationships to close into a visually comprehensible whole. He may have extracted from the programme a set of interdependent relationships adding up to a unity of the biological kind, but he still has to face up to the ordering of a vast number of variables, and how he does this is a question. There is no common theoretical agreement as to what happens or should happen at that point. There is a hiatus. One may even be justified in speaking of a missing architectural language.

I show here how architectural languages[1] can be established, interpreted, and used.

To deploy such a language to solve functional problems is to build. But if there is, in addition, rhetorical intent and a concern for formal qualities, then building becomes architecture. (Hence Nikolaus Pevsner's famous dictum that a bicycle shed is a building but Lincoln Cathedral is a piece of architecture.) So I am concerned with both practical and poetic uses of architectural languages.

My approach builds on some ideas of modern logic, and I draw on some recent artificial intelligence and cognitive science research, but I do not assume any background in these fields. The technical apparatus that I introduce is, for the most part, elementary and informal. I begin by considering how buildings may be described in words and showing how such descriptions may be formalized using the notation of first-order predicate calculus. This leads to the idea of a critical language for speaking about the qualities of buildings.

Turning to the question of depiction by drawings and scale models, I develop the notion of design worlds that provide graphic tokens which can be manipulated according to certain grammatical rules. I then view design processes as computations in design worlds with the objective of satisfying predicates of form and function stated in a critical language.

There are three main parts to the central thesis. First, I propose that the relationship of criticism to design may be understood as a matter of the truth-functional semantics of a critical language in a design world. Second, I show how design worlds may be specified by formal grammars. Third, I argue that the rules of such grammars encode knowledge of how to put together buildings that function adequately. Thus the relation of form to function is strongly mediated by the syntactic and semantic rules under which a designer operates.

I hope that this discussion will be of general interest to architects and architecture students concerned with the theoretical foundations of their discipline, but I have a more directly practical aim as well. Computer technology is revolutionizing the way that architectural design is done, but the theoretical pressuppositions underlying computer-aided architectural design systems are rarely made explicit—and when they are, they often turn out to be shaky and inconsistent. There is an urgent need for a comprehensive, rigorously developed computational theory of design that can provide an adequate basis for practical software development work. I cannot claim to have produced such a theory fully fledged, but I raise what seem to me to be the relevant questions about it, and I explore some of the starting points in a quest for answers.

ACKNOWLEDGMENTS

This book grew out of seminars on design theory conducted at Harvard, UCLA, Carnegie-Mellon, and Cambridge, and I am grateful to my students and colleagues at these universities for raising many stimulating questions. Chapter 8 draws extensively on work conducted in collaboration with George Stiny, and my discussions with him over the years have been a fruitful source of insight. My particular thanks go to Claudia Knauer, who produced the illustrations, Yasuyo Iguchi, who designed the book, and Debra Edelstein, my editor at The MIT Press.

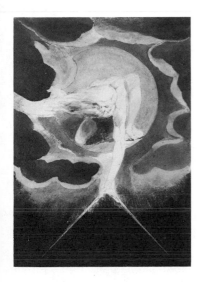

1.1
The creator as an architect bringing
order out of chaos. William Blake,
The Ancient of Days, frontispiece to
Europa, a Prophecy, 1794. The
Lessing J. Rosenwald Collection,
Library of Congress, Washington,
D.C.

DISTINCTIONS

The beginning of architecture is empty space—characterized by Plato in the *Timaeus* as "the mother and receptacle of all created and visible and in any way sensible things." Architecture is an art of *distinctions* within the continuum of space, for example between solid and void, interior and exterior, light and dark, or warm and cold.

When such distinctions are made an amorphous world is transformed into a world that has distinct parts organized in some particular way. Thus creation myths frequently recount successive acts of distinction from which the form of the world emerges. The book of Genesis, for instance, describes the world before creation as "without form, and void," then tells how God "divided the light from the darkness" and "divided the waters which were under the firmament from the waters which were above the firmament." The sea and the dry land then appeared and became the habitations of different creatures. On a more modest scale, architects also make distinctions in space to produce habitable form, and numerous illustrators of creation (most notably William Blake) have found it natural to depict the deity as an architect, with dividers in hand, bringing form out of chaos by separating and distinguishing (figure 1.1).

So the means of architecture are basically given by our capabilities to make and sense physical distinctions in space. Frequently, then, architecture is classified with painting and sculpture as a visual art concerned primarily with optical distinctions in light and color and surface. This tendency is encouraged when we look at drawings and photographs of buildings, rather than directly experience the real thing. But it can be misleading: distinctions between warm and cold, still and breezy air, in scent and sound, in the feel of surfaces on the skin, and in sensations of movement may be equally important components of architectural experience. It is with sensitivity to the dimensions, nuances, and subtleties of spatial distinction that the abilities to understand, to be moved by, and eventually to create architecture originate.

Distinctions in space present themselves to us as differences in stimuli reaching our receptor organs. An array of such stimuli (for example, an array of patches of light falling on the back of the retina) constitutes a perceptual field.[1]

Aristotle recognized five distinct sensory modalities: visual, auditory, tactual, olfactory, and gustatory. Today we usually add the kinesthetic (the sensation of bodily movement), and it is sometimes suggested that the tactual should be further subdivided into the modalities of warmth, cold, pressure, and pain. The standard modern view is that the differentiation of modalities follows directly from the way our nervous systems are organized: for each modality there is a receptor system that transduces physical stimuli into brain states.

Psychophysicists usually distinguish four sensory attributes within each modality: quality, intensity, extension, and duration. When a colored patch appears on a movie screen, for example, a viewer senses its qualities of hue and saturation, its brightness (intensity), its area (extension), and the time during which it is present (duration). By contrast with qualitative attributes (such as hue, pitch, and odor), the attributes of intensity, extension, and duration are quantitative—they vary in magnitude.

For our purposes here we can think of the input to a receptor as an array of physical stimuli and the output as a corresponding array of symbols, stored in memory and recording qualitative and quantitative attributes. A laser scanner, as used for input of images to a computer, provides a clear model of this. The scanner treats the visual field as an array of small, square cells (pixels) and scans it to produce a corresponding array of numerically encoded intensity levels (figure 1.2).

1.2
A visual field sampled on a square grid to yield an array of intensity levels

THE LOGIC OF ARCHITECTURE

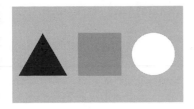

a. A visual field

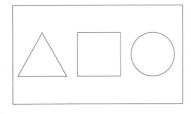

b. The corresponding primal sketch

1.3
Extraction of a primal sketch

1.4
Open and ambiguous contours

The segmentation of perceptual fields (particularly visual fields) into distinct parts which we regard as "things" is one of the most basic of the processes performed by our perceptual systems.[2] Consider, for example, the visual field (that is, array of intensity levels) shown in figure 1.3a. We can easily draw contours to divide this field into continuous areas of similar intensity (figure 1.3b). This produces a maplike representation of the visual field known to researchers in image analysis as a "primal sketch" (Marr, 1979). Computer programs have been developed for extracting primal sketches, and some recent theories of the human visual system suggest that it employs analogous mechanisms at a preconscious level (Fischler and Firschein, 1987).

Extraction of edges from a visual field does not always divide it into simple closed regions, however. Open contours will sometimes result, as shown in figure 1.4. Furthermore, where there are gradual transitions rather than sharp discontinuities, the locations of edges can become indefinite: using different edge-extraction algorithms and setting different thresholds at which the "similar" becomes the "dissimilar" will often produce different configurations of edges and different divisions of the field into regions. Even at this very low level of visual information processing, different observers may interpret a scene in different ways.

A visual field

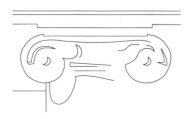

Primal sketch

A further step in the processing of sensations is to differentiate figures from the backgrounds against which they appear. We naturally interpret the facade of Gunnar Asplund's Villa Snellman (figure 1.5), for example, as a collection of well-defined figures (windows and decorative motifs) arranged on the ground of the wall surface. But the distinction between figure and ground is not always so clear. Rudolf Arnheim (1974) has noted that we can interpret solids and voids in a facade in several different ways (figure 1.6). Small windows may appear as discrete figures upon a continuous ground of wall. If we enlarge the ratio of opening to wall surface, as in Gothic architecture, we can reach a point where we interpret a facade as an alternation of open and solid elements, neither of which is unambiguously figure or ground. If we carry this process still further, as perhaps in the glazed wall of a modern office building, we eventually produce the figure of a structural frame seen against a continuous ground of window surface.

In addition to distinguishing elementary figures, we often give further structure to our perceptions of surface and space by grouping elementary figures into higher-order figures. For example, we immediately interpret the cluster shown in figure 1.7a as a circle. Rather more surprisingly, we interpret the cluster shown in figure 1.7b as a pair of overlapping triangles. Such phenomena were studied extensively by the Gestalt psychologists, who formulated various "Gestalt

1.5
Figures of openings on the ground of a wall: elevation of the Villa Snellman by Gunnar Asplund, 1917–18

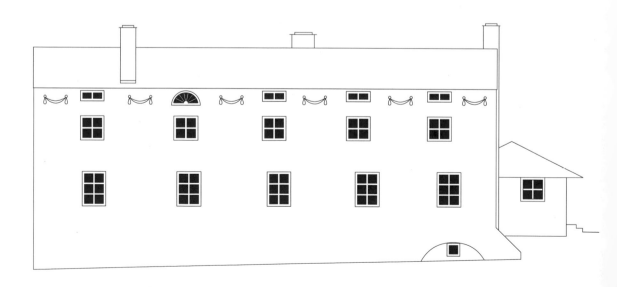

THE LOGIC OF ARCHITECTURE

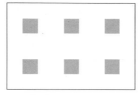

Punched openings

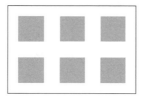

Ambiguous

Frame

1.6
Different figures appear as
proportions of solid and void
in a wall are varied

a. Circle

b. Overlapping triangles

1.7
Grouping of elementary figures
into higher-order figures

a. Proximity creates columns

b. Similarity creates diagonals

c. Both rows and columns

1.8
Grouping by proximity and
similarity

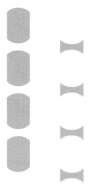

1.9
Enclosed shapes tend to be read
as figures

laws" governing figure perception.[3]   They observed that figures close to each other tend to be grouped into a unit: the law of proximity (figure 1.8a).   According to the law of similarity, like figures tend to be grouped (figure 1.8b).   And these effects may combine, as shown in figure 1.8c.

Another well-known Gestalt law, the law of closure, suggests that shapes with closed contours tend to be seen as units (figure 1.9), while the law of good continuation notes that relatively smooth, uninterrupted contours also help to define units (figure 1.10).   And the law of symmetry asserts that symmetrical objects tend to be seen as units (figure 1.11).   The theoretical framework of Gestalt psychology is no longer widely accepted, but the Gestalt laws remain useful empirical generalizations.

Notice how Asplund knowingly manipulated all these effects to inject a restless vitality into the apparently simple facade of the Villa Snellman.   Proximity and similarity allow us to read horizontal and vertical rows of openings, but this reading is subverted by the complex rhythm of the top row and the variation of window sizes from story to story.   The effects of the law of good continuation are disrupted (but not totally destroyed) by introduction of slight horizontal and vertical offsets.   The closed figures of arched openings are contrasted with the open curves of the decorative motifs.   Overall symmetry is clearly enough suggested to lend an apparent classical unity (much like that of a Renaissance palace) to the composition, but this begins to dissolve on closer inspection.   The overall effect is to engage us in a fascinating game of expectation and surprise as we attempt to organize our perceptions.

A figure is something in the visual field to which we direct our attention, and the Gestalt laws describe how we tend to do this.   But we can often shift our attention (particularly when the effects of the Gestalt laws are weak or contradictory), so that what is a figure at one moment becomes part of the background at another, and we become aware of new figures.   The elementary design exercise of figure-ground reversal exploits this possibility (figure 1.12).   And it is part of the fascination of Islamic tile patterns that they allow us to pick out a variety of different figures within them (figure 1.13).   Thus, at this higher level of visual information processing, different observers of a scene may be attending to quite different things.

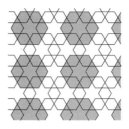

1.10
Good continuation: we perceive
the organization that interrupts
fewest lines—a rectangle and a
square

1.11
Symmetry: we perceive the
symmetrical T-shapes rather than
the asymmetrical L-shapes

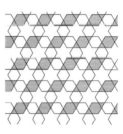

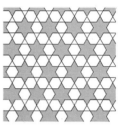

1.13
Some of the figures that can be
found within a tesselation

1.12
Figure-ground reversal

When perceived things are substantial, spatially coherent, and persist over time, we usually regard them as physical objects. Such things maintain their identity (that is, we can recognize them when we see them again), and we use verbal or other labels to identify them. To recognize an object is to correctly apply a label to a figure in a perceptual field (figure 1.14). Not only human beings, but also advanced computer vision systems can perform this task.[4]

The question of how object-recognition mechanisms actually work has long been a focus of epistemological debate (Daley, 1982). Cartesian rationalists have insisted that the human capacity for object recognition must be innate, while empiricists have tried to demonstrate how it can arise from sensory experience. Empiricists have often maintained that we must begin by discriminating objects then sort these into classes according to their observed similarities and differences, but others (for example Goodman and Elgin, 1988) have argued that "beliefs and expectations supply systems of categories or kinds that structure what we perceive." Whatever stance we take on these issues, though, we surely must grant that object recognition is a crucial step in the process of understanding and describing what we see. It provides the basis for interpreting visual fields as collections of physical objects, for predicating properties of these objects, and for specifying relationships of objects.

Later we shall see how designers look at things in different ways, recognize different objects, and follow profoundly different paths of design exploration and critical analysis as a result.

1.14
Recognition is the correct
application of labels

triangle

square

circle

white (Parthenon)

1.15
An object and a simple description

We can refer to an object by pointing at it, or by assigning it a label and subsequently using that label. And once we can refer to objects, we can go on to describe them. Consider, for example, the simple sentence:

The Parthenon is white.

The reference of this sentence is carried by the proper name *The Parthenon*, and the phrase *is white* ascribes a physical property. Thus the sentence refers to its subject and applies a predicate. The complete sentence constitutes a very simple physical description of the building shown in figure 1.15.[5]

When such a sentence is used in some definite context, it makes a claim that may be either true or false. That is, it expresses a proposition. If the sentence is employed appropriately with respect to the subject, then it is true; otherwise it is false. The sentence may be true on one occasion and false on another. For example, it is true as I write that the Parthenon is white. But it was once brightly colored.

Instead of making claims in English we can do so in the terser and more uniform notation of first-order logic. We can write, for example:

white (Parthenon)

Under the notational conventions followed here the symbol denoting the subject of the assertion (the topic) is written between parentheses, and the symbol expressing the content of the assertion (the comment) is written in front of the parentheses. The complete expression is called a predicate, the symbol in front of the parentheses is called the predicate symbol, and the symbols between the parentheses are called the arguments of the predicate. (This corresponds to the usual grammatical distinction between subject and predicate of a sentence.) Our example expression is a predicate with one argument, but, in general, a predicate is an *n*-tuple of arguments grouped between parentheses and prefixed by a predicate symbol. It has a value of either true or false. Our example asserts that the object *Parthenon* is in the set of white objects. This, of course, assumes that we have some clear interpretation for the predicate symbol. For the moment we shall take it that predicate symbols have roughly the same meanings as their English cognates.

Now let us consider the slightly more complicated sentence

The color of the Parthenon is white.

Here we have the ascriptive phrase *is white* as before, but the referring expression has been made more precise. It specifies not only a particular physical object, but also the aspect of that object that is of concern to us — specifically, its color. In first-order logic we can express the referring expression as:

color (Parthenon)

Here *color* is used as a function symbol, and the expression is a function with one argument. Although functions are written like predicates, they work quite differently. Unlike a predicate, a function does not express a complete thought, and it can have a value other than *true* or *false* (figure 1.16). In this case, the function's value is *white*. We can complete the thought by specifying the value picked out by the given argument, thus:

color (Parthenon) = white
color (grass) = green
color (sky) = blue

An alternative notational approach is to use a predicate symbol to characterize the nature of the relation between the individuals *Parthenon* and *white*. We want to say that the relation is of *color* (not, for example, of *size* or of *shape*). Thus we might write:

color (Parthenon, white)
color (grass, green)
color (sky, blue)

1.16
Arguments and values of a function and a relation expressing the same information

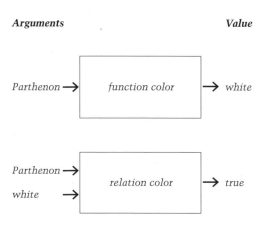

Here the predicate symbol *color* serves as a binary relation symbol, and we use it to assert that ordered pairs of arguments such as ⟨*Parthenon, white*⟩ are in the relation to which it refers. The relation is a mapping from physical objects to colors. The mapping happens to be a function, and the value of the function appears as the final argument. In general, a function of *n* arguments can be converted into a relation of (*n* + *1*) arguments in this way. (However, relations cannot always be converted into functions.)

By substituting other symbols in place of *color* we can construct a set of referring expressions that identify physical properties of the Parthenon that interest us, for example:

length (Parthenon)
width (Parthenon)
numberofcolumns (Parthenon)
cubiccapacity (Parthenon)
material (Parthenon)

Then, by associating values, we can produce a more extensive physical description of the Parthenon. We can use function symbols and the equality operator, thus:

material (Parthenon) = marble

Alternatively, we can use relation symbols and write two-place predicates, thus:

material (Parthenon, marble)

Sometimes we may need predicates of more than two places. Consider, for example, the English sentence:

The color of the material of the Parthenon is white.

This might be expressed as a three-place predicate:

color (material, Parthenon, white)

Indefinitely many predicates might, in principle, be applied to buildings and parts of buildings. In practice, though, the predicates that concern us when we consider the physical properties of buildings are quite well defined. Usually we are interested in shape (rectangular, triangular, circular), size (length, width, height, diameter), mass and volume properties (density, volume, weight), color (red, yellow, blue), other surface properties (rough, shiny, transparent), and material (steel, brick, concrete, marble). English has a wide variety of predicate adjectives for specifying such properties.

Let us further extend our elementary logical framework by considering the following "incomplete sentence":

The color of the Parthenon is _____.

We can turn it into a variety of different meaningful (though not always true) complete sentences by substituting words like *white*, *red*, *purple*, and so on for the blank. Each such sentence specifies an imaginable state of the Parthenon. The range of imaginable states specifiable in this way is given by the extension of our concept of color. (Substitution of something other than a color word yields a meaningless string of words, to which no truth value can be assigned and which does not specify an imaginable state.)

Linguists and ethnologists define the words that can be substituted for a blank, in this way, as a contrastive set (Conklin, 1962; Frake, 1962; Lyons 1963). The words in a contrastive set all come under some superordinate term (such as *color*), and they exclude one another. That is, only one of them can be applied at a time: the Parthenon cannot simultaneously be white and red.

To express this point a little more formally, we can put a symbol in place of the blank, as follows:

*The color of the Parthenon is **X**.*

Now we say that **X** is a variable standing for color. The range of **X** is the set of all colors. By substituting[6] a specific value from this range for **X**, for example *white*, we specify one imaginable state of the Parthenon. The variable, then, stands for a domain of imaginable possibilities, and we select one specific possibility from this domain when we substitute a value for the variable. The sentence thus expresses a parameterized proposition: it can be instantiated to a proposition by substituting a value for **X**. (We will, throughout this book, make extensive use of the idea of a parameterized expression and its instantiations.)

It is straightforward to generalize to use of more than one variable in the following fashion:

*The color of the Parthenon is **X**.*
*The length of the Parthenon is **Y**.*
*The material of the Parthenon is **Z**.*

The different variables (**X**, **Y**, and **Z**) stand for different dimensions of variation, and the range of possible states is the set of all possible combinations of values (that is, the Cartesian product[7] of the ranges of **X**, **Y**, and **Z**).

This description can also be expressed in the notation of first-order logic, as follows:

*color (Parthenon, **X**)*
*length (Parthenon, **Y**)*
*material (Parthenon, **Z**)*

Alternatively, using functions instead of predicates, we can write:

*color (Parthenon) = **X***
*length (Parthenon) = **Y***
*material (Parthenon) = **Z***

Since both constants (*Parthenon*) and variables (**X**, **Y**, and **Z**) appear in these expressions, we need some way to distinguish the two. I shall follow the typographic convention of showing variables in boldface.

These expressions are not complete sentences in first-order logic, since they contain free variables and are neither true nor false. However, we can turn them into sentences with truth values by substituting values for the variables. If substitution of a value for a variable argument of a predicate yields a true sentence, we say that the variable satisfies the predicate. Thus substitution of the value *marble* for the variable **Z** yields the true claim:

material (Parthenon, marble)

But substitution of the value *steel* yields the false claim

material (Parthenon, steel)

Thus the value *steel* fails to satisfy the predicate. Similarly, values may or may not satisfy sentences constructed with functions.

STORAGE OF VALUES IN DATA STRUCTURES

This format for expressing descriptions is not as compact and uniform as it might be. Instead of writing a set of expressions to describe the properties of the Parthenon one by one, we might write a single expression as follows:

*properties (Parthenon, **Length**, **Width**, **Color**)*

An even more general scheme for describing any object in terms of its length, width, and color is:

*properties (**Name**, **Length**, **Width**, **Color**)*

Here the value of **Name** picks out the individual object to be described. In other words, we have a key followed by descriptors.

	Name	Length	Width	Color
Record 1				
Record 2				
.				
.				
.				
Record n				

A structure of this type is known, in computational jargon, as a record. A sequence of records is a file. We can think of files as tables, in which rows correspond to objects that are to be described, columns correspond to descriptor variables, and cells are spaces for recording the values of variables, as shown in figure 1.17, for example. This constitutes a simple data structure suitable for storing descriptions in computer memory.

In general, then, the properties of objects can be specified in at least three different ways: by writing English sentences, by writing expressions in the notation of first-order logic, or by filling the slots in a data structure with appropriate values. It is usually possible to translate from any one of these formats to any other.

PARTS AND WHOLES

So far we have considered the properties of the Parthenon taken as a whole, but we can also direct our attention to parts of the Parthenon. This reveals a hierarchy (figure 1.18). We might first regard the Parthenon as a set of fairly large parts, such as columns. Then we might say that a column is, itself, broken down into parts such as capital and shaft. These parts might then be still further subdivided.

More formally, we can say that the Parthenon can be broken down into some set of elementary parts, which we choose to regard (for our purposes at hand) as indivisible.[8] Elementary parts may then be grouped into various subsets, and subsets may be included within larger subsets. The set of all subsets of a set is its power set. The power set forms a lattice under the relation of inclusion. To exemplify this, figure 1.19 illustrates the lattice formed by the subsets of elements of a classical entablature.

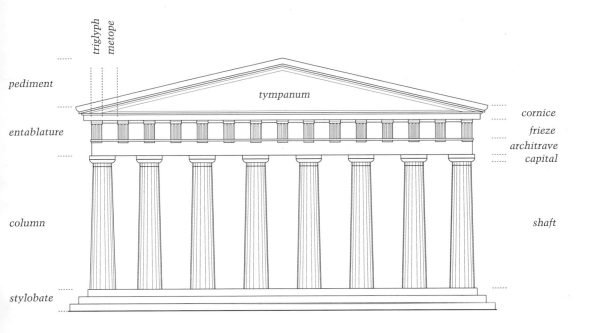

1.18
Decomposition of the Parthenon into primary and secondary parts

1.19
The lattice formed by the parts of an entablature under the relation of inclusion

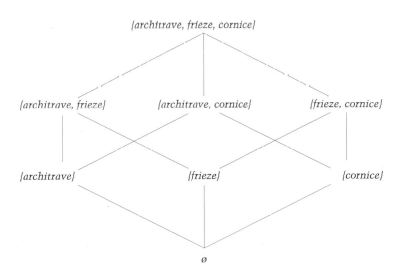

BUILDING DESCRIPTIONS

Part	Length	Height	Color
architrave			
frieze			
cornice			

.
.
.

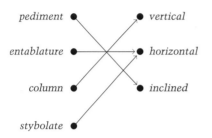

Not all of the subsets in the power set of the elements of a building will be of interest to us. Indeed, most will not. But those that are may be identified and referred to by name (such as *capital*) or indirectly picked out by a function (such as *thingabove (shaft)*).

This opens up the possibility not only of ascribing physical properties to the Parthenon as a whole, but also of ascribing physical properties to its parts. We might, for example, express a description of the Parthenon as a file of part records, as shown in figure 1.20. An alternative approach is to define **Part** as a variable ranging over the parts of the Parthenon, and to consider functions such as:

*length (**Part**)*
*height (**Part**)*
*color (**Part**)*

Then we can express a description by recording values of these functions for particular parts or (more compactly) by providing general rules or procedures for evaluating them. In general, such functions are one-to-one or many-to-one mappings from a set of parts to a contrastive set of properties. Figure 1.21, for example, illustrates a function mapping from a set of parts to a set of possible orientations.

We might also write sentences, such as:

The pediment is triangular.
All columns are fluted.
Some columns are broken.

Translation of the first sentence into logical notation is straightforward. We can write:

triangular (pediment)

The second sentence, however, contains the universal quantifier *all*: it makes a claim not just about one column, but about all columns (figure 1.22). By convention, in logic, the universal quantifier is written ∀ and pronounced "for all." Using this symbol and a variable **Column** we can now write:

*∀ **Column** (fluted (**Column**))*

This is a sentence in which the variable **Column** is bound by the universal quantifier. Since the variable is bound the claim made is either true or false. (We could demonstrate its falsity by finding an unfluted column—a column that does not satisfy the predicate *fluted (**Column**)*.) Similarly, the existential quantifier is written ∃ and pronounced "there exists." Using it we can write:

*∃ **Column** (broken (**Column**))*

This sentence is either true or false. (We could demonstrate its truth by finding a broken column—one that satisfies the predicate *broken (**Column**)*.)

1.22
Quantified assertions about the
columns of the Parthenon

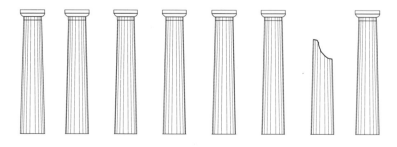

*∀ **Column** (fluted (**Column**))*
*∃ **Column** (broken (**Column**))*

The expressive power of first-order logic is greatly enhanced by allowing the use of variables, in quantified sentences, to make assertions about sets of objects. If we were to extend this idea, and also allow variables to stand in place of predicate and function symbols (that is, quantification over predicates and functions), we would obtain a second-order logic. Consider the sentence:

The Parthenon has a mysterious quality.

We might express it, in logical notation, as:

∃ X (X (Parthenon) and mysterious (X))

Here, though, we will not take the step of introducing second-order logic; first-order will suffice for our purposes.

We might also consider introduction of additional quantifiers to allow construction of modal assertions, as for example the sentence:

Most columns are intact.

This would also take us beyond standard first-order logic, so we will not further pursue the elaboration of quantification.[9]

PHYSICAL RELATIONS AND INTERNAL PHYSICAL STRUCTURE

In addition to specifying the properties of the parts of an object, we can also specify the relationships in which those parts stand to each other. Consider, for example, the following sentences:

The capital is above the shaft.
The shaft is below the capital.
The column is between the plinth and the entablature.
The cella is inside the colonnade.
The colonnade is outside the cella.
The portico is in front of the cella.
The cella is behind the portico.

Here various positional relationships are specified by employing prepositions of place.[10] Translations into logical notation are as follows (figures 1.23, 1.24):

above (capital, shaft)
below (shaft, capital)
between (column, plinth, entablature)
inside (cella, colonnade)
outside (colonnade, cella)
frontof (portico, cella)
backof (cella, portico)

THE LOGIC OF ARCHITECTURE

1.23
Some spatial relationships among
the construction elements of the
Parthenon

beside (metope, triglyph)

between (column, plinth, entablature)

above (capital, shaft)

below (shaft, capital)

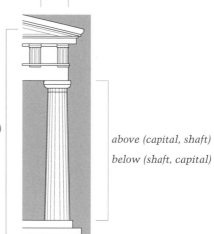

1.24
Some spatial relationships in the plan
of the Parthenon

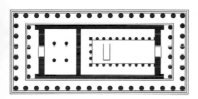

inside (naos, peristyle)

front of (pronaos, naos)

back of (opisthodomos, naos)

BUILDING DESCRIPTIONS

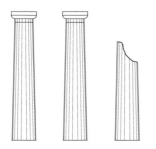

equal (leftcolumn, middlecolumn)
taller (leftcolumn, rightcolumn)
shorter (rightcolumn, leftcolumn)

1.25
Some comparatives

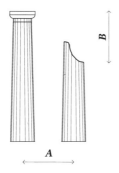

spacing (leftcolumn, rightcolumn, A)

1.26
Specification of numerical intervals

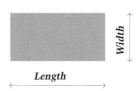

R = Length/Width
proportion (plan, R)

1.27
Specification of numerical ratios

We can also specify relationships of inclusion, for example:

The shaft is part of the column.

In logical notation this becomes:

part (shaft, column)

Furthermore, we can write comparatives (figure 1.25):

equal (leftcolumn, middlecolumn)
taller (leftcolumn, rightcolumn)
shorter (rightcolumn, leftcolumn)

Variables can be introduced into claims about relationships, for example:

*above (**Part**, entablature)*

The variable **Part** ranges over all the parts of the Parthenon. Substitution of the value *pediment* for **Part** yields the true claim:

above (pediment, entablature)

But substitution of the value *plinth* yields the false claim:

above (plinth, entablature)

All the terms can be variables, for example:

*above (**Part**, **Part**)*
*between (**Part**, **Part**, **Part**)*

Thus the subset of ordered pairs of values in the Cartesian product **Part x Part** that satisfy the predicate *above (**Part**, **Part**)* constitutes the relation *above* in the set of parts of the Parthenon, and the subset of ordered triples of values in the Cartesian product **Part x Part x Part** that satisfy the predicate *between (**Part**, **Part**, **Part**)* constitutes the relation *between* in the set of parts of the Parthenon.

Sometimes it is useful to introduce numerical descriptors (figure 1.26), as for example in:

spacing (leftcolumn, rightcolumn, A)
heightdifference (leftcolumn, rightcolumn, B)

Here the variables **A** and **B** take numerical values on some measurement scale. Not only intervals, but also ratios can be specified with numerical parameters, for example (figure 1.27):

proportion (plan, R)

In general, relations in sets of objects (such as the parts of the Parthenon) can be recorded in tabular files. For example the relation *above* can be expressed as a two-column table (figure 1.28). Every pair of parts in the relation appears as a record. Similarly, the relation *heightdifference* can be

Part	Part
cornice	frieze
frieze	architrave
architrave	capital
capital	shaft
shaft	stylobate

1.28
A file expressing the relation
above in a set of parts

expressed as a three-column table. In this case there is a record for every pair of parts, and their height difference is recorded in the third column.

Thus we can specify the internal relationships between an object's parts by writing English sentences, by writing *n*-place predicates in first-order logic, or by entering values in data structures. In any case, when we do so, we describe the object's physical structure. We can also specify the external relationships of an object—of the Parthenon to the Erechtheion, for example. These begin to establish the internal structure of some more inclusive object, such as the city of Athens.

COMPOUND CLAIMS

To form more complex claims than we have so far we can use logical connectives to combine sentences. First-order logic provides for negation, conjunction, and disjunction, as illustrated by the following examples:

not color (Parthenon, green)
material (Parthenon, marble) and color (Parthenon, white)
*∀ **Column** (broken (**Column**) or unbroken (**Column**))*
*∃ **Column** (not unbroken (Column))*

It also allows formation of conditionals and biconditionals, but it will be convenient to defer consideration of these until later.

These connectives enhance the expressive power of first-order logic by allowing us to form compound sentences from simple ones without specifying the truth or falsity of the constituent sentences. Then, when the truth-values of the constituent sentences are known, the truth-values of compound sentences can be determined by applying the well-known Boolean laws.[11] These laws are usually expressed by means of truth-tables. Where **S1** and **S2** are sentences, for example, the truth-table for conjunction is:

S1	S2	S1 and S2
true	true	true
true	false	false
false	true	false
false	false	false

The truth-table for disjunction is:

S1	S2	S1 or S2
true	true	true
true	false	true
false	true	true
false	false	false

And the truth-table for negation is:

S1	*not S1*
true	*false*
false	*true*

Truth-tables for more complex combinations can be built up from these.

CONCEPTUALIZATIONS AND DESCRIPTIONS

The threads of this discussion can now be drawn together into some unifying definitions.

In a given context, the set of objects to which we can refer, and about which we can express comments, is the universe of discourse. In discourse about a building the universe invariably includes the parts of the building to which we choose to give attention. Different people may decompose a building into parts in different ways and so include different collections of parts in a universe of discourse.

The universe of discourse may be extended to include various contrastive sets of properties that interest us. There might, for example, be a contrastive set of colors:

{red, orange, yellow, green . . .}

There might be a contrastive set of textures:

{rough, smooth}

There might be a set of lengths (expressed in numbers of feet), and so on. Different people may be concerned with different properties and may draw distinctions within contrastive sets in different ways.

A function is a particular kind of interrelationship among the objects in a universe of discourse. Specifically, a function takes an object or objects in the universe of discourse as its arguments and has an object in the universe of discourse as its value. A function may map from parts to parts, as for example:

*above (**Part**) = **Part***

Or it may map from parts to properties, thus:

*texture (**Part**) = **Texture***

By naming all the functions that we want to consider, for a specified universe of discourse, we establish a functional basis set.

A relation is a second kind of interrelationship among the objects in a universe of discourse. Unary relations have one argument, as in:

round (A)

Binary relations have two arguments, for example:

above (B, C)

In general, a relation symbol takes n arguments. When values are substituted for all the arguments, as for example in

above (capital, shaft)

an assertion about an n-tuple of objects in the universe of discourse results. This assertion may be true or false. The extension of the relation is the set of all ordered n-tuples of objects in the universe of discourse which satisfy the predicate.[12] As with functions, we can establish a relational basis set by naming all the relations that we want to consider. In architecture, for example, we are frequently concerned with relations of position, shape, scale and proportion, tone, color, and texture among the parts of a composition.

A conceptualization (Genesereth and Nilsson, 1987) consists of a universe of discourse, together with a functional basis set and a relational basis set for that universe. By establishing a suitable conceptualization, we can lay the foundation for describing buildings.[13] That is, we can establish the building parts to which we may directly and indirectly refer, the properties and relationships that we can ascribe to those parts, and the aspects of internal physical structure that we can specify. When we describe by means of English sentences, the conceptualization is implicit in the vocabulary and sentence constructions that we employ. In first-order logic the conceptualization is usually made explicit by declaring the constant, variable, function, and relation symbols that we intend to use. And in a computer data structure the conceptualization establishes the slots that are to be filled with values.

Within the framework of a conceptualization, a description is a collection of assertions about a building. These assertions may be expressed as English sentences, as first-order logic sentences, or as entries in a data structure. A description is complete (relative to the conceptualization) if it allows evaluation of any function in the functional basis set, or determination of whether any relation in the relational basis set is satisfied, for any arguments. Otherwise (and more usually) it is incomplete: a particular description of the Parthenon might not tell us the material of the columns or the shape of the pediment or whether the pronaos is adjacent to the opisthodomos—even though the conceptualization provides for this.

SUMMARY

If we want to develop a discourse about some body of architectural work, we must establish an appropriate conceptualization within which that discourse can unfold. We must have a strategy for segmenting architectural compositions into parts and a way to refer to parts by name. (In the tradition of classical architecture, for example, there is a standard system of segmentation and naming.) We must also have a sufficiently extensive and finely differentiated vocabulary of relation and function symbols for use in specifying the properties and interrelationships of parts. Finally, we need a system for constructing assertions from names of parts, relation symbols, and function symbols: we might assign values to variables in a data structure, we might construct a set of first-order logic sentences, or we might allow the discourse to unfold as a sequence of English sentences.

ARCHITECTURAL FORM

A DEFINITION OF FORM

On the foundation established in chapter 1 we can now lay out a reasonably clear and precise definition of "form." We shall take it, for our purposes here, that the form of a building is its internal physical structure, as described under some appropriate conceptualization. Indefinitely many aspects of internal physical structure might be considered and described, but the conceptualization always defines the scope of our interest.

This definition is in the spirit of the general usage of the term in aesthetics. Clive Bell (1914), for example, claimed that "relations and combinations of lines and colors" in a painting could constitute "significant form." Another early modernist critic, R. H. Wilenski (1927), insisted that an architect's "business as artist" was with "the definition, organization and completion of his formal experience by creating a concrete object." He went on to propose that "the architect experiences, synthesizes, and creates; he experiences proportion, balance, line, recession and so on, he coordinates and organizes his experience, and he gives it definite form in a building. . . . He is concerned from first to last with problems of formal relations." A more recent text, Monroe Beardsley's *Aesthetics* (1958), suggests that "the form of an aesthetic object is the total web of relations among its parts." The commonality of these definitions is captured by one of the usual dictionary senses of "form." *Webster's*, for instance, defines the form of a work of art as its "structural element," specifically "the combinations and relations to each other of various components (as lines, colors, and volumes in a visual work of art or themes and elaborations in an aural work of art)."

Under this definition we can find no form in the elementary particles of matter (leptons and quarks) since, as described in current physical theory, they have no detectable shape or structure (though some physicists have speculated that they might eventually turn out to be composite objects). But we can find form in all higher-level particles, such as atoms and molecules, since relationships between their constituent parts can be described. Similarly, in Euclid's geometry, a point is an elementary, formless object. But lines, polygons, etc. have form.

The ancient Greeks were fascinated by the concept of form, and in their consideration of the forms of things they drew a fundamental distinction between *chaos* and *kosmos* (that is, order). In science they attempted to discover a cosmology—an underlying system of order in the form of the world—and in the arts they developed an explicit concern for formal regularities and disciplines in compositions. This gave rise, ultimately, to an influential tradition of formalist criticism—criticism that concerns itself primarily with the properties of form rather than with the external relations of works. A formalist critic might, for example, begin with a simple observation about form, such as:

round (column)

When the observation is expressed in this way, however, it is not possible to add a further comment about "roundness" for the technical reason that *round* is a predicate symbol, not the identifier of an object in the universe of discourse. This situation can be remedied by treating *round* as the value of a function, thus:

shape (column) = round

Now the shape of the column can be the subject of comments, for example[1]:

symmetrical (shape (column))

We can carry this sort of construction further, for example:

symmetry (shape (column)) = rotationalsymmetry
graceful (symmetry (shape (column)))

This is a comment on the symmetry of the shape of the column. We can unpack its meaning by evaluating functions, thus:

graceful (symmetry (round))
graceful (rotationalsymmetry)

In other words, the symmetry of roundness is graceful or, alternatively, rotational symmetry is graceful.

This strategy is one of reification[2]—of introducing into the universe of discourse constructs such as *shape* and *symmetry* to serve as topics of critical comment. Then, by adding predicates such as *graceful* that apply to these things, we can extend the corresponding critical language to provide not only for expression of observations about the physical properties and relations of architectural elements, but also for expression of value judgments about architectural form.

We might begin to develop a vocabulary of formalist criticism by noting that, in most buildings, there is repetition of elements such as columns. We might comment on the repetition of columns in the Parthenon:

rhythmic (repetition (columns))

The predicate, here, originates from the Greek term *rhythmos* (figure 2.1)[3]—originally associated with the idea of regular movement, as in dance.

Secondly, we might observe that the dimensions of parts of a composition are in certain ratios. Thus, for example, we might want to comment:

well-proportioned (shape (portico))

The predicate used here derives from the Greek concept of *symmetria*. Use of this concept in artistic theory and criticism can be traced back at least to the well-known *Canon*[4] of the fifth-century BC Greek sculptor Polyclitus. *Symmetria* was achieved, according to Polyclitus, by relating the dimensions of all parts of a statue to each other, and to the whole, by means of an appropriate system of ratios. Hence his famous remark that "perfection arises through many numbers."

Vitruvius drew much of his aesthetic theory from earlier Greek sources, so it is not surprising to find that he propounded similar ideas. He suggested that there should be "a correspondence among the members of an entire work, and of the whole to a certain part selected as standard." He then went on to discuss the ratios governing the dimensions of the human body and to propose that the dimensions of a building should be derived from the basic module by use of a system of ratios related to that of the body.

Much of the theory concerned with ratios and proportion in architectural composition can be traced back, ultimately, to the Pythagoreans. They observed that the pitch of the note sounded by a plucked string was proportional to its length and that harmonious combinations of notes resulted when the lengths of the strings formed certain ratios of small whole numbers, particularly 1:2 (octave), 2:3 (fifth), and 3:4 (fourth). So there emerged the compelling idea, with the authority of Pythagorean and Platonic philosophy behind it, that harmony and beauty followed from ratios of small whole numbers. These ratios should govern not only the musical scale, but also the proportions of buildings.[5] This idea was discussed by Vitruvius, though not in a very coherent way. Later it was taken up by medieval thinkers, notably

2.1
Rhythmos: repetition of elements at
regular intervals

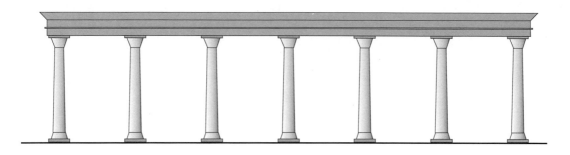

aaa. . . rhythm

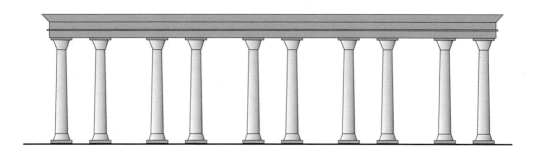

aba. . . rhythm

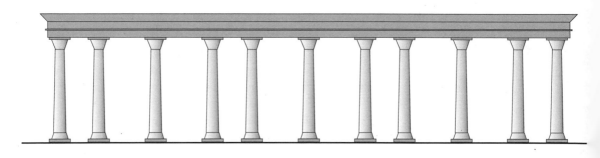

abba. . . rhythm

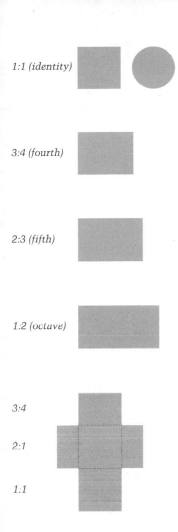

1:1 (identity)

3:4 (fourth)

2:3 (fifth)

1:2 (octave)

3:4

2:1

1:1

2.2
Symmetria: harmonic proportions for rooms as recommended by Palladio

2.3
Bilateral symmetry: reflection across an axis is the symmetry operation

Augustine and Aquinas, with the result that the use of harmonic ratios became an important formal ordering principle in medieval religious architecture. And it was to flower most spectacularly in the Italian Renaissance, particularly in the work of Palladio, who used harmonic ratios to interrelate length, width, and height within a room and to coordinate the proportions of different rooms (figure 2.2). Palladio would presumably want a critic to comment:

harmonious (proportion (room))

The idea of harmonic governing ratios lost favor during the eighteenth century, when theorists like Edmund Burke and William Hogarth (in his *Analysis of Beauty*) denied that ratios could be beautiful in themselves and argued that the sense of harmony was a purely subjective matter. But interest in systems of proportioning rules that allegedly guarantee the harmony of architectural compositions has periodically revived: Le Corbusier, for example, proposed a system based on Fibonnaci sequences and the golden ratio.[6]

The English word "symmetry" also derives from the Greek *symmetria*, but it has come, by a gradual process of differentiation of concepts, to refer to a different kind of formal regularity from that connected to modules, ratios, dimensioning disciplines, and progressions.

In general usage today, "symmetrical" most commonly refers to bilateral symmetry—the kind of symmetry possessed by the human body (figure 2.3). This was an important principle of classical architectural composition, and we might, for example, comment of the Parthenon:

bilaterallysymmetrical (shape (pediment))

Renaissance architectural theorists frequently suggested the desirability of bilateral symmetry. Alberti remarked in his *Ten Books of Architecture* that "if a dog had one ear like that of an ass, or if a man had one foot bigger than the other, or one hand very large, and the other very small, we should immediately pronounce such a one deformed." He then drew the moral that the parts of an architectural composition should be disposed "with an exact correspondence as to the number, form, and appearance; so that the right may answer to the left, the high to the low, the similar to the similar, so as to form a correspondent ornament in that body whereof they are parts." Similarly, in a well-known letter, Michelangelo[7] commented that "the nose, that is in the middle of the face, is neither obligated to one nor to the other eye, but one hand is altogether obligated to be like the other, and one eye like the other, with respect to the sides and of the corresponding parts." He proposed that architecture

2.4
A composition in which rotation is
the symmetry operation

2.5
A composition in which translation
is the symmetry operation

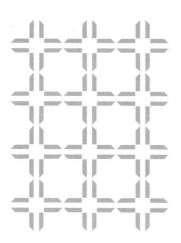

2.6
A composition with translations,
rotations, and reflections as symmetry operations

should follow the same principle "because it is a certain thing, that the members of architecture derive from the members of man. Who has not been or is not a good master of the human body, and most of all of anatomy, cannot understand anything of it."

Despite the ancient tradition of bilaterally symmetrical composition and these fifteenth- and sixteenth-century discussions of the idea, it was not until well into the seventeenth century that the concepts of proportion and symmetry, as we understand them today, were clearly distinguished. Pascal, for example, apparently thought of them as synonymous. And when Claude Perrault published his French translation of Vitruvius (1673), he rendered *symmetria* as "proportion." But in a footnote he commented that, in everyday speech, the word *symétrie* referred to "the relationship which parts on the left side have with those on the right, those high up with those low down, those in back with those in front." By the eighteenth century we can find the English architect Sir William Chambers writing, "This column . . . must have a pilaster by its side, to make a symmetry with that on the other side of the window."

Modern mathematics has further generalized and formalized the concept of geometric symmetry, grounding it upon the idea of a group[8] of geometric transformations. We now say that an architectural composition is symmetrical to the extent that it has symmetry operations, that is, isometric transformations (translations, rotations, reflections, and compositions of these) that transform the composition into itself: symmetry is defined as a property of a set of transformations. For example, a bilaterally symmetrical plan is transformed into itself by reflection across its axis; a pinwheel is transformed into itself by rotation (figure 2.4); any regular frieze pattern (if we take it to be of unlimited length) is transformed into itself by translation through an appropriate increment along its axis (figure 2.5); and regular plane patterns may have translations, rotations, and reflections as symmetry operations (figure 2.6). This definition is broad enough to encompass not only symmetry about axes passing through a point, but also all kinds of repeating linear patterns, repeating two-dimensional patterns, and repeating three-dimensional patterns.

From ancient times onward many critics have claimed that the predicate *beautiful* is correctly applied to compositions that have the classical formal qualities of rhythm, proportion, and symmetry. Vitruvius, for example, made frequent use of the Greek term *eurythmy*. (A reasonably good English equivalent is "grace.") He defined it as

. . . beauty and fitness in the adjustments of the members. This is found when the members of a work are of a height suited to their breadth, of a breadth suited to their length, and, in a word, when they all correspond symmetrically.

In St. Augustine's aesthetic theory, formal order is regarded as the source of beauty, and in one passage from *De Vera Religione* (trans. Burleigh, 1953) Augustine suggested that the application of this principle to architecture was self-evident:

If I ask a workman why, after constructing one arch, he builds another like it over against it, he will reply, I dare say, that in a building like parts must correspond to like. If I go further and ask why he thinks so, he will say that it is fitting, or beautiful, or that it gives pleasure to those who behold it.

Alberti, in his *Ten Books*, was to define the sought-after quality of harmony in architectural form in rather similar fashion. His very elegant formulation (which draws directly upon Aristotelian ideas) runs as follows:

Just as all the individual members harmonize in an animal organism, so all the separate parts of a building should harmonize. . . . Each part of a building must correspond to all the others so as to contribute to the success and beauty of the whole. The building cannot be beautiful in only one of its parts while the others are neglected; all must harmonize in order to appear as a single, well-articulated body, not a jumble of unrelated fragments.

In his influential essay *Inquiry into the Origin of Our Ideas of Beauty and Virtue* (1725) the British philosopher Francis Hutcheson attempted to show *how* beauty depends on formal qualities. He suggested, in a much-quoted passage, that "what we call beautiful in objects, to speak in the mathematical style, seems to be in compound ratio of uniformity and variety: so that where the uniformity of bodies is equal, the beauty is as the variety; and where the variety is equal, the beauty is as the uniformity." Later in the essay, he gave the more concise formula for beauty as "uniformity amidst variety." Thus, according to Hutcheson's doctrine, richly varied compositions that are organized in accordance with some underlying unifying principle are beautiful. So are mathematical theorems that apply to extensive sets of apparently diverse figures or curves, and the forms of plants and animals.

Owen Jones, the great nineteenth-century theoretician of ornament, gave a psychological interpretation to the "unity and variety" formula and explored its practical implications in the decorative arts. In the introduction to his *Grammar of Ornament* (1856) he asserted the general principle that "all ornament should be based upon a geometrical construction." But the principles of construction should not be too readily apparent. Of proportion, for example, he wrote:

As in every perfect work of Architecture a true proportion will be found to reign between all the members which compose it, so throughout the Decorative Arts every assemblage of forms should be arranged on certain definite proportions; the whole and each particular member should be a multiple of some simple unit.

However, he went on:

Those proportions will be the most beautiful which it will be most difficult for the eye to detect. Thus the proportion of a double square, or 4 to 8, will be less beautiful than the more subtle ratio of 5 to 8; 3 to 6, than 3 to 7; 3 to 9 than 3 to 8; 3 to 4 than 3 to 5.

(Note the contrast, here, with the Pythagorean views discussed earlier.) Later, in his chapter on "Moresque Ornament," he explicitly related aesthetic value to the degree of "mental effort" required to discover an underlying order:

All compositions of squares or of circles will be monotonous, and afford but little pleasure, because the means whereby they are produced are very apparent. So we think that compositions distributed in equal lines or divisions will be less beautiful than those which require a higher mental effort to appreciate them.

Then, in some remarks on the use of curves, he related this "mental effort" to the economy with which a composition can be described:

Those compositions of curves will be most agreeable, where the mechanical process of describing them shall be least apparent; and we shall find it to be universally the case, that in the best periods of art all mouldings and ornaments were founded on curves of the higher order, such as the conic sections; whilst, when art declined, circles and compass-work were much more dominant.

In this century, numerous variants of the "uniformity and variety" (alternatively, "unity and variety" or "order and complexity") formula have been put forward,[9] leading ultimately to various efforts to quantify aesthetic value. The mathematician George Birkhoff (1933) made an interesting but in the end unconvincing attempt to measure aesthetic values of visual and musical compositions by a formula of the form $m = o/c$, where m is aesthetic value, o is an objective measure of order, and c is an objective measure of complexity.[10] Following the publication of Shannon and Weaver's *Mathematical Theory of Communication* (1949), there were some attempts to identify uniformity and variety with information redundancy and entropy (as formulated in statistical information theory), and thus to find an information-theoretic measure of aesthetic value.[11] During the 1960s an alternative formulation of information theory, based upon the theory of algorithms rather than upon concepts of probability, was developed (Kolmogorov, 1968). This appears to provide a rather more promising foundation for analysis of aesthetic value, and at least one rigorously developed exploration of the approach (much in the spirit of Owen Jones's analyses) has appeared (Stiny and Gips, 1978).

The uniformity and variety formula applies quite convincingly to classical architecture, with its regular rhythms, disciplined proportions, and strict symmetries enlivened by freer decorative elements and the subtle asymmetries of shade and shadow. And early modernist play of irregular forms and placements within a framework of regular structural rhythms, symmetrical enclosure, and regulating lines (as at the Villa Savoye) seems consistent with it too. But the Russian constructivists inverted the definition, preferring random assemblage to rhythmic placement, asymmetrical and occluded fragments to symmetrical closed forms, and arbitrary proportions to the regulation of simple ratios (figure 2.7). Thus we should not look for a universal definition of aesthetic value in terms of particular formal qualities, but should recognize instead that different people, at different times, will seek and value different formal qualities in compositions. This will be reflected in differing critical terminology and in differing usages of predicates such as *beautiful*.

A composition by El Lissitzky that achieves its drama through negation of classical principles

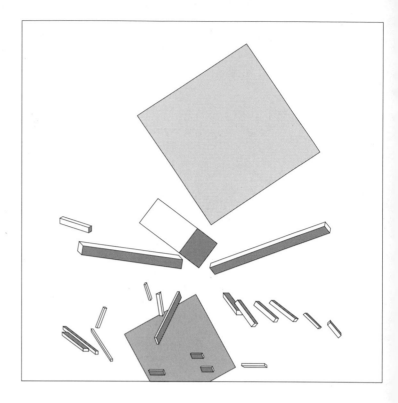

FORMALIST CRITICISM

Many theoreticians and critics have distinguished between aesthetic value that is held to derive from the formal qualities of a work (for example, regular rhythm, good proportions, symmetry, underlying uniformity, and an appropriate amount of variety) and aesthetic value that supposedly has other sources. In a well-known passage contained in *Parentalia*, for example, Sir Christopher Wren gave the following analysis:

There are two causes of Beauty, natural and customary. Natural is from Geometry, consisting in Uniformity (that is Equality) and Proportion. Customary Beauty is begotten by the use of our senses to those objects which are usually pleasing to us from other causes, as Familiarity or particular Inclination breeds a Love to Things not in themselves lovely. Here lies the great Occasion of Errors; here is tried the architect's Judgement: but always the true test is natural or geometrical Beauty.

Various other seventeenth- and eighteenth-century figures suggested variations of this dichotomy. Claude Perrault, in his treatise on the orders of architecture (1683), had distinguished positive beauty, which derived from formal and material qualities, from arbitrary beauty, which followed from fashion, custom, and usage.[12] In his *Elements of*

Criticism (1761) the British philosopher Henry Home (Lord Kames) proposed a distinction between intrinsic and relative beauty. Intrinsic beauty, much like Wren's "natural" beauty and Perrault's "positive" beauty, was a property derived directly from the formal and material qualities of a work and could be appreciated without reference to any other thing. But relative beauty, on the other hand, "is that of means relating to some good end or purpose." Thus appreciation of relative beauty requires consideration of a work's role relative to other things. Natural forms, according to Kames, possess both kinds of beauty, and please "partly from symmetry and partly from utility."

Certainly the most celebrated version of the distinction was that drawn by Kant in his *Critique of Aesthetic Judgement* (1790).[13] He distinguished between free and dependent (or pure and adherent) beauty. Free beauty is an entirely formal matter, divorced from all considerations of function, depiction, or content. Kant assigned this kind of beauty to decorative patterns and arabesques, shells, crystals, and the like. Appreciation of dependent beauty, on the other hand, follows from a knowledge of ends, as when we judge an artifact well adapted to some purpose or a picture as a good likeness. So, Kant suggested, a well-designed building appeals both to our sense of pure form and to our sense of aptness or fitness.

Nineteenth- and twentieth-century aestheticians have typically distinguished formal values from material values on the one hand and from associational values on the other.[14] Material values are said to follow directly from pleasurable colors, textures, sounds, scents, tastes, and so on, without consideration of form. That is, they are based upon recognition of physical properties only and do not require the recognition of physical relations. But associational values are said to relate to content, as when the form evokes ideas or emotions or serves to convey some meaning.

The critical attitude of formalism is grounded on the belief that formal values, rather than material or associational values, are of paramount importance in a work of art. The theoretical foundations of this position received articulate expression from the Viennese critic Eduard Hanslick, who argued in his book *On the Musically Beautiful* (1854) that music should be valued for its own sake, without consideration of external associations or purposes: the critic's primary concerns are with patterns of melody, harmony, rhythm, and instrumentation.

On the face of it, rigorous formalism seems less tenable in the visual arts, where representation has traditionally been a central concern. But the English critics Clive Bell (1914, 1922) and Roger Fry (1926, 1937, 1939) consistently took and strongly defended formalist positions. This had the merits of focusing critical attention on issues other than representational accuracy in painting and of providing a basis for understanding abstract painting and sculpture. It also proved congenial to the kind of architecture that is concerned primarily with formal experience, rather than with immediate sensual pleasures, sentimental associations, or historical references, as for example the severely geometric, white-painted compositions of the early modern movement. And indeed, we find Jeanneret (the young Le Corbusier) and Ozenfant insisting in the pages of *L'Esprit Nouveau* 4 (1920) that the primary aesthetic value of architecture derived from the composition of elementary geometric solids, while the association of ideas was a secondary matter.

Thus it is useful to qualify the predicate *beautiful* and to distinguish the usages of *formally beautiful*, *materially beautiful*, *associationally beautiful*, and so on. In formalist criticism *beautiful* is normally taken to mean *formally beautiful*, but in other critical traditions the predicate *beautiful* may be applied in different ways.

SUMMARY

Formalist criticism attends to rhythms, ratios, symmetries, and other aspects of the form of a building. It makes use of a vocabulary of descriptive predicates: rhythms may be regular or irregular, ratios may be harmonic, symmetries may be dihedral, and so on. It also employs predicates such as *graceful*, *harmonious*, and *beautiful*, which express judgments of aesthetic value. In the next few chapters I shall treat design primarily as a matter of formal composition—of constructing rhythms, ratios, symmetries, asymmetries, contrasts, harmonies, and so on, in order to produce beauty. Then I shall expand the discussion (as suggested by Kant's conception of beauty) to deal not only with pure form, but also with design that concerns itself with aptness or fitness for practical or representational ends.

GIVING FORM TO MATERIALS

In his *Poetics of Music* (1942) Stravinsky pointed out that isolated natural sounds such as "the murmur of the breeze in the trees, the rippling of a brook, the song of a bird" are not music, but merely "promises of music." Then he argued that "tonal elements become music only by virtue of their being organized." To generalize, an artist *gives* form to his or her materials.

The notion that an artist gives form to materials can be traced back directly to the Platonic doctrine of ideas.[1] Plato suggested that physical objects imperfectly imitate perfect, abstract ideas. Aristotle, in the *Metaphysics*, developed a modification of this doctrine, according to which a form first exists in the mind of the artist, then it is given by the artist to matter. Numerous later commentators elaborated this theme and discussed its application to painting, sculpture, and architecture. In a particularly famous passage in *Summa Theologia* St. Thomas Aquinas suggested that "the house pre-existed in the mind of the architect: and this can be designated as the Idea of the house, because the artist intends to assimilate the real house to the same form that he has conceived in his mind."

Alberti echoed this, in his *Ten Books of Architecture*, when he carefully distinguished between the "design" and the "structure" of a building. He added:

Nor has this design any thing that makes it in its nature inseparable from matter; for we see that the same design is in a multitude of buildings, which have all the same form, and are exactly alike as to the situation of their parts and the disposition of their lines and angles; and we can in our thought and imagination contrive perfect forms of buildings entirely separate from matter, by settling and regulating in a certain order, the disposition and conjunction of the lines and angles. Which being granted, we shall call the design a firm and graceful pre-ordering of the lines and angles, conceived in the mind, and contrived by an ingenious artist.

DESIGN MEDIA AND DESIGN WORLDS

We need not commit ourselves completely to such Platonism.[2] It is sufficient for our purposes here to recognize that when we describe the forms of buildings we refer to extant constructions of physical materials in physical space, but when we describe designs we make claims about something else—constructions of the imagination. More precisely, we refer to some sort of model—a drawing, physical scale model, structure of information in computer memory, or even mental model—rather than to a real building.[3] Just as an assertion in a critical language consists of verbal tokens (words) forming a one-dimensional string (a sentence), so a model is a collection of graphic tokens, such as points, lines, and polygons, forming a two-dimensional or three-dimensional arrangement. We can think of the space populated by these tokens, for example a drawing surface or a three-dimensional Cartesian coordinate system, as a specialized, delimited microworld—the design world. Tokens can be inserted into the design world, deleted from it, geometrically transformed, and otherwise manipulated. We assume that some procedure exists for translating graphic tokens, and their properties and relations, into corresponding objects, properties, and relations in the larger world. In this sense, the design world is used to depict possibilities in the larger world. But the potential translation into physical reality may or may not actually take place or have any prospect of taking place; it suffices that such translation is possible in principle.

Designers often establish design worlds implicitly, through their choices of design media and instruments. A drawing board and traditional drafting instruments, for example, establish a Euclidean design world populated by two kinds of graphic tokens—straight lines and circular arcs—that can vary in size and position and be related to each other as parallels, perpendiculars, and so on. A designer toying with a cardboard working model enters a design world populated by plane polygons that can be shaped in different ways and translated and rotated in three-dimensional space. Designers shaping clay with their fingers, or cutting polystyrene blocks with hot wires, enter yet other kinds of design worlds.

When a computer-aided design system is used, the data structure and its associated operations establish the design world. There might, for example, be records to store information specifying points, vectors, arcs, polygons, and other kinds of graphic tokens. Fields might be provided for specification of properties such as thicknesses of lines and colors of polygons. Procedures exist for translating information in the data structure into a screen display, and there is some repertoire of operations for inserting, deleting, transforming, and combining graphic tokens to produce compositions.

The first step in precise formulation of a design world is to specify the primitives (kinds of elementary graphic tokens) out of which designs may be assembled. Let us briefly and informally consider some of the basic possibilities.

POINT WORLDS

To take points as the primitives of a design world is to initiate an exploration of formal possibilities in a very low-level, atomistic way—much like considering the physical world purely at the atomic and molecular level, painting in a pointillist style like that of Seurat, or examining a building in brick-by-brick fashion.

The idea of a point world follows closely from that of a Cartesian coordinate system. Consider, for example, a two-dimensional, rectangular, coordinate system as shown in figure 3.1a. A point in such a system is a structured object with two components—an x-coordinate and a y-coordinate. We can express the combination of these components into a single object by writing, for example:

point (10, 20)

Space can be filled, at any density, with a square array of such points (figure 3.1b). Thus a picture plane can be described as an array of points, and any one of these points can be specified by substituting values for **X** and **Y** in:

*point (**X**, **Y**)*

A kind of graphic primitive known as a pixel may now be defined as an array point with an associated state, described:

*pixel (point (**X**, **Y**), **State**)*

The value of the variable **State** describes the corresponding square cell of the picture plane (figure 3.1c). In the simplest case **State** is a binary variable specifying whether the cell is filled or unfilled. If there are n pixels in the bitmap, then 2^n different patterns can exist in the design world.

Bitmaps are widely used for encoding images and storing them in computer memory.[4] Raster display devices have equivalent grids of pixels on their screens and display bitmapped images by intensifying pixels or not according to the corresponding stored values. The technique can be extended to deal with halftone and color images by elaborating the description of states, for example:

*pixel (point (**X**, **Y**), color (**Hue**, **Saturation**, **Value**))*

One of the simplest types of computer graphics systems used by artists and designers, a paint system, is based directly on the idea of bitmapping. A paint system displays a

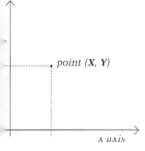

a. Representation of a point

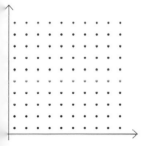

b. A square array of points

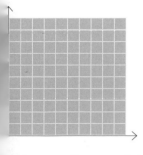

c. Corresponding array of pixels

3.1
Establishment of a point world

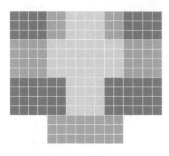

bitmapped image on the screen and provides "tools" (actually operations on the bitmap) for performing various graphic manipulations. Some computer programs used to perform floor-plan layout tasks represent plans, in closely analogous fashion, as sets of square modules (figure 3.2). An architect working with any of these systems has entered a two-dimensional point world.

In a three-dimensional Cartesian coordinate system, space can be filled, to any desired density, with a cubic array of points. When states are associated with these gridpoints they are known as voxels—volumetric elements:

*voxel (point (**X**, **Y**, **Z**), **State**)*

A binary array of voxels can be used to represent three-dimensional solid shapes (figure 3.3), and in medical imaging voxel arrays are frequently used for three-dimensional representation of anatomy.[5] In this case the description of states is elaborated to allow representation of spatial distribution of material, thus:

*voxel (point (**X**, **Y**, **Z**), **Material**)*

Architectural theorists have occasionally noted that building forms might be represented in this fashion: in his discussions of modular coordination, for example, Albert Farwell Bemis (1936) showed how architectural forms could be built up from four-inch cubes (figure 3.4). But in practice it rarely proves useful to adopt such an extreme atomistic viewpoint.

3.2

Bitmap representation of a floor plan: rooms are modeled by collections of adjacent pixels

3.3

A three-dimensional solid represented by a voxel array

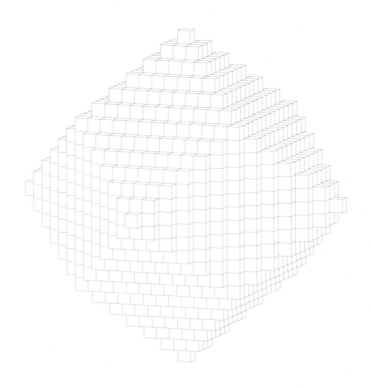

3.4
A house represented as a collection of
four-inch cubes (after Bemis, 1936)

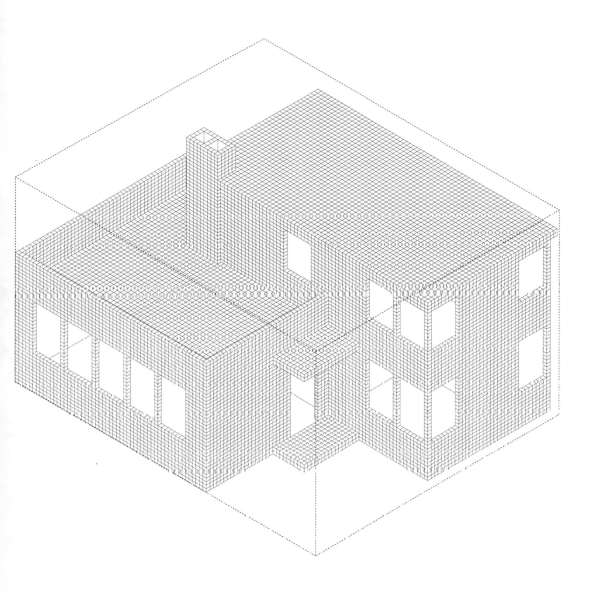

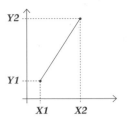

line (point (**X1**, **Y1**), point (**X2**, **Y2**))

3.5
Representation of a straight line by
its endpoint coordinates

Circular arc

Elliptical arc

Spline

Fractal

3.6
Different types of lines connecting
the same two points

A famous passage from Alberti's *Ten Books of Architecture* suggests the usefulness of taking lines as primitives. Alberti proposed that "the whole force and rule of the design consists in a right and exact adapting and joining together of *the lines and angles* which compose and form the face of the building" (my italics). In other words, lines are the elements of architectural compositions, and design is a matter of forming relationships (such as angles) between lines.

An architect who takes up drafting instruments such as parallel rule, triangles, dividers, and compasses to construct plans, sections, and elevations enters the kind of world that Alberti had in mind. The associated theory is that of Euclid's geometry, so it is not surprising that this has figured prominently in the history of architectural thought. The "secrets" of the medieval masons consisted, in large part, of Euclid-based procedures for construction of line figures (Frankl, 1945). Renaissance architectural treatises, such as Serlio's *Five Books of Architecture* (1545), typically introduced points, straight lines, and arcs as basic compositional elements, then surveyed line figures and constructions. And the first significant discussion of architectural theory in English was contained in Dr. John Dee's preface to an English translation of Euclid's *Elements* (1570).

In a two-dimensional Cartesian coordinate system, a straight line segment can be represented by its endpoint coordinates (figure 3.5). In other words, we can describe it as a relationship of two points:

*line (point (**X1**, **Y1**), point (**X2**, **Y2**))*

Arcs, splines, fractals, and other types of curved lines can also be represented by associating coefficients specifying shape between the endpoints (figure 3.6).[6] Thus the database of a two-dimensional, line-based, computer graphics system consists of records describing lines, and display software translates this information into corresponding marks on a screen or plotting surface. Various relations in the set of lines, such as connection at endpoints, might also be recorded. Associated editing operations usually allow the user to insert, delete, extend, trim, divide, reshape, and move lines of various types. Thus a line world is established in much the same way that traditional drafting instruments do so, and computer-aided design systems of this type are consequently called two-dimensional drafting systems.

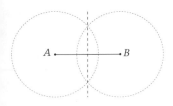

Perpendicular bisector of line AB

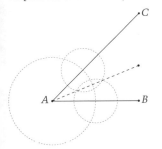

Bisector of angle CAB

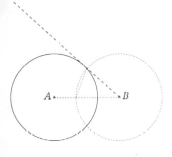

*Tangent from point B
to circle centered at A*

3.7
Some Euclidean constructions of
straight lines and arcs

Euclid's *Elements* is mostly concerned with the types of relations into which straight lines and arcs can be put; that is, with the construction of parallels and perpendiculars to straight lines, bisectors of angles, tangents to circles, and so on (figure 3.7). Drafting instruments and Euclid's theorems provide the means to form such relationships, and computer drafting systems provide analogous capabilities. Composition in a two-dimensional line world thus becomes a matter of using the available construction tools to build up structures of such relationships.

The development of perspective construction methods encouraged Renaissance architects to explore not only two-dimensional line worlds, but also three-dimensional worlds in which building designs became "wire frames" of lines in space—depicted by projecting these lines onto a plane (figure 3.8). Line-based computer graphics techniques can be extended from two dimensions to three in a similar way: a three-dimensional coordinate system is introduced, endpoints are now represented by coordinate triples instead of coordinate pairs (figure 3.9), and the display software must appropriately project lines onto the screen or plotting surface before drawing them (figure 3.10). Systems organized like this are usually known as wire-frame modeling systems.

To work in a line world (either two dimensional or three-dimensional) is to direct attention constantly to discontinuities of color or material, boundaries and silhouettes of shapes, edges of spaces, and the profiles defined by the intersections of surfaces (figure 3.11). Everything else is implicit and must, literally, be read between the lines. Translation from a line world to three-dimensional physical reality is largely a matter of cutting along specified lines, painting up to specified lines, and so on.

3.8
A wire-frame perspective drawing
of a three-dimensional form (after
Serlio's *Five Books of Architecture*,
1545)

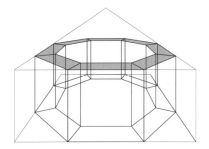

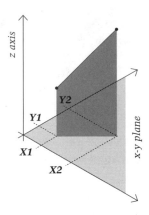

*line (point (**X1**, **Y1**, **Z1**), point (**X2**, **Y2**, **Z2**))*

3.9
Representation of a straight line by
coordinate triples

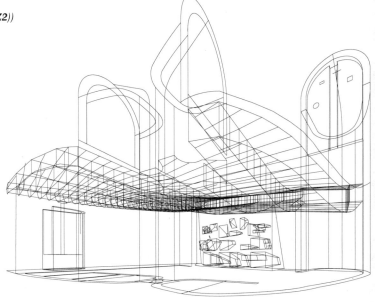

3.10
A computer-generated wire-frame
perspective

3.11
Lines defining edges and inter-
sections of surfaces (after Guarini's
Architettura Civile, 1737)

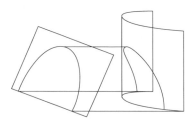

Just as zero-dimensional endpoints bound one-dimensional line segments, so one-dimensional line segments can become the edges bounding two-dimensional polygons (figure 3.12). A triangle, for example, might be described as a relationship of lines:

*triangle (line (point (**X1**, **Y1**), point (**X2**, **Y2**)),*
*line (point (**X2**, **Y2**), point (**X3**, **Y3**)),*
*line (point (**X3**, **Y3**), point (**X1**, **Y1**)))*

Circles (figure 3.13) and ellipses (figure 3.14) are also closed planar shapes. A colored circle, for example, might be described:

*circle (location (**X**, **Y**),*
*size (**Diameter**),*
*color (**Hue**, **Saturation**, **Value**))*

More complex closed planar shapes can be produced by using a variety of curved lines as edges (figure 3.15). When closed colored shapes are arranged in the plane (figure 3.16), an image related to the traditions of painting, rather than to those of line drawing, is produced.

3.12
The vertices, edges, and surface of a plane polygon

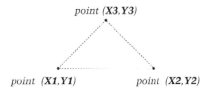

*triangle (point (**X1**,**Y1**), point (**X2**,**Y2**), point (**X3**,**Y3**))*

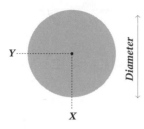

3.13
Description of a circle by three
variables

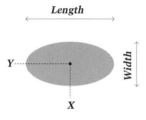

3.14
Description of an ellipse by four
variables

3.15
Some examples of closed planar
shapes with both straight and
curved edges

Designers frequently take two-dimensional colored shapes as the primitives of design worlds. An architect might, for example, cut shapes from cardboard to represent rooms or furniture items, then shuffle them around on a plane surface to explore alternative configurations. Similarly, a painter might cut shapes from colored paper and arrange them to produce a collage.

The data structure of a computer graphics system for manipulating this sort of world has records for the various kinds of closed planar shapes that are admitted—polygons, circles, ellipses, and so on. Usually each record stores shape, position, color, and pattern information. Associated editing operations typically provide for shaping and positioning the graphic elements and for assigning colors and patterns to them.

Closed planar shapes can also be arranged in three-dimensional space. A cube, for example, is twelve edges in a line world, but is six square surfaces in a three-dimensional surface world (figure 3.17).

Once surfaces are liberated into three-dimensional space they can become curved as well as planar. An architect's design world might, for example, admit of cylindrical, spherical, and conical surfaces (figure 3.18). An automobile stylist's design world needs to be populated with warped and spline surfaces as well.

Traditionally, architects have explored surface worlds by constructing physical models of cardboard, clay, or fabric, or through use of painters' surface-rendering techniques. More recently, however, computer-aided design systems with the capacity to model and render surfaces have become increasingly commonplace.[7] The data structure of such a system records vertex coordinates, the associations of edges to vertices, the associations of surfaces to edges, and coefficients specifying edge and surface curvatures. There are operations to insert, delete, reshape, and move surfaces. Usually, as well, there is software to render surface compositions with hidden edge lines removed or with shading (figure 3.19).

To work in any such surface world, and to consider the visual effects that illuminated surfaces produce, is to heed Le Corbusier's admonition that architecture is "the masterly, correct, and magnificent play of masses brought together in light." Translation from a surface world to three-dimensional physical reality usually involves producing specified surface shapes (by such methods as bending, lofting, milling, and so on) and specified surface qualities (by painting, polishing, etc.).

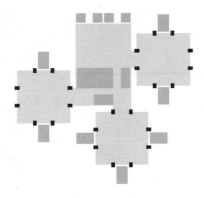

3.16
A floor plan schematically
represented as a collection of closed
colored shapes in the plane

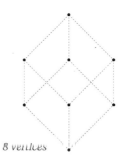

8 vertices

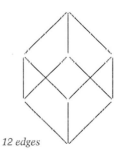

12 edges

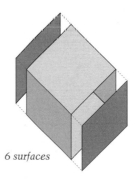

6 surfaces

3.17
Point, line, and surface
boundary models of a cube

DESIGN WORLDS

3.18
Examples of curved surfaces

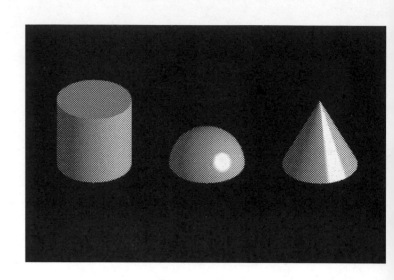

3.19
Hidden-line and shaded-surface
views of a surface composition

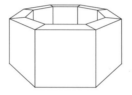

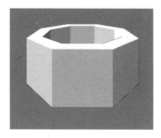

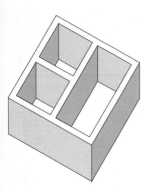

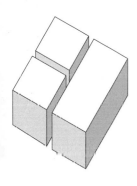

In the same way that lines can bound surfaces, so surfaces can bound closed volumes such as cubes and spheres. In architecture, closed volumes appear both as solid construction elements (columns, beams, etc.) and as bounded voids (rooms, for example). Thus a building can always be understood, in complementary ways, as an assemblage of solids or as an assemblage of voids (figure 3.20).[8]

Just as points bound lines and lines bound polygons, so polygons bound polyhedra. Thus, for example, a cube can be represented as a relationship of surfaces. The three-dimensional volume is bounded by six two-dimensional surfaces, each two-dimensional surface is bounded by four one-dimensional lines, each one-dimensional line is bounded by two zero-dimensional points, and each point is specified by a triple of numbers. (It is straightforward but tedious to write out the corresponding symbolic expression.)

Architects sometimes use three-dimensional volumes directly, as the primitives of composition. Le Corbusier suggested this in a well-known sketch (figure 3.21): he introduced a vocabulary of basic volumetric elements, then showed how these might be assembled into a complex architectural composition. As a child, Frank Lloyd Wright played with Froebel blocks (figure 3.22), and many of his mature architectural compositions clearly emerge from a process of taking simple volumes and intersecting them in space to produce something richer (MacCormac, 1974; figure 3.23).

3.20
The complementarity of solids and voids in a building

3.21
A sketch by Le Corbusier from *Vers une architecture* (1923), showing how architectural compositions can be assembled from simple volumetric solids

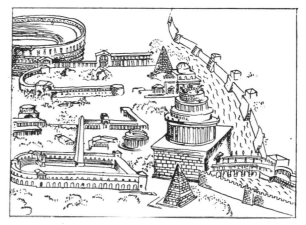

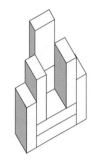

Throne

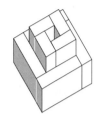

Well

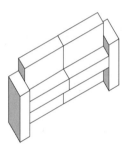

Garden bench

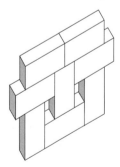

Monument

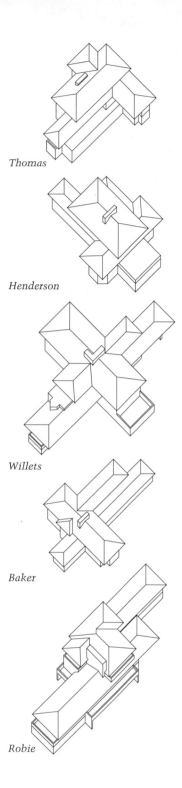

Thomas

Henderson

Willets

Baker

Robie

3.22
Composition of closed volumes:
some forms constructed with
Froebel blocks

3.23
The combination of simple hip roofs
to produce more complex volumes in
Frank Lloyd Wright's prairie houses
(after Koning and Eizenberg, 1981)

THE LOGIC OF ARCHITECTURE

Pixel shape

Line shape

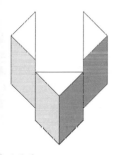

Surface shape

Solid shape

3.24
Shapes are collections of primitives

Wooden or polystyrene building blocks of various sizes and shapes can be used for exploration of volumetric worlds. Brunelleschi reportedly carved large turnips, and modern architects have sometimes (with unfortunate results) turned to sugar cubes. The techniques of stereotomy provide a way to explore three-dimensional volumetric worlds by using drafting instruments to construct projected views.[9] But such media and techniques have obvious disadvantages, and the computer offers an increasingly attractive alternative.

Computer-aided design systems that take closed volumes as their primitives are usually known as solid modelers.[10] They provide vocabularies of closed volumes (boxes, cylinders, spheres, etc.), together with operations for inserting, deleting, reshaping, and positioning them. Advanced solid modelers also provide operations for combining simple shapes to produce more complex shapes.

The data structures of solid modelers are more complex than those of line or surface modelers since they must keep track of more associations: not only of edges to their endpoints and faces to their bounding edges, but also of volumes to their bounding faces. Furthermore, variables describing volume, mass, and material properties may be associated with solids.

Translation from a volumetric world to physical construction is usually more direct and less problematic than it is for the other types of worlds that we have considered. Two-dimensional design worlds have inherent ambiguities of interpretation in the third dimension, line worlds are ambiguous about surface, and surface worlds can be ambiguous about the disposition of solids and voids; but volumetric worlds leave little missing information to be filled in and few inconsistencies to be resolved in the translation process. It is even feasible, in some contexts, to automatically translate solid models into numerical-control cutter paths for production of actual three-dimensional objects (Grayer, 1977).

SHAPES

In any design world a shape may be defined as a collection of primitives—such as a collection of pixels, a collection of straight lines and arcs, a collection of polygons, or a collection of solids (figure 3.24). Any primitive is, itself, a shape. The empty shape contains no primitives.

It is tempting to go a step further and say that a shape is not merely a collection, but a *set* of primitives. Thus primitives become atoms of compositions—definite, discrete parts

Collection of lines

8 primitives

12 primitives

3.25
Alternative decompositions of
a shape into primitives

that retain their identity. Sometimes this is appropriate, and most computer-aided design systems treat shapes as sets of primitives. But it can lead to difficulties. If we assume, for example, that the shape shown in figure 3.25 consists of eight primitive lines, then we are not recognizing the existence of the small central square. On the other hand, if we assume that the shape consists of twelve primitive lines, then we are not recognizing the existence of the two larger rectangles. To avoid this sort of difficulty I shall not insist that shapes are sets of primitives, and I shall use the more general term "collections."[11]

FUNCTIONS AND RELATIONS OF SHAPES

In general, we will be interested not only in shapes themselves, but also in functions and relations of shapes. So the specification of a design world must provide for this.

Consider, for example, the function *length (**Line**)*. We can reasonably say that a design world represents this function when there is some way to evaluate it for any line picked out by a value of the argument **Line**. If a graduated scale is associated with a design world of drafted lines, for example, the designer has a simple way to find the required value. But the scale does not provide a way to evaluate the function *circumference (**Circle**)*: to accomplish this task the designer must be able to measure diameter and must know the formula for calculating circumference as a function of diameter.

In a similar way, a design world represents a relation of shapes if and only if there is some way to determine whether specified shapes are in the relation. In a world of colored cardboard polygons, for example, a designer can determine the truth of assertions such as the following by visual inspection:

color (square, red)
adjacent (square, triangle)

Computer-aided design systems typically represent various relations of shapes in their databases by structures of pointers or by tables in a relational database system (Codd, 1970; Chen, 1976). Thus they can provide facilities for querying the relations of a specified shape or the shapes in a specified relation.

Methods of evaluating functions and relations of shapes in a design world by visual inspection, use of measurement instruments, or execution of computer programs provide a designer with the capacity to make observations about a design. Then, as we shall see in chapter 5, these observations can be combined with other knowledge to yield useful inferences. The practical usefulness of a design world is largely determined by the range of observations that it allows.

SPECIFICATION AND IMPLEMENTATION OF DESIGN WORLDS

The informal characterization of design worlds on which I have relied so far can now be made precise. Let us summarize what must be done to specify a design world.

First, we must create some working space. This can be done by assuming a Cartesian coordinate system or by taking a clean sheet of paper on which to draw.

Next, we must define the primitives from which designs are assembled. The simplest of these objects are points. Usually it is useful to introduce various kinds of lines: straight segments, arcs, conics, splines, fractals, and so on. We might add a variety of closed planar objects: circles, ellipses, polygons, etc. In a three-dimensional design world we might allow curved surfaces, such as spherical, cylindrical, conical, ruled, and spline surfaces. Finally, we might allow closed solids such as spheres, cylinders, cones, and polyhedra.

Once the primitives have been established, we can define shapes as collections of primitives. Any primitive is a shape, and any arrangement of primitives is a shape. To describe such collections we need a binary relation *member* associating primitives with shapes, so that we can construct sentences like:

member (line3, square2)

The next step is to specify the functions and relations of shapes that we will want to be able to evaluate. Often we will be interested in measuring geometric properties such as lengths of lines, areas of closed planar shapes, and volumes of closed solids. We may want to inspect colors and textures of shapes. And we will usually be concerned with various binary relations of shapes—inclusion, adjacency, overlap, disjointness, and so on.

A specification of a design world is made practically useful to a designer by implementing it in some way. The implementation might, for example, employ paper and drawing instruments and rely on the graphic expression of properties, functions, and relations. Grouping of lines into shapes might be expressed by drawing different shapes on different overlays of transparent paper. Special instruments, such as scales, protractors, and planimeters, might be introduced to evaluate certain functions. Alternatively, the implementation might employ wooden or polystyrene blocks, together with cutting and shaping tools. In this case, functions and relations are expressed spatially and by joining (with glue, hinges, pins, etc.). In a computer implementation, geometric primitives are typically stored as records. Grouping of primitives into shapes might be expressed by providing pointers from primitive records to shape records, or by setting up appropriate tables. Functions and relations of shapes might be expressed explicitly by storing tables in a relational database or implicitly by providing procedures that can be executed to return values of functions or lists of shapes in specified relations. In any case, the implementation establishes a physical symbol system. It provides some kind of memory structure in which shape tokens (embodied as cardboard polygons, blocks of wood, pencil lines on paper, or bits in computer memory) can be stored, and some way of interrogating that memory structure to make observations of designs.

AXIOMATIZATION OF DESIGN WORLDS

Once we have established the space, shapes, primitives, properties, functions, and relations that will concern us in a design world, we can go a step further and axiomatize that world. That is, we can state necessary relationships between shapes that exist within it. A world of wooden blocks, for example, is governed by the axiom that two blocks cannot be in the same place at the same time. And a two-dimensional line world manipulated with drafting instruments is governed by the axioms of Euclid's geometry. Sometimes axioms express arbitrary conventions, for example that all dimensions are modular (figure 3.26) or that rectangular cuboids can only be arranged orthogonally to each other (figure 3.27).

When designers work with conventional graphic and physical modeling media, much of the axiomatization of the design world is implicit in the physical properties of the materials and instruments that are used. Similarly, in a computer-aided design system, the axiomatization is usually implicit in the organization of the data structure and the definition of the procedures used to operate on the data structure. In principle, though, the axioms of a design world may be stated formally and rigorously as a set of logical assertions.

3.26
Schematic plan of Children's Home,
Amsterdam, 1958, by Aldo Van Eyck.
A composition in a design world
strictly governed by an axiom of mod-
ularity.

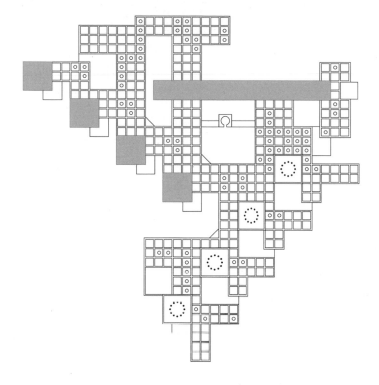

3.27
A composition by Van Doesburg
and Van Eesteren, 1925. De Stijl
designers often worked in design
worlds governed by axioms that
allowed cuboids to intersect but
required them to remain strictly
orthogonal.

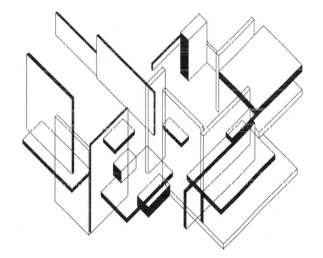

Just as variables have ranges of states so too do complete design worlds. In a world of wooden blocks or cardboard cutouts, a state is simply a particular arrangement of the pieces. In a world of lines drawn on a surface, a state is a particular line pattern. And in a computer-aided design system, a state is a particular binding of values to the variables in the data structure.

A design operation (such as moving a wooden block or inserting a line) changes a design world from one state to another. The set of all states reachable by performing design operations, then, becomes the universe of possibilities that a designer explores (usually very partially) in search of design solutions. This universe may be pictured as a state-action tree (figure 3.28), in which the root is the initial state, internal nodes are possible states (not necessarily unique), and branches are available design operations. By performing manual operations on a drawing or scale model a designer traverses a state-action tree. By quickly executing design operations a computer-aided design system provides a high-speed way to move around in a state-action tree. In practice, state-action trees usually branch luxuriantly and rapidly become inconceivably enormous. But they are always limited to the territory staked out by some set of assumptions about shape primitives and their possible properties and relationships.

A designer's exploration of formal possibilities can be thought of as a path traced through the state-action tree—like Ariadne's thread strung through the Cretan labyrinth. The sequence of nodes along this path describes the evolution of the designer's knowledge about the form of a design proposal, and sometimes this evolution is recorded by preserving sequences of sketches, snapshots of models in progress, or backup copies of a computer-aided design system's database.[12] The tree may not always be traversed in a

3.28
Part of the state-action tree for a design world, and a designer's path through it from the initial state to a final state. Circles represent states and arrows represent available actions.

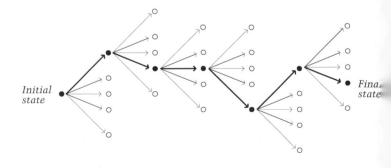

forward direction: sometimes a designer decides that a line of exploration is not fruitful and so retracts some design moves to return to a former node, perhaps even to the root of the tree.

The intermediate states of a design world need not be complete, consistent depictions of the three-dimensional form of a building: designers make extensive use of incomplete and ambiguous sketches and models as they try to discover and pin down formal possibilities. But we require completeness (in some reasonable, practical sense) and consistency of the final state, which we are to understand as a proposal for the form of an actual building.

SUMMARY

In summary, selection of the primitives and axioms for a design world establishes some domain of formal possibilities for a designer to explore, and the designer must be concerned that the domain is appropriate to the task at hand. The process of exploration is supported by implementing the formal specification of the world with graphic media and instruments, with physical modeling media and tools, or as the database and associated procedures of a computer-aided design system.

We have now seen how an architectural discourse can unfold as a sequence of assertions in a critical language or as a sequence of depictions constructed from graphic tokens in a design world. It remains to show how these verbal and graphic discourses are related.

INTERPRETATION OF FIRST-ORDER LOGIC IN DESIGN WORLDS

Critical language

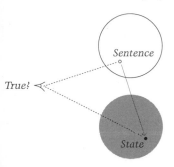

Design world

4.1
Observation of how a critical language relates to the design world

Once we have established a design world and put it into some state, we can make claims about it. These claims may or may not be true of that world, and we need some way of determining whether they are or not. In other words, we need a way to interpret sentences in the design world. We might interpret English sentences, but here we shall concern ourselves with interpretation of sentences in first-order logic, as introduced in chapter 1.

We shall adopt the viewpoint of the observer shown in figure 4.1. On one hand we have a language with a vocabulary (names for shapes and for function and relation symbols) of our choosing and the syntax of first-order logic. The language is the set of sentences which can be constructed with the specified vocabulary according to the specified syntactic rules. On the other hand we have a design world, which has some set of possible states. We assume that the symbols of the sentences refer in some consistent way to the shapes, functions, and relations of the design world. Thus the sentences can be regarded as claims about states of the design world. For any given sentence, and any given state, we can ask: "Is this sentence true or false?" We know the meaning of a sentence if we know what the design world would have to be like in order for the sentence to be true—that is, the conditions under which it is true (or false).

A straightforward (but uninteresting) way to establish the semantics of a critical language, then, is to enumerate all the possible sentences in the language, to enumerate all the possible states of the design world, and to associate a value of true or false with each sentence/state pair in the Cartesian product of the two sets. We can display the result of this in the form of a matrix, as shown in figure 4.2. Rows correspond to states, columns correspond to sentences, and the symbols T or F indicate whether a given sentence is true or false for a given state. By scanning down a column we can find all the states for which a sentence is true—in other words, what it takes to make it true. By scanning across a row we can find all the true sentences about a state—everything that can be truly said about that state.

The pattern of T and F symbols in the matrix establishes an interpretation I of the critical language in the design world. Clearly it is possible to establish many different

	Sentence 1	*Sentence 2*	*Sentence 3*	...
State 1	T	F	T	
State 2	F	F	F	
State 3	T	T	T	
⋮				

4.2
A matrix that establishes an interpretation I of a critical language in a design world

interpretations *I, J, . . .* etc. by deploying *T* and *F* symbols in different patterns within the matrix, and a given sentence may be true under one interpretation and false under another. Usually, though, we are not particularly interested in arbitrary interpretations: we want, instead, to establish some interpretation *I* that accurately expresses our intuitive grasp of the meanings of vocabulary elements and sentences in the language.

Another way to formulate this view of semantics is to say that each sentence is a truth function—that is, a function mapping from states of the design world to the set of values *{T,F}*. A column of the matrix defines this function by explicitly giving its value for every state of the design world.

The obvious problem with this approach is that explicit construction of the matrix is, in any interesting case, impractical. It would be inconceivably enormous. But the approach becomes much more interesing and useful if, instead of defining all the truth functions explicitly, we provide concise and efficient rules for evaluating them. In other words, we specify general truth conditions.

To specify truth conditions we must first specify how vocabulary elements in the critical language refer to the design world, then give rules by which the truth-values of sentences are determined from the truth-values of their parts. This idea was first rigorously and comprehensively developed by the philosopher Alfred Tarski, then carried further by Rudolf Carnap in his extensive writings on semantics. It has become the foundation of the modern theory of model-theoretic semantics.[1] Detailed, rigorous exposition of theory requires introduction of some fairly formidable technical apparatus and use of a highly abstract style of argument that will seem strange and tedious to most designers. This is best left to the standard texts on formal logic and model theory. But the basic idea can be grasped through consideration of a simple example, and this will suffice for our purposes here.

Consider a two-dimensional design world populated by straight lines described by their endpoint coordinates. One possible state of that world is illustrated in figure 4.3. Let us assume that, for referring to individual lines, the critical language has a set of proper names:

{line1, line2, line3 . . . lineN}

The first step, in establishing an interpretation *I*, is to define a one-to-one mapping of proper names to lines; that is, an interpretation of proper names as lines. This can be done by

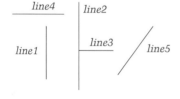

4.3
A design world populated by lines

writing names on lines as shown, or in a data structure by using the names as keys of records storing endpoint coordinates.

Next, consider one-place predicates such as:

vertical **(Line)**
horizontal **(Line)**

The extension of such a predicate in the design world may be defined as the set of lines for which the predicate holds. Thus, in our example, the extension of *vertical* **(Line)** is given by the list of names:

{line1, line2}

and the extension of *horizontal* **(Line)** is given by the list:

{line3, line4}

In this way we interpret one-place predicates as sets of lines. Furthermore, we can write simple rules for determining whether arbitrary lines are in the extensions of these predicates. A line is vertical if and only if its endpoint x-coordinates are the same. And a line is horizontal if and only if its endpoint y-coordinates are the same.

Two-place predicates can be handled in a similar way. Consider, for example:

parallel **(Line, Line)**
perpendicular **(Line, Line)**

The extension of *parallel* **(Line, Line)** in the design world is given by the list of ordered pairs:

{⟨line1, line2⟩, ⟨line2, line1⟩, ⟨line3, line4⟩, ⟨line4, line3⟩}

And the extension of *perpendicular* **(Line, Line)** is given by:

*{⟨line1, line3⟩, ⟨line1, line4⟩, ⟨line2, line3⟩, ⟨line2, line4⟩,
⟨line3, line1⟩, ⟨line3, line2⟩, ⟨line4, line1⟩, ⟨line4, line2⟩}*

The language might include three-place predicates such as:

triangle **(Line, Line, Line)**

And it might include four-place predicates like:

square **(Line, Line, Line, Line)**

In general, an *n*-place predicate is interpreted as a set of ordered *n*-tuples of lines, and we need a rule or procedure for determining whether the predicate holds for an arbitrary *n*-tuple of lines.

To interpret a function symbol we provide a method for evaluating the function. Consider the function:

length **(Line)**

We know how to interpret this if we can place a scale against an arbitrary line and read off its length or if we can perform appropriate arithmetic operations on endpoint coordinates. Then, if we have a way of determining whether one number is less than another, we can interpret sentences of the form:

*lessthan (length (**Line**), length (**Line**))*

The next step is to extend the rules of interpretation to cover not only simple sentences, but also compound sentences formed with the connectives *and*, *or*, *not*. For example, we might want to interpret sentences like:

*parallel (**Line**, **Line**) and not perpendicular (**Line**, **Line**)*

We simply use the standard Boolean laws, as expressed in truth-tables, to determine the truth-values of compound sentences from the truth-values of their constituent sentences.

A further step is to extend the rules to cover sentences with quantifiers, such as:

$\forall$ ***Line*** *(straight (**Line**))*

We can say that this is true if and only if all individual lines in the design world are elements in the extension of the predicate *straight (**Line**)*. Similarly, we can say that the sentence:

$\exists$ ***Line*** *(short (**Line**))*

is true if and only if there is at least one line in the design world that satisfies the predicate *short (**Line**)*. In a computer-aided design system, we might provide for interpretation of quantified assertions by writing procedures to search through lists of line records and perform tests for straightness, shortness, and so on.

A final step would be to extend the rules to cover, in general, *n*-place quantified assertions. This, however, requires introduction of more extensive logical apparatus, so I shall not pursue it here.

A computer game for teaching first-order logic, known as Tarski's World (Barwise and Etchemendy, 1987), strikingly dramatizes this idea of interpretation of first-order logic sentences in a design world. Tarski's World presents two windows (figure 4.4), one for entering sentences in first-order logic and one for manipulating a three-dimensional design world of polyhedra. The world is populated by tetrahedra, cubes, and dodecahedra. There are operations for inserting, deleting, naming, sizing, and moving polyhedra. For describing relations of polyhedra the system provides a selection of

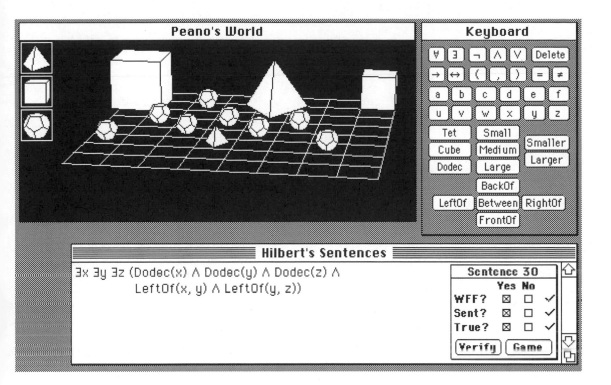

4.4
Tarski's World: first-order logic
sentences are interpreted in a world
of three-dimensional blocks on a grid

relation symbols: *small, medium, large, smaller, larger, leftof, between, rightof, backof,* and *frontof.* The system tests and reports whether sentences are syntactically correct and whether they are currently true or false in the world.[2]

CRITICAL LANGUAGES AND OBSERVATIONS

We can now provisionally define a critical language as a language with an interpretation *I* in a given design world. Thus, for example, Tarski's World has a highly simplified critical language. The vocabulary has names for a few kinds of polyhedra and a few kinds of relations. The syntax is that of first-order logic, and it allows the construction of sentences about polyhedra, their sizes, and their spatial relations. Nothing else can be said.

Different critics may, and sometimes do, have different interpretations of a critical language in a design world; in this case they may mean different things by the same critical assertion. In practice, there is not likely to be much argument about observations like:

adjacent (square, circle)

There is good consensus about what it takes for this to be true. But there is less consensus about assertions like:

graceful (juxtaposition (square, circle))

Critics may differ considerably in their conceptions of the conditions for correct application of the predicate *graceful* to a juxtaposition of shapes.

In this book I shall begin with very simple design worlds and critical languages, then progressively elaborate them to allow for more sophisticated exploration and discourse. For the most part I shall use two-dimensional and three-dimensional worlds of lines, polygons, and polyhedra, and I shall use standard first-order logic for making assertions about those worlds. First-order logic has some strict limitations, but it will suffice for our purposes here.[3]

DESIGN PROBLEMS

So far we have a completely hermetic system. The critical language refers to a design that is bounded and self-contained. This will not do, since design (as opposed to abstract pattern-making in a microworld) is undertaken with the intention of changing the real world. We must extend the framework that has been developed by considering the way in which a design world depicts possible states of the real world.

Under a depiction relation, shapes in the construction world stand for objects in the real world. Furthermore, properties of shapes in the design world stand for properties of objects in the real world, and relations of shapes in the design world stand for relations of shapes in the real world. A triangular pattern of reference thus develops (figure 4.5): sentences in the critical language refer directly to shapes in the design world and indirectly to objects in the real world.

Now we can give precise definition to the intuitive notion of a design problem. In general, a problem exists when you want something but cannot immediately see how to get it: intellectual effort is required to find a solution. More specifically, a design problem exists when you can say what you want in the critical language but cannot immediately see how to produce a state of the design world that depicts what you want. The task is to manipulate the design world to produce such a state and to demonstrate that this state satisfies the predicates of the formulation. There is an implicit subjunctive: if the real world were as depicted in a successful design, then you would actually have what you want.

Critical language

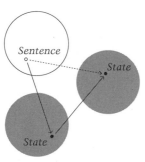

Design world

4.5
A triangular pattern of reference: sentences in the critical language refer directly to states of the design world, states of the design world depict possible states of the real world, so sentences refer *indirectly* to the real world

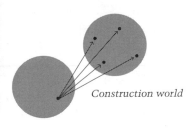

Construction world

Design world

4.6
A state of the design world may
have multiple realizations in the
construction world

CONVENTIONS OF DEPICTION

In order to understand precisely how architectural depiction works we must first dispose of an ontological question. We must ask what exists, in the real world, to be depicted. The usual architect's answer (with which I have no reason to quarrel for our purposes here) is that a site and some repertoire of construction components and materials exists. The possible states that concern us are the possible configurations of components and materials on the site. A design world does not need the capacity to depict anything except the site and an arrangement of components and materials on it.

In different contexts, though, the nature of the site, of the construction repertoire, and of the design problem formulation may require depiction of different sorts of things. To keep this clear, I shall no longer speak of the "real" world but of a "construction world" that encompasses everything that may need to be depicted and reasoned about in the exploration of a particular design problem. This greatly simplifies the problem of establishing a satisfactory system of depiction.

Formally, a depiction of a construction world in a design world is the value of a function or partial function D mapping from physical objects in the construction world to shapes in the design world, from functions in the construction world to functions in the design world, and from relations in the construction world to relations in the design world. In general, D will be a many-to-one mapping: many states of the construction world will have the same depiction in the design world. Conversely, there is a one-to-many mapping (the inverse of D) from states of the design world to states of the construction world (figure 4.6). Any state of the construction world corresponding, under this inverse mapping, to a state of the design world is a realization of that design.

Thus the notion of truth-functional meaning is extended. For any state of the design world and state of the construction world we can ask whether we have a true depiction in the design world. Or, if we want to look at it in the other way, we can ask whether we have a true realization in the construction world. A surveyor might begin with an existing building and attempt to produce a true depiction (an accurate measured drawing, say) in the construction world. Conversely, a contractor might begin with a state of the design world and attempt to produce a true realization (a corresponding actual building) in the construction world. In the case of an unrealized design we will be interested in the question of whether a true realization *can* be produced in the construction world.

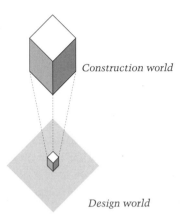

4.7
Three-dimensional scale modeling:
shapes in the design world stand
for similar but larger shapes in the
construction world

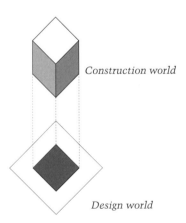

4.8
Plans: two-dimensional shapes in the
design world are parallel projections
of shapes in the construction world

The usual systems of architectural depiction are well
known, but it will be useful to review them briefly here. Any
such system is grounded on rules establishing the references of graphic tokens.[4] In a plan or elevation, for example,
lines usually stand for boundaries—edges of solids, or divisions between different materials. Often there are conventions under which colors and patterns stand for materials.
And, in a plumbing or electrical layout drawing, various special symbols (which need not "look like" their referents) may
indicate different types of fixtures. (In chapter 6 I shall
examine these kinds of rules more closely).

Secondly, in order to convey spatial relationships, there
must be some function mapping from coordinates of objects
in the construction world to coordinates of corresponding
graphic tokens in the design world. The techniques of scale
modeling, plan, elevation, and section drafting, axonometric
projection, and perspective rendering employ different functions of this sort.[5]

For example, the simplest (and probably the most ancient)
of depiction techniques is to make, in the design world, a
scaled-down three-dimensional model of the proposed building in the construction world (figure 4.7). Technically, the
depiction function D becomes a similarity transformation
from points in the construction world to points in the design
world: three-dimensional shapes in the design world stand
for similar but larger shapes in the construction world.

A second standard technique is to compose plans,
elevations, and sections in the design world. In this case,
two-dimensional shapes in the design world are parallel projections of three-dimensional shapes in the construction
world[6] (figure 4.8).

Axonometric projections generalize this principle (figure
4.9). Under the conventions of plan, elevation, and section
drawing we usually position the projection plane so as to
minimize foreshortening of shapes, but in an axonometric
we rotate the projection plane so that perpendicular lines and
surfaces can be shown—at the cost of producing some foreshortening. Technically, shapes in the design world become
affine transformations of shapes in the construction world.

Yet another convention, which was known to the Romans
and then rediscovered in Renaissance Italy, is to replace
parallel projection by perspective projection. The essential
difference between parallel and perspective projection is
illustrated in figure 4.10: in parallel projection the projection
rays are imagined to be parallel (like rays of sunlight casting
shadows), while in perspective projection they are imagined

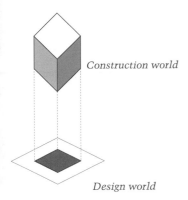

Construction world

Design world

4.9
Foreshortening of shapes in
axonometric due to the rotation
of the projection plane

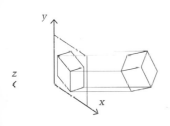

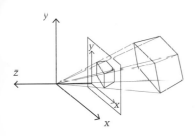

4.10
Comparison of parallel and
perspective projections

to diverge from the viewer's eye. From an arithmetic view-point (as when these projections are calculated in a computer graphics system), we can say that a parallel projection on the xy picture plane is made simply by discarding the z (depth) coordinates, while a perspective projection is made by dividing by the z coordinates, so that shapes are scaled down in proportion to their depth back from the xy picture plane. This division has the effect of encoding additional depth information in the drawing at the cost of further shape distortion: shapes in the design world are now perspective transformations of shapes in the construction world.

Figure 4.10 also shows one of the reasons why mappings from the design world to the construction world are, in general, one-to-many instead of one-to-one: any point on the picture plane corresponds to many points in the construction world along the projection ray passing through it. Thus different three-dimensional arrangements in the construction world may collapse onto the same image in the picture plane (figure 4.11). Architects often work with such ambiguous views; this can be a strategy for concentrating on certain design issues and relationships while postponing consideration of others. Later, as more design decisions are made, the depiction may be disambiguated—for example, by providing a wall section to clarify the depth relationships in an elevation.

Sometimes a designer wishes to specify the connectivity, but not the precise sizes and shapes, of elements in a composition. An architect might, for example, draw a rough "bubble diagram" of a floor plan, and an electrical engineer might produce an undimensioned network diagram. In this case, shapes in the design world become nonlinear continuous transformations of shapes in the construction world.

Figure 4.12 shows how the standard depiction conventions form a hierarchy according to the generality of the transformations involved. If full-scale, three-dimensional mock-ups are composed in the design world, then shapes in the design world are isometries of shapes in the construction world. If three-dimensional scale models or plans and elevations are composed, then shapes in the design world are similar to shapes in the construction world. When axonometrics are drawn, we can say that shapes in the design world have affinity to shapes in the construction world; and when perspectives are drawn, we can say only that the shapes in the design world are linearly related to shapes in the construction world. Other conventions of depiction, such as those

Similarity

Affinity

Linearity

Nonlinearity

4.11
An Ames room demonstrates that
different architectural compositions may collapse onto the same
perspective image

4.12
Transformations of a square
under different depiction
conventions

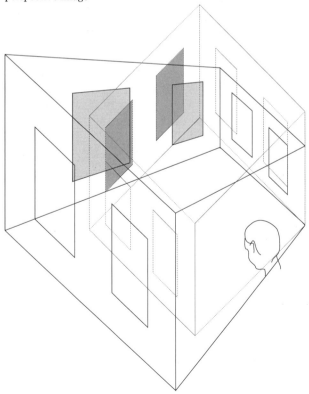

followed by cubist painters, may involve nonlinear transformations.

A depiction (like a verbal description) is usually incomplete: it does not show everything that *could* be shown. A small-scale sketch plan might depict walls by single lines, thus not showing their thickness. Plans do not show height relationships, and elevations do not show depth relationships. Line drawings do not show colors and textures. Drawing, as has often been remarked, is the art of knowing what to leave out.

ANNOTATIONS

An architectural drawing may consist not only of graphic tokens specifying shapes and positions of objects, but also textual annotations associated with the graphic tokens. These annotations may serve to fix reference more precisely, as when some plumbing fixture symbol is supplemented with a serial number from a manufacturer's catalogue. They may also specify material properties, as when a graphic token depicting a wall is labeled "brick" or "concrete." (Colors and patterns may be used to encode the same information if appropriate coding conventions exist.)

Sometimes annotations are physically separated from a drawing but logically connected to it by means of some cross-referencing scheme. Typically, for example, an architectural design is expressed jointly by a set of plan and elevation drawings and a set of cross-referenced text documents (specifications, door and window schedules, and so on).

THE DATABASES OF COMPUTER-AIDED DESIGN SYSTEMS

When a computer-aided design system is used (in place of conventional drawings or scale models), the pattern of reference becomes even more complex: the number of worlds to consider grows from three to four, and the interpretation links grow from three to six. The structure of the situation is diagrammed in figure 4.13. The database of the computer-aided design system contains records (or other structures) storing symbolic descriptions of physical components and assemblies in the construction world. In the graphic interface of the computer-aided design system this information is interpreted as a graphic display depicting those components and assemblies. An expression in the critical language may

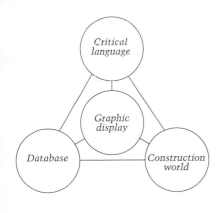

4.13
Paths of reference in computer-aided design

refer directly to graphic tokens in the display, indirectly to the database records from which the display is generated, and even more indirectly to the components and assemblies in the construction world described by those records.

Each of these worlds has an associated vocabulary and syntax. In the construction world there is some vocabulary of physical components, which can be put together in compositions in certain ways. In the database there are records of various types, which can be put together in files, arrays, lists, and so on. In the graphic display there are pixels, lines, and polygons, which can be put together in graphic compositions. And finally, in the critical language, there are object names, predicate symbols, and function symbols, which can be put together in sentences.

Conventions of interpretation define mappings between these worlds. We can, for example, consider the conventions for interpretation of the critical language in the graphic display, in the underlying database, or in the construction world that the database represents. We can consider how the design encoded in the database is interpreted as a graphic display or realized as a physical construction. And we can consider how graphic displays depict the construction world. These conventions of vocabulary and syntax in the various worlds, and for mapping between worlds, define a framework within which design reasoning takes place.

EVALUATION OF CONSTRUCTION WORLD PREDICATES

Given such a framework of conventions, a critic may want to make observations not only about the formal properties of the design itself, but also about the state of affairs that *would* result if the design *were* to be executed. The building that is depicted might, for example, be buildable or unbuildable, economical or expensive, structurally adequate or inadequate. To provide for this, the critical language must be extended by addition of appropriate predicate and function symbols, and the meanings of these must be established by specification of truth conditions.

4.14
Flow of data in an integrated computer-aided design system that automatically determines whether a design requirement has been satisfied

Predicate

Project database → Analysis function → Verification procedure → true or false

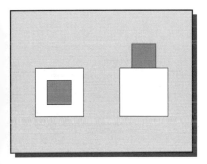

color (bigcube, white)
color (smallcube, gray)
above (smallcube, bigcube)
below (bigcube, smallcube)

Critical language window

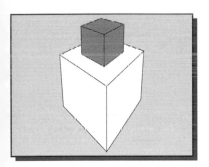

Design world window

Construction world window

4.15
Windows into different domains

Since the time of Galileo the standard way to specify such truth conditions has been to provide formulae and procedures for calculating the values of functions, or for determining whether predicates are satisfied, from information recorded in the design world. These formulae and procedures encode knowledge about the construction world. Let us imagine that a designer has drawn a rectangular cantilever beam in elevation and cross section and specified its material. The question is whether this beam is strong enough to support the loads to which it will be subjected. In his *Dialogues Concerning Two New Sciences* (1632) Galileo showed how to calculate the strength of a cantilever beam as a function of its section, length, and material properties, and thus how to evaluate the predicate *strong enough*. The succeeding centuries have seen the development of an enormous repertoire of techniques, based on classical physics and theorems of analysis and calculus, for calculating various measures of technical performance as functions of geometric and material properties (Cowan, 1977).

Today these calculations are usually executed by computer. In "integrated" computer-aided design systems, values for input variables of analysis routines are extracted directly from the database that represents the design[7] (figure 4.14). For example, there might be routines to perform area take offs, cost analyses, structural analyses, and thermal analyses. The values that they output can be used in automatic verification procedures that report whether or not specified design requirements are satisfied.

SUMMARY

We have now seen how expressions in critical languages are interpreted in design worlds and how designs in design worlds are realized in construction worlds. (The relationships among these three domains can be summarized by imagining "windows" into each one, as shown in figure 4.15.) Design problems are formulated by specifying, in the critical language, predicates to be satisfied. The designer's basic task, then, is to find a state of the design world which depicts a state of the construction world satisfying the predicates. The critic's basic task is to identify predicates left unsatisfied by the designer's proposal. And the designer can respond to criticism by adapting the proposal to satisfy those predicates.

KNOWLEDGE BASES ABOUT CONSTRUCTION WORLDS

Really interesting critics do not confine themselves to obvious, direct observations and algorithmic analyses of a design. They go a step further and combine their observations with facts and rules about the construction world to derive comments that are not self-evident and that we may take to be surprising and insightful. This process of critical inference is schematically diagrammed in figure 5.1.

The sum total of what a critic knows about a construction world is that critic's knowledge base. Its content might be expressed in many different formats—as English sentences, diagrams, code of computer programs, and so on—but it will be convenient for our purposes here to think of it as a set of declarative sentences in the syntax of first-order logic. This is not unrealistic, since first-order logic is sufficiently powerful to capture a great deal of useful, nontrivial design knowledge.[1] Furthermore, there is available a well-developed theory of resolution in first-order logic; that is, determination that a statement is consistent with or derivable from another set of statements (Robinson, 1965). This considerably facilitates reasoning with knowledge represented in first-order logic.[2]

Some critics operate with large knowledge bases and some with small ones. Some knowledge bases contain accurate knowledge of a construction world, while others may be incomplete and inaccurate. Closed-minded critics refuse to alter their knowledge bases, whereas open-minded critics are willing to add and retract facts and rules. Some take their knowledge to be categorical, and others admit of degrees of uncertainty. At any moment, though, the current knowledge base provides the foundation for making and justifying critical comments.

In order for a critic to make useful comments about a design, the critic's conceptualization of the construction world (which forms the basis for expression of facts and rules about that world) and the designer's conceptualization (which forms the basis for depiction) must be similar. That is, the critic must have facts and rules about the objects and relationships that the designer depicts. This permits the critic to make observations of the design world, then to draw inferences from them. Different kinds of definition allow

5.1

Derivation of critical comments from
observations of a design proposal and
facts and rules about the construction
world

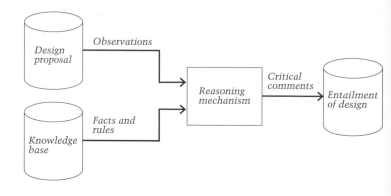

different kinds of observations and therefore different inferences: a plan does not provoke the same comments as a
section.

The set of true assertions about a design that can be
derived from observations of it, together with the facts and
rules in some critical knowledge base, by the application of a
reasoning mechanism, constitute that design's entailment.
Generally a design will entail economic, social, and cultural
consequences of interest. It is the critic's task to explore the
entailment. An epistemological problem must, however, be
faced here. In practice, the entailment of any design will
tend to be very large and complex. How does the critic focus
on relevant implications and ignore the vast number of irrelevant ones (for example, that painting the walls green will
not cause a neighboring building to explode)? This is an
aspect of the well-known "frame problem" in artificial intelligence (Dennett, 1984). There is considerable anecdotal evidence to suggest that critics usually deal with it by coming
to their task with an agenda of issues to be pursued.
Consequently, designers must be on the alert for critical
agendas that are too narrow or otherwise inappropriate.

In general, an effective critic must know what to look for
in a design, bring an adequate knowledge base and an appropriate agenda to bear, and apply sound, efficient reasoning
strategies to derive useful comments.[3]

AXIOMS, FACTS, AND RULES

It is an ancient idea (going back at least to Euclid) that a
knowledge base about some topic can usefully be structured
as a collection of axioms, facts, and rules. We can think of
the axioms as fundamental assumptions or basic definitions,
such as those set forth at the beginning of Euclid's geometry.

We then expect the corpus of facts to be consistent with these axioms and derivable from them through the application of rules. Facts can be proved by directly or indirectly deriving them from the axioms, or they can be disproved by demonstrating inconsistency with an axiom. This became the paradigm for Newton's mechanics and for Spinoza's axiomatized metaphysics. More recently it has served as the foundation for the development of "knowledge-based" computer systems that perform reasoning in various specialized domains.

The axioms, facts, and rules of an adequate knowledge base for architectural criticism are extensive. They include those of physical geometry and classical physics (since a critic must be concerned with basic feasibility), of relevant areas of economics (since a critic must be concerned with cost and financial feasibility), of aspects of the social sciences (since a critic must be concerned with the relations of buildings to human behavior patterns), and of the relevant cultural framework. Thus the education of an architect involves not only development of facility in manipulation of design worlds, but also development of a sufficiently extensive knowledge base to allow derivation of an adequate picture of what those proposals entail.

INFERENCE

The mechanism by which critical comments are produced can be described as one of inference—deriving conclusions from premises. Each step in a logically sound inference process must be sanctioned by one of the rules of inference that logic provides.[4] Rules of inference associate sentence patterns called conditions with sentence patterns called conclusions. Whenever we have sentences that match the conditions, we can infer sentences that match the conclusions.

A particular type of compound sentence called an implication plays a crucial role in most inference processes. Implications are formed with the material conditional symbol, which is written → and pronounced "if . . . then." The following, for example, is an implication:

below (column, beam) → *supports (column, beam)*

This asserts, "*If* the column is below the beam *then* the column supports the beam." Whenever the antecedent (on the left) is true, the consequent (on the right) is true.

Implications are used as premises in inference according to the rule of *modus ponens* (which, in fact, follows from the definition of "implies"), for example:

premise 1	*below (column, beam) →*
	supports (column, beam)
premise 2	*below (column, beam)*
conclusion	*supports (column, beam)*

They are also used in inference according to the reverse rule of *modus tolens*, for example:

premise 1	*below (column, beam) →*
	supports (column, beam)
premise 2	*not supports (column, beam)*
conclusion	*not below (column, beam)*

Bidirectional implications play a closely related role. These are sentences formed with the material biconditional symbol, which is written ↔ and pronounced "if and only if ... then." The following is a bidirectional implication:

below (column, beam) ↔ above (beam, column)

This asserts, "If and only if the column is below the beam, then the beam is above the column." This can be understood as an abbreviation for:

below (column, beam) → above (beam, column) and
above (beam, column) → below (column, beam)

In a bidirectional implication the sentences on the left and right are said to be equivalent. Whenever one is true the other is true. And whenever one is false the other is false.

One rule of inference that does not involve implications is called elimination. This applies to conjunctions, for example as follows:

premise	*stone (column) and round (column)*
conclusion 1	*stone (column)*
conclusion 2	*round (column)*

Conversely, the rule of introduction licenses us to reason:

premise 1	*stone (column)*
premise 2	*round (column)*
conclusion	*stone (column) and round (column)*

Frequently we want to reason from the general to the particular by using the rule of universal instantiation, for example:

premise 1	$\forall$ *X polyhedron (X)*
premise 2	*X = column*
conclusion	*polyhedron (column)*

Similarly, we can replace variables in existentially quantified sentences according to the rule of existential instantiation, but this introduces some technical complexities that we will not pursue here.

If we restrict ourselves to certain simplified forms of expression (as is the practice, for example, in Prolog programming[5]), we can omit explicit quantification in implications containing variables to yield concisely stated general rules, for example:

*below (**X**, beam) → supports (**X**, beam)*

This says that anything below the beam supports the beam—a fact about all the objects in the universe of discourse. According to the rule of universal instantiation we can, by instantiating **X** to suitable values, derive facts such as:

below (column, beam) → supports (column, beam)
below (wall, beam) → supports (wall, beam)
below (bracket, beam) → supports (bracket, beam)

In other words, a rule implicitly encodes a set of facts, and any fact in this set can be made explicit by instantiation.

In general, critics take as their premises observations of the design and facts and rules about the construction world and derive their conclusions through a multistep process—by constructing chains of inference from intermediate conclusion to intermediate conclusion and eventually to the final conclusion. Some critic might, for example, work by the rules:

*triangle (**Shape**) → dynamic (**Shape**)*
*dynamic (**Shape**) and color (**Shape**, pink) →*
*postmodern (**Shape**)*

Now, when he detects a three-sided pink polygon in a design world, he can conclude from the first rule that this shape is dynamic, and from the second rule he can derive the critical conclusion that the shape is postmodern.

FORWARD-CHAINING AND BACKWARD-CHAINING

Reasoning can proceed in two directions. A critic might, for example, begin with a set of observations and, by constructing chains of inferences, attempt to derive a useful set of conclusions: this is called forward-chaining inference (Davis and King, 1977). Alternatively, a critic might state a fact as a hypothesis and attempt to prove or disprove it: this is called backward-chaining inference.

Typically, at any step in such a process, there are several (perhaps many) possible inferences to consider. So just as design worlds have associated state-action trees, so do critics. In this case, though, each state is a state of the critic's working memory (which we take to be a collection of sentences), and each branch is a legal inference. Strategies for efficiently finding paths through those trees to useful conclusions are known as inference procedures.

Procedures for both forward-chaining and backward-chaining inference may be executed manually. Alternatively, it is now possible to build efficient automatic inference engines. A "knowledge-based" or "expert" computer system consists, essentially, of a knowledge base of facts and rules about some domain of interest, together with an inference engine that can be applied to the knowledge base.[6] Knowledge-based systems that provide design criticism began to appear in the 1980s and seem certain to be of increasing practical importance.[7]

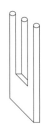

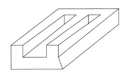

5.2
Drawings of unrealizable "nonsense figures"

CONSISTENT, FEASIBLE, AND GOOD DESIGNS

A basic task of critical inference is to establish whether or not a given design proposal makes consistent sense. A proposal is nonsensical if contradictory facts can be derived from observations of it. Some well-known examples of such proposals are illustrated in figure 5.2: observations of these lead to inconsistent conclusions about their three-dimensional geometry. If a design can be shown to be nonsensical, then there is no further entailment to consider.

A design may be geometrically consistent but unrealizable. In a strong sense, a proposal is unrealizable if it can be shown to be inconsistent with physical laws. At best, we can imagine its realization in a construction world governed by physical laws that are different from those of the world in which we live. In a weaker sense, a proposal may be technologically or economically unrealizable in a particular construction world (the necessary materials and processes may not be available, or may cost too much), but realizable at some other time or place. For example, modern architects can assume that steel-framed highrise buildings are realizable, but ancient Greek architects could not. Finally, realizability may be socially or historically contingent. We might see that a proposal would be realizable if social conditions were different, or would have been realizable had history taken a different course.

Among design proposals that can be shown to be realizable, a critic will usually be interested in discriminating the good from the bad. This requires knowledge of rules of valuation—that is, conditions for correct application of predicates such as *commodious* and *delightful*. In different contexts, at different moments, critics may operate under different rules

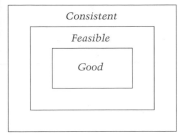

5.3
Nested classes of design proposals

of valuation, thus yielding different conclusions as to whether a design proposal is good or bad.

In general, then, there will be many possible construction worlds, each governed by a set of axioms and described by a corpus of facts and rules. Interpretation of critical comments about consistency, feasibility, and quality of designs is a matter of possible-world semantics.[8] Some critical comments (tautologies) may be true in all construction worlds, others may be true in some but not all construction worlds, and others (contradictions) may be true in no construction worlds.

However we relate critical comments to construction worlds, these comments divide design proposals that are produced for consideration into nested classes, as shown in figure 5.3. The designer's problem is to produce proposals that are consistent, feasible, and good.

COMPUTATIONAL EFFICIENCY

In summary, a design problem is represented by predicates stated in a critical language, a design world which depicts some construction world, a knowledge base about that construction world, and procedures for deriving inferences. Two such representations are informationally equivalent if all the information in the one is also inferable from the other, and vice versa (Simon, 1978). In other words, each could be constructed from the information in the other.

Informationally equivalent representations are not necessarily computationally equivalent, however: one may be more efficient than the other. According to a definition cogently stated by Larkin and Simon (1987): "Two representations are computationally equivalent if they are informationally equivalent and, in addition, any inference that can be drawn easily and quickly from the information given explicitly in the one can also be drawn easily and quickly from the information given explicitly in the other, and vice versa." In general, computational efficiency depends on how the information describing design requirements, the design, and the construction world is organized in a data structure, and on the procedures that are available for operating on the data structure.

A designer must find a design problem representation of sufficient computational efficiency to allow the problem to be solved within practical time and resource limits. The traditional approach to this has been to represent design requirements in the form of a written list (the program, or brief), to represent the design primarily by means of drawings, and to represent the construction world by means of facts and rules stored in reference books and in the designer's head. Historically, developments in the technology of design have mostly been directed at improving on the computational efficiency of this approach. First, formalized procedures were developed for evaluating functions used in reasoning about cost and performance. Next, calculators and computers were used to execute these procedures more efficiently. More recently, it has become common to model designs in the databases of computer-aided design systems rather than in the form of drawings on paper and to gain further efficiency by integrating cost- and technical-analysis procedures with these databases. And more recently still, there has been growing interest in the application of general-purpose automatic inference techniques in design reasoning.

CAVEAT: THE MONOTONICITY ASSUMPTION

The theory that I have outlined here commits us to the so-called monotonicity assumption.[9] We must assume that the addition of new facts and rules to the critical knowledge base does not falsify any fact already in the knowledge base. Or, to put this in another way, the knowledge base cannot accept any new fact or rule if it contradicts something already known. This is not an entirely satisfactory description of human critics, who undoubtedly have the ability to accept and sort out new and perhaps contradictory information.

Consider, for example, a critic who reasons about a design as follows:

observation	*possesses (room, window)*
rule	*possesses (room, window) →*
	ventilated (room)
conclusion	*ventilated (room)*

But now the critic makes another observation:

observation	*inoperable (window)*

This leads to the revised conclusion:

conclusion	*not ventilated (room)*

Then a third observation leads, by a different route, back to the original conclusion:

observation	*airconditioned (room)*
rule	*airconditioned (room) →*
	ventilated (room)
conclusion	*ventilated (room)*

Such nonmonotonic reasoning is very important, since critics often seek to observe designs in original ways, to bring new facts about them to light, to uncover contradictions, and to challenge beliefs. Furthermore, the problem is fundamental, since monotonicity follows directly from the fundamental properties of traditional first-order logic. So it seems likely that development of a more generally satisfactory theory of design reasoning will await the outcome of current attempts to find useful formalizations of nonmonotonic modes of reasoning.

DESIGN GAMES

According to the view of design reasoning I have now laid out, the roles of designer and critic (which may, of course, be combined in one person) are symmetrical. A critic may stake some claims expressed as sentences in the critical language, setting the designer the task of satisfying them by manipulating the design world. Conversely, the designer may produce a proposal expressed as a state of the design world, setting the critic the task of deriving conclusions that establish whether or not it is satisfactory and why. The initiative may be on either side, or proposals and goals may evolve together.

Design, then, is a complex game in which exploration of formal possibilities in some world and critical inference from some knowledge base proceed in parallel and eventually reach a reconciliation. There is also a meta-game, in which the axiomatization of the design world, the rules for interpreting the critical language in that world, the conventions of depiction of the construction world, and the contents of the critic's knowledge base are established.

A logician might ask why it is necessary to separate the facts depicted in the design world from those in the critic's knowledge base (and not be satisfied with the answer that designers and critics have always done this). After all, a design might be regarded simply as a collection of facts about building form. The data structure of a computer-aided design system expresses these facts symbolically. It might even express them as sentences of first-order logic—just like the critic's assertions.

One part of the answer is that the separation provides conceptual clarity by resolving an ancient paradox. In the *Meno*, Plato had his protagonist formulate this paradox for Socrates:

And how will you inquire, Socrates, into that which you do not know? What will you put forth as the subject of inquiry? And if you find what you want, how will you ever know that this is what you did not know?

More specifically, how do we know what to look for when we search for the solution to a design problem? And how do we know when we have found a solution? If we carefully distinguish between the graphic design world and the critic's verbal assertions, we can reply that we are looking for a state of the design world. And we will know when we have found the sought-after state because we will be able to demonstrate that it satisfies predicates stated in the critical language. A second part of the answer is that we can gain computational efficiency: some of the inference processes required in design are best supported by graphic depictions and some are best supported by collections of verbally expressed facts and rules.[10] So, *pace* Mies van der Rohe, designers must draw *and* talk.

THE EXPRESSIVENESS OF CRITICAL LANGUAGES

A useful critical language must have sufficient expressive power to capture relevant knowledge of the construction world that is under consideration and to allow complete and precise formulation of the requirements for solution of a design problem—that is, the predicates that the designer seeks to satisfy by manipulating the design world. The vocabulary of common nouns provided by a critical language plays a crucial role in this. Let us consider how such a vocabulary might be established.

INDIVIDUALS, CLASSES, AND INHERITANCE

In the early decades of this century many artists and designers—Constructivists, Suprematists, members of the de Stijl group, and others—were interested in worlds of abstract geometric elements and in exploration of formal relations in these worlds. Related approaches to design education, such as that pursued in the famous Bauhaus introductory course, also emphasized formal relations of abstract elements. When critical discourse is cast purely in these terms, however, it soon becomes strained and tedious. Consider, for example, the design by Peter Eisenman shown in figures 6.1 and 6.2, and the following commentary (Eisenman, 1982)—in which the only element recognized is an el form and the only predicates used are "equal width," "same shape," "inverted," "deeper than," and "similar":

In an orthogonal or frontal reading of the two north quadrants, the el forms can be read as equal, they can be called A-A, a notation about the equality of the width of both elements, or 0-0, a notation about the equality of their width in relationship to a neutral base condition. If reading occurs from the west, the el forms are seen to be the same size and shape, and although they are in inverted positions with respect to each other, they can also be given an A-A notation (or 0-0 as a base condition). However, from the northwest corner, it is obvious that the horizontal element of the north face is deeper than the horizontal element of the west face of the quadrant. This, then, gives the north face a (+) notation and the west face a (-) or (0) notation in relation to the north face; or, conversely, the north face can be seen as (0), in which case the west face becomes (-). At the same time, when viewed from the northeast corner, the north and east faces appear similar, and they both can be given a (+) or (0) notation. The same shifting condition is evident in the relative sizes (widths) of both the vertical and horizontal elements of these elevations.

6.1
Peter Eisenman, House X, Scheme F

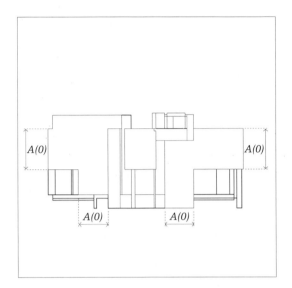

North elevation

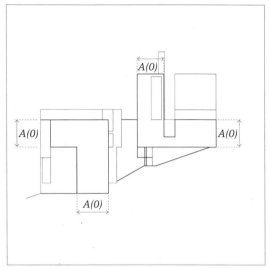

West elevation

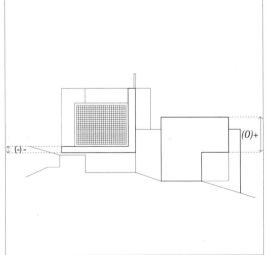

East elevation

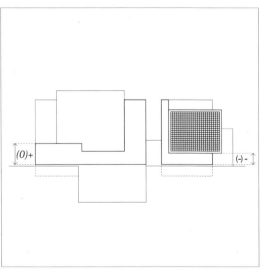

South elevation

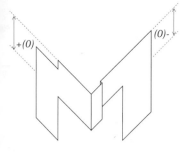

Northwest corner

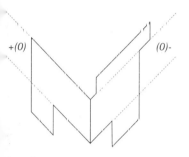

Northeast corner

6.2
Axonometric diagrams of House X corners

This sort of close formal analysis is not entirely unilluminating, but something, clearly, is missing (no doubt deliberately excluded, in this case, for polemical purposes).

What is eschewed as far as possible, in all these cases, is the interpretive step of classifying the elements under consideration in conventional ways. We are not supposed to ask of an element "What *is* it?"

Some definitions are needed to make this clear. When we speak of the *Parthenon, Plato*, or the *Queen Mary*, we employ proper nouns to refer to individual objects. But when we speak of *temples, philosophers*, and *ships*, we employ common nouns to refer to classes of objects. We can specify class membership by writing English sentences:

The Parthenon is a temple.
Plato is a philosopher.
The Queen Mary is a ship.

And we can do the same in logical notation:

temple (Parthenon)
philosopher (Plato)
ship (QueenMary)

In architectural discourse we frequently use common nouns such as *column, beam, wall, floor, door*, and *window* when speaking of construction elements. Similarly, we use common nouns like *bedroom* and *kitchen* when speaking of spaces and common nouns like *house* and *temple* when speaking of complete buildings.

Classes and common nouns are useful because they allow us to structure our knowledge not just as facts about individuals, but also as generalizations about entire classes. We might take it as a fact, for example, that philosophers are clever. Thus we can write the rule:

philosopher (X) → clever (X)

Thus if **X** is Plato, we can infer that Plato is clever. Similarly, the rule:

ship (X) → floats (X)

allows us to infer from the fact that the Queen Mary is a ship the fact that the Queen Mary floats. Technically, these individuals *inherit*[1] certain properties by virtue of their class membership.

When we label a shape in a design world with a common noun such as *column* or *kitchen* we are saying that we want that shape to represent a member of a class. If we know some facts about the class, then this knowledge can enter into the critical discourse, direct design intentions, and guide design explorations. But if we want to break free from preconceptions, or avoid well-trodden paths of critical discourse, then we must confine ourselves to labels such as *square* or *el-shape* that come very lightly freighted with architectural knowledge.

TYPES AND INSTANCES

What classes do we want to recognize in conceptualizations of buildings and critical discourse about them? How should we characterize and label members of classes? What properties do we want design elements to inherit by virtue of class membership? The approach that I shall take to answering these questions is based upon a distinction originally drawn by the American philosopher C. S. Peirce (1931) between types of objects and tokens or instances.[2] Briefly, a token instantiates or is an instance of a type. Thus, for example, the word *architecture* instantiates the letter *r* twice, the letter *a* once, and contains no token that instantiates the letter *z*. Similarly, the Doric column is instantiated repeatedly in the Parthenon. Tokens are unique physical entities that we find located in a particular place at a particular time. Tokens may be of the same type by virtue of having something, for example, shape, in common.[3] Each such token conforms to the type that it instantiates.

Hence complex constructions of various kinds may be understood as assemblages of instances drawn from some specified set, or vocabulary, of simpler types of objects. For example, a word instantiates various characters from an alphabet, a sentence instantiates various words from the vocabulary of a language, and a simple melody instantiates various notes from a scale. Often we can recognize that a physical system instantiates various types of artifacts. And, most relevant to our concerns here, a building instantiates various recognizable types of architectural elements (columns, beams, walls, etc.). A drawing of that building instantiates various types of abstract shapes (such as squares, circles, and triangles), and the given conventions of depiction establish some mapping between shape tokens in the design world and physical instances in the construction world.

ESSENTIAL AND ACCIDENTAL PROPERTIES

A further distinction following from this concept of type is that between essential and accidental properties of an object. (The word "accidental" is here used in a technical sense, in which it carries no pejorative connotations.) Essential

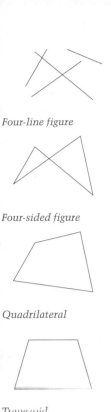

Four-line figure

Four-sided figure

Quadrilateral

Trapezoid

Parallelogram

Rectangle

Square

6.3
A typical hierarchy of subtypes
defined by successively more
restrictive definitions

properties are those that it shares with others of its type.[4] Accidental properties, on the other hand, may vary from instance to instance within a type. For example, we might choose to say that bilateral symmetry is an essential property of a classical portico, but that classical porticos may have various different colors. Thus the bilateral symmetry of the portico of the Parthenon is an essential property, while its white color is an accidental property. If it were to be painted in bright colors (as indeed it once was), we would still regard it as a classical portico. But if it were altered in some way that destroyed the bilateral symmetry (say the removal of the last three columns on one side), then we would no longer regard it as a classical portico. The essence of being a classical portico would not be preserved under such an operation.

Another way to put this point is to note that formation of a type is an act of abstraction; we identify what is the same about all members of some class of objects and disregard what varies. The invariants, then, are the essential properties. Thus, for example, we see that all classical porticos are bilaterally symmetrical but that the colors of classical porticos vary from instance to instance.

Types may be divided into subtypes by specifying additional essential properties. Thus, for example, we might divide classical porticos into Doric, Ionic, and Corinthian subtypes. Conversely, we may generalize type definitions by deleting properties, as when we generalize from squares to rectangles, and from rectangles to quadrilaterals. In general, then, we may construct hierarchies of subtypes within subtypes (figure 6.3). Where such a hierarchy spans a universe of discourse, it provides a comprehensive classification scheme for elements in that universe. Such schemes are often referred to as typologies.

These technical definitions of type and essence are more precise than, but reasonably consistent with, the influential early definition of architectural type that was given by Quatremère de Quincy in his *Dictionnaire historique d'architecture* (1832). Quatremère took great pains to distinguish between concrete models, to be replicated "exactly," and types, regarded as "more or less vague" intellectual constructs, after which one can "conceive works which do not resemble each other." However, works that conform to a type all have some kind of common "elementary principle." It does not seem to be stretching things too far to identify Quatremère's "elementary principle" with the essence of a type and to identify his lack of "resemblance" with variation in accidental properties.

TYPES AND VOCABULARIES

If we grant the validity and usefulness of the essential/accidental distinction, there remains the question of the basis upon which it should be put. Conflicting positions have been advanced on this point; some philosophers argue that essences are absolute, while others take them to be relative.

The former position is that essences are, in some sense, given and unchanging. Thus revelation of the essence of an object is akin to revelation of a scientific or mathematical truth. Indeed the task of science, on this view, is to cut through superficialities and errors to reveal the *real* essences of things, and it is generally held that the successes of modern science are bringing it closer to this goal. Thus, for example, modern science has a better definition of what it is to be a whale or a lemon or a man than did ancient science.

A closely related view lies at the root of classical attitudes toward artistic form; the artist's task is taken to be the elimination of accidents and imperfections in order to reveal an object's essence. To put this another way, an artist represents universals rather than depicts particulars. For example, Sir Joshua Reynolds stated forcefully, in the fourth of his *Discourses on Art* (1771), that "perfect form is produced by leaving out particularities and retaining only general ideas." He developed his point in considerable detail, suggesting, for example, that the painter should not "debase his conceptions with minute attention to the discriminations of Drapery." Instead, he should abstract and generalize, so that "the cloathing is neither Woollen, nor linen, nor silk, sattin, or velvet: it is drapery: it is nothing more." In summary, the painter must "consider nature in the abstract, and represent in every one of his figures the character of its species."

Neoclassical sculptors took Reynolds's precept one step further and abstracted away from "accidents" of color to produce monochromatic statues of white marble or natural metal. And they also preferred to abstract away from the details of clothing, either to reveal the essential human form naked or to clothe it in the stylized folds of classical drapery. Similarly, architects of the early modern movement (following a distinct classicizing tendency) preferred to leave their buildings white. If they allowed colors at all, they were saturated primaries: the "essential" colors. And they either refused to clothe their buildings with surface decoration or, like Louis Sullivan, employed decoration that related to underlying structure in much the same way that classical drapery relates to the underlying anatomy.

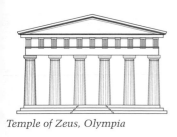

Temple of Zeus, Olympia

Temple of Poseidon, Paestum

The Parthenon, Athens

6.4
Realizations of the essential Greek temple form

These attitudes, like so many classical attitudes in the arts, can be traced back to the Platonic doctrine of Ideas and Aristotle's theory of forms. Plato took the aim of art to be *mimesis* (imitation), and in a famous passage of the *Republic* he illustrated this notion with the example of a bed—distinguishing between the unchanging, perfect, abstract idea of a bed; the imperfect imitation of the idea by a craftsman who constructs a bed; and the still more imperfect imitation of the imitation by a painter who depicts the bed. But Cicero in the *Orator* and Plotinus in his *Enneads* modified this doctrine to accord a higher status to art. The modified theory claims that an artist does not just hold up a mirror to nature, but imitates a general idea (for example of a bed) which he or she has in mind. The task of a craftsman or painter, then, was to seek the right and perfect form for an object.

Rhys Carpenter has persuasively argued, in *The Esthetic Basis of Greek Art* (1959), that for the Greeks the underlying essences of things were always conceived of visually: "For the Greek mind there was always a concrete visual image somehow attached to the abstract universal concept." Thus the Greeks "regarded the world of objects as a series of typical forms displayed and embodied in individual instances" (figure 6.4). This leads the architect to a very conservative view of form:

If he plans a temple, his most conspicuous artistic duty will be to consider afresh the adequacy and rightness of the temple-form as his predecessors have sought it out and embodied it. What criteria can he use for scrutinizing their success or failure? Only those of that inner necessity by which a form is recognized as right and true. Whatever is unessential, whatever is not necessary to the temple for its purpose or stability or durability, is irrelevant to the form; it is not a part of the temple. The expense and labor and time incident to the processes of building conspire to encourage the architect in eliminating the superfluous. How then could there logically be different temple-plans, when there is only one purpose for which temples are used, one identical force of gravitation to combat and master, one rain and sun to oppose? There should only be variety insomuch as there might be inadequacy in expressing, or incompleteness in discovering, the true and right form. The Parthenon is not a different building from the temple of Poseidon at Paestum: it is the same building grown closer and truer to its proper and perfect semblance. Iktinos invented nothing: he merely saw more clearly how things should be.

One of the clearest and most celebrated statements of this sort of attitude in architectural theory is that set forth by Marc-Antoine Laugier in his *Essai sur l'architecture* (1753).[5] For Laugier, the essence of a work of architecture was represented by a "primitive hut" of certain construction. He introduced this notion with an anecdote of a "savage" seeking shelter:

He wants to make himself a dwelling that protects but does not bury him. Some fallen branches in the forest are the right material for his purpose; he chooses four of the strongest, raises them upright, and arranges them in a square; across the top he lays four other branches; on these he hoists from two sides yet another row of branches which, inclining towards each other, meet at their highest point. He then covers this kind of roof with leaves so closely packed that neither sun nor rain can penetrate. Thus, man is housed.

This, Laugier suggested, provided a universal architectural prototype:

All the splendors of architecture ever conceived have been modeled on the little rustic hut I have just described. It is by approaching the simplicity of this first model that fundamental mistakes are avoided and true perfection is achieved. The pieces of wood set upright have given us the idea of the column, the pieces placed horizontally on top of them the idea of the entablature, the inclining pieces forming the roof the idea of the pediment.

Just these few parts form the essence:

From now on it is easy to distinguish between the parts which are essential to the composition of an architectural Order and those which have been introduced by necessity or have been added by caprice. The parts that are essential are the cause of beauty, the parts introduced by necessity cause every license, the parts added by caprice cause every fault.

(In Laugier's usage "introduced by necessity" means introduced for circumstantial practical reasons.) Thus, according to Laugier, in order to qualify as a true work of architecture, a building must, in some sense, instantiate the type represented by the primitive hut. Furthermore, accidents of form (that is, parts "introduced by necessity" or "added by caprice") should be rigorously suppressed, the better to reveal the absolute essence. This turned out to be a rather inconvenient prescription in practice, since the primitive hut had no walls; Laugier was forced to admit that walls might be introduced "by necessity" and that this was an allowable "license."

The idea of an architectural archetype is closely related to very similar ideas in biological thought.[6] Goethe (writing later in the eighteenth century than Laugier) postulated a plant archetype, the essence of which was to be found in every plant instance (figure 6.5). Similarly, he imagined such an archetype of vertebrate anatomy and wrote, in his *First Draft of a General Introduction to Comparative Anatomy* (1795): "On this account an attempt is here made to arrive at an anatomical type, a general picture in which the forms of

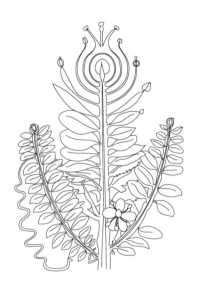

6.5
Goethe's *Urpflanze*: an image of a universal plant archetype (after Thompson and Geddes, 1931)

all animals are contained in potentia, and by means of which we can describe each animal in an invariable order." (Ironically enough, though, Goethe had no sympathy for Laugier's architectural theory; he violently attacked it and took the side of gothic against classic.) In the nineteenth century the French biologist Etienne Geoffroy Saint-Hilaire attempted to found a science of morphology based upon the idea of "one uniform type," and the British biologist Richard Owen published a famous volume entitled *On the Archetype and Homologies of the Vertebrate Skeleton* (1848).

RELATIVE ESSENCES

The relativist position, by contrast, is that there are *no* absolute essences and that essential/accidental distinctions may be drawn in various ways. Properties are of the same basic kind, and what we take to be the essence of something simply depends on our interests of the moment or on quirks of vocabulary. John Dewey (1938) provided a cogent statement of this position:

As far as present logical texts still continue to talk about essences, properties and accidents as something inherently different from one another, they are repeating distinctions that once had an ontological meaning and that no longer have it. Anything is "essential" which is indispensable in a given inquiry and anything is "accidental" which is superfluous.

An example of a more recent statement is that given by Nicholas Rescher (1975):

Our essentialism adopts the posture of a pragmatic *pluralism*. For we shall maintain that there are various different and *alternative* bases upon which the essential/accidental distinction can be placed, and that one cannot establish any one of these as uniquely and universally *correct*, but rather can only maintain one or another of them as functionally suitable within the concrete setting of a particular problem-context. Viewing the distinction between the essential and the accidental as one to be developed along *various distinct lines*, no one of which is specially privileged, we regard the implementation of one or another of these as a matter not to be settled at the theoretical level of general principles, but at the concrete level of specific contexts of application.

As Rescher points out, this interpretation of essentialism allows for different people, with different interests, to regard different features of some given object as essential and to classify objects according to alternative type definitions. In other words, typologies should properly be regarded as situational rather than universal. He offers the following example:

Suppose some item is introduced into the framework of discussion as, e.g., "this wooden kitchen chair." Then from the carpenter's perspective it would be essential that it be a wooden piece of furniture (whether a chair or table might be incidental); from the home decorator's perspective it would be essential that it is a kitchen chair (that it is wooden might be incidental); from the fire marshal's perspective that it be something wooden; and so on.

That is, the carpenter, the home decorator, and the fire marshal all follow different habits or conventions of abstraction (as appropriate to their interests), resulting in classification of the object under different types.

It seems to me that consideration of the history of architecture tends to cast the relativist position in a favorable light, since it reveals wide variation in the ways that essences have been defined, even within the classical tradition. Let us consider, for example, a set of apparently clear, well-defined and unchanging architectural types: the five orders of classical architecture. John Summerson (1963) has traced the history of their type definitions as follows (my italics):

Let us be quite clear about how variable or how invariable the orders are. Serlio puts them before us with a tremendous air of authority, giving dimensions for each part as if to settle the profiles and proportions once and for all. But in fact, Serlio's orders, while obviously reflecting Vitruvius to some extent, are also based on his own observation of ancient monuments and thus, by a process of personal selection, to quite a considerable degree his own invention. It could hardly be otherwise. Vitruvius's descriptions have gaps in them and these can only be filled from knowledge of surviving Roman monuments themselves. The orders as exemplified in these monuments vary considerably from one to the other *so it is open to anybody to abstract what he considers the best features of each in order to set out what he considers his ideal Corinthian, Ionic or whatever it is.* All through the history of classical architecture speculation as to the ideal types of each of the orders has continued, oscillating between antiquarian reverence on the one hand and sheer personal invention on the other.

Parallels of the orders illustrate Summerson's point: they compare alternative abstractions of the essences of the Tuscan, Doric, Ionic, Corinthian, and composite orders Figure 6.6 compares the Doric as defined by seven eminent authorities.

6.6
Alternative abstractions of the
essence of the Doric (after Chitham,
1985)

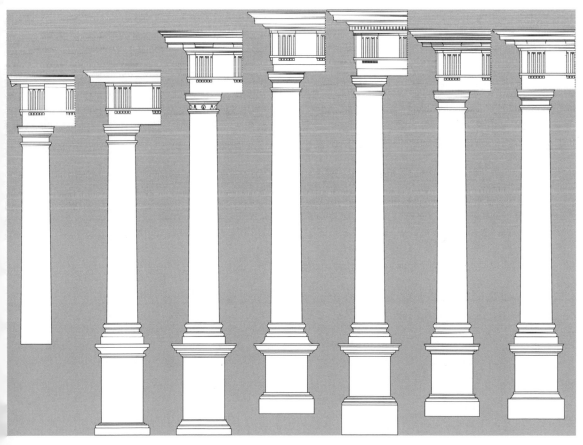

Vitruvius   Serlio   Vignola   Palladio   Scamozzi   Perrault   Gibbs

The dispute between the absolutists and the relativists turns on whether the meanings of common nouns are a matter of nature (and thus to be sought through scientific investigation) or a matter of language (to be established through definition and analysis). This led John Locke, in *An Essay Concerning Human Understanding* (1690), to distinguish between *real* essences (which he claimed exist in things themselves, are made by nature, and are unknowable) and *nominal* essences—definitions that determine what things may properly be called by names. Following from this, it may be argued that the essence/accident distinction is drawn relative to the vocabulary of the language that we use. C. I. Lewis (1946), for example, has suggested:

Traditionally any attribute required for application of a term is said to be of the essence of the thing named. It is, of course, meaningless to speak of the essence of a thing except relative to its being named by a particular term.

Or, as Locke himself put it, "boundaries of species are as men, and not as nature, make them."

Such a language-oriented view serves well our particular purposes here.[7] I shall take it that the essence of an architectural type is a matter of convention and that this can be made explicit by formally stating a definition. A classically-minded architect might want to argue for stability and permanence of such definitions—leading to an architecture concerned with imitating and perfecting established forms. An anti-classicist, on the other hand, might want to argue that traditional definitions are always up for renegotiation and that traditional forms can be reinterpreted in radically new ways as concerns and interests change.

TYPE DEFINITIONS

How can type definitions be stated? In order to establish the semantic properties of a critical language we must have some way to define the necessary and sufficient conditions for objects to be instances of types.

One approach is to employ diagrams (figure 6.7)—to *show* what a square or triangle is. This runs into the philosophical puzzle of how a single diagram may stand for many different things. Kant formulated this in his *Critique of Pure Reason* (1781), as follows:

6.7
Essential properties depicted by
a graphic schema

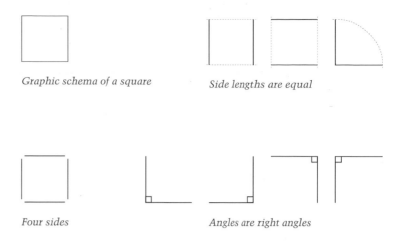

Graphic schema of a square   *Side lengths are equal*

Four sides   *Angles are right angles*

In truth, it is not images of objects, but schemata, which lie at the foundations of our pure sensuous conceptions. No image could ever be adequate to our conception of triangles in general. For the generalness of the conception it never could attain to, as this includes under itself all triangles, whether right-angled, acute-angled, etc., while the image would always be limited to a single part of this sphere.

The problem, in short, is to ascertain which of the indefinitely many properties displayed by the diagram are to be taken as essential and which may be varied to generate other instances subsumed under the type. A way around the difficulty is to implicitly or explictly dissect the diagram into partial diagrams that illustrate propositions, as shown in figure 6.7, and to specify the essence of the type by taking the conjunction of these propositions. This results in a verbal schema. Each proposition (feature) of such a schema is necessary for an object to be an instance of the type, and the schema taken as a whole is sufficient to determine whether an object is an instance. Schemata are conveniently expressed in the form of recognition rules, for example:

*sides (**Polygon**, 4) and*
*regular (**Polygon**) → square (**Polygon**)*

Application of this rule to polygons enables us to classify them as squares or not.

If a necessary condition is not satisfied, then an object cannot be an instance of the type. But satisfaction of a necessary condition might not guarantee that it is an instance, since other necessary conditions might remain unsatisfied. A condition might be sufficient to guarantee that it is an instance but not necessary, since satisfaction of other conditions might independently suffice. For example, a recognition rule for classical columns might be stated:

*Tuscan (**Column**) or*
*Doric (**Column**) or*
*Ionic (**Column**) or*
*Corinthian (**Column**) → classical (**Column**)*

No one of these conditions is necessary, but any one is sufficient. Finally, a condition might be necessary and sufficient: an object is an instance if and only if this condition is satisfied.

Often, as noted earlier, it is convenient to structure our knowledge in the form of taxonomic hierarchies, in which subtypes inherit the properties of subsuming types. The following rules, for example, define such a hierarchy:

*polygon (**X**) → thing (**X**)*
*quadrilateral (**X**) → polygon (**X**)*
*rectangle (**X**) → quadrilateral (**X**)*
*square (**X**) → rectangle (**X**)*

In other words: **X** is a thing; all polygons are things; all quadrilaterals are polygons; all rectangles are quadrilaterals; all squares are rectangles. Now consider an additional fact about polygons:

*polygon (**X**) → planefigure (**X**)*

By inheritance, through the taxonomic hierarchy, this property is associated with quadrilaterals, rectangles, and squares as well.[8]

EXCEPTIONAL INSTANCES

This scheme runs into difficulties where there are exceptions to consider. As a general rule, classical columns have bases, so we can write:

*classical (**Column**) → possesses (**Column**, base)*

But Parthenon Doric columns, while undoubtedly classical, do not have bases. The difficulty can be overcome by allowing for the abnormality, thus:

*classical (**Column**) and not Parthenon (**Column**) →*
*possesses (**Column**, base)*

In practice, our knowledge must often be qualified in this way. A problem, though, is that attempts to produce precise and rigorous definitions typically yield lengthy, cumbersome lists of exceptions, as a glance at almost any building code will confirm.

Another way to handle the problem of exceptional instances is to abandon insistence on necessary features and sharp, well-defined type definitions and to develop instead an approach based on family resemblances. The principle here is that some instances will be very "typical" because they share many features with many other "family members," while other instances will be very "atypical" because they share only a few features with other "family members." On this view, type schemata (such as that for classical columns) and the boundaries of types are fuzzily defined. Parthenon Doric columns count as slightly atypical classical columns. There is linguistic and psychological evidence that human beings do, indeed, often structure their knowledge of things in this way. Lakoff (1972) has noted the frequent use of "hedges" such as "technically," "loosely speaking," and "strictly speaking" to suggest degrees of membership in sentences such as "Strictly speaking, the Doric column is not classical." Rosch (1973) has studied people's ability to judge distances of instances from the "most typical" of its kind and has suggested that the "most typical" instance should be regarded as the "prototype" that defines the type.

The frame formalism as introduced by Minsky (1975) provides a particularly general and flexible way to take account of these complexities in the formulation of type definitions. A frame consists of slots and slot fillers. A slot may be filled or unfilled. The filler of a slot can be an actual value, a default value, a procedure for finding a value, or another frame. An actual value is one that we know to be true, while a default value is one that we assume to be true until we learn otherwise. Thus default values encode expectations that can be adjusted, if necessary, in specific contexts. A frame for chairs might be written[9]:

Chair
    Specialization of: *furniture*
    Number of legs:
    Default: *4*
    If needed: *use procedure count*
    Number of arms: *0, 1, or 2*
    Seat:
    Back:
    Default: *same as seat*
    Style:
    Good for: *sitting*

Then, a frame representing a particular instance of a chair might be:

Dining chair
> **Specialization of:** *chair*
> **Number of legs**:
> **Number of arms**: *2*
> **Seat:** *woven*
> **Back:** *bent wood*
> **Style**: *Thonet*
> **Good for**: *sitting at table*

These strategies all challenge the basic empiricist assumption that a type is an abstraction formed by dropping details that vary idiosyncratically from one exemplar to the next and retaining only the residue of commonality. They eliminate rigid insistence on necessary and sufficient conditions for falling under a type and substitute, instead, the notion of typical characteristics that can be illustrated by displaying prototypes. For our purposes it is not necessary to enter further into the controversy over how types should be defined[10]: I shall simply assume, henceforth, that we can make use of some sort of classification scheme and associated property inheritance mechanism, based either on necessity or on default.

ARCHITECTURAL VOCABULARIES

The types of architectural elements recognizable in a specified corpus of architectural compositions constitute the vocabulary of that corpus, just as a spoken vocabulary is a set of word types, the tokens of which are found in a specified corpus of sentences. It is commonplace, for example, to characterize architectural styles in terms of their vocabularies: the vocabulary of classical architecture includes the Doric column, the round arch, and the triangular pediment; that of the Gothic includes the pointed arch and the flying buttress; and so on. Sir Banister Fletcher's *History of Architecture on the Comparative Method* (1896), which is still being reissued in successive editions, compares vocabulary elements across different cultures and periods in much the same way that a work of comparative philology might compare words.

It has also been standard practice for architectural texts to set forth recommended vocabularies which, they propose, students should learn and then employ in the production of compositions (figures 6.8, 6.9). Francesco Milizia's *Principj di Architettura Civile* (1832) displays various types of

6.8
A classical vocabulary of window
treatments (after Chitham, 1985)

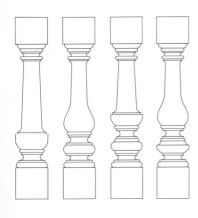

6.9
A classical vocabulary of balusters
(after Swan, 1758)

construction elements and explores their variants. Julien Guadet's vast compendium of beaux-arts design lore, his *Eléments et théories d'architecture* (1894), exhaustively lists and describes both elements of composition (major volumetric elements) and elements of construction (physical components). Guadet described the elemental forms of walls, doors, windows, pilasters, columns, vaults, ceilings, and stairs as "the arsenal of architecture." The catalogues of modern industrialized component building systems are even more systematic and rigorous.

Some theorists have suggested the existence of a universal architectural vocabulary. Guadet claimed that his "arsenal" existed independently of individual architects, cultures, and climates. More recently, Thiis-Evensen (1988) has argued that "creativity is primarily related to the way in which certain basic forms are combined and varied," and he attempts to show "that there is a common language of form which we can immediately understand, regardless of individual or culture." This leads him to an elaborate taxonomic hierarchy in which elements are first divided into three broad classes: floors, walls, and roofs. Within each class, "general solutions to problems of form" are catalogued. Thus the themes of dome, barrel vault, gable, shed roof, and flat roof are suggested for roofs (figure 6.10), stairs (treated as a special kind of floor) come in the basic varieties shown in figure 6.11, and so on.

Whether we see a Babel of vocabularies or believe that we can discern universal commonalities, use of the concept of an architectural vocabulary seems indispensable in the conceptualization and description of buildings. We take instances of vocabulary elements to be the objects that an architect specifies and disposes, and we couch architectural discussion and criticism in terms of names for different types of elements. In practice, a vocabulary need not be fixed, explicit, or well-defined, but in principle the types comprising the vocabulary can be enumerated, named, and specified by type diagrams, recognition rules, or frames.

READING DRAWINGS

Organization of knowledge within the framework of some system of types enables us to read architectural drawings, scale models, and other depictions constructed within design worlds. We do so by recognizing instances of abstract shape types (squares, triangles, circles, and so on) and applying our knowledge of depiction conventions to see them as standing for instances of architectural vocabulary elements (or parts of

Dome

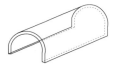

Barrel vault

Gable

Shed

Flat

6.10
A vocabulary of roof themes
(after Thiis-Evensen, 1988)

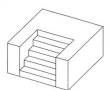

Plateau

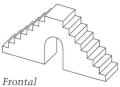

Frontal

Fan

Divided

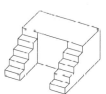

Side

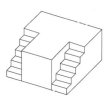

Overlapping

6.11
A vocabulary of stair motifs
(after Thiis-Evensen, 1988)

A composition of discrete shapes

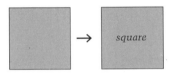

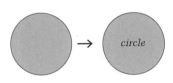

Labeling rules

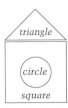

Labeled composition

such elements) in the construction world. For purposes of analysis it is convenient to consider this as a two-step process: shape recognition then interpretation.

Where shapes are discrete, recognition is relatively straightforward. We can simply apply recognition rules, such as those shown in figure 6.12, to label the instances appropriately. The task of recognizing discrete alphabetic characters is of this nature.

More often, though, a drawing presents a complex scene, and the task becomes one of subshape recognition—breaking the scene down into parts and searching through the collection of parts to find those that qualify as instances of the shape type that interests us. This too is straightforward (though potentially laborious) if we treat shapes, as most computer-aided design systems do, as sets of discrete, indivisible primitives, such as vectors and arcs. This allows the task to be formulated as one of enumerating subsets of primitives and matching each subset against the type definition—a process similar to that of finding substrings in character strings. But human designers often do something more sophisticated than this; they recognize emergent subshapes. If we overlay two squares as shown in figure 6.13, for example, a third (smaller) square and two L-shapes emerge. Or, if we overlay two equilateral triangles as shown in figure 6.14, a hexagon, a star, and six more equilateral triangles emerge. We have no difficulty in recognizing these emergent shapes, but it is obvious that we could not do so if we defined a square as four "atomic" vectors or a triangle as three "atomic" vectors.[11]

For generality, then, we must abandon the assumption that shapes have "atomic" parts. Once we do this, combinatorial explosions of emergent form can quickly develop. Combination of eight straight lines as shown in figure 6.15, for example, yields nine one-unit squares, four two-unit squares, and one three-unit square.

The emergent shapes in a figure are not, in general, all immediately evident to us: sometimes we must actively search for them. Gottschaldt (1926) studied this phenomenon by asking subjects to find "hidden" shapes in line drawings (figure 6.16) and found that some such shapes can be extremely difficult to discover. Not surprisingly, then, computer algorithms for performing similar tasks turn out to be computationally complex.[12]

The complete structure of a shape is given by all its subshapes—an infinite number of them if we assume that a shape does not have atomic parts, and usually a very large number if we assume that it does. But a designer pays atten-

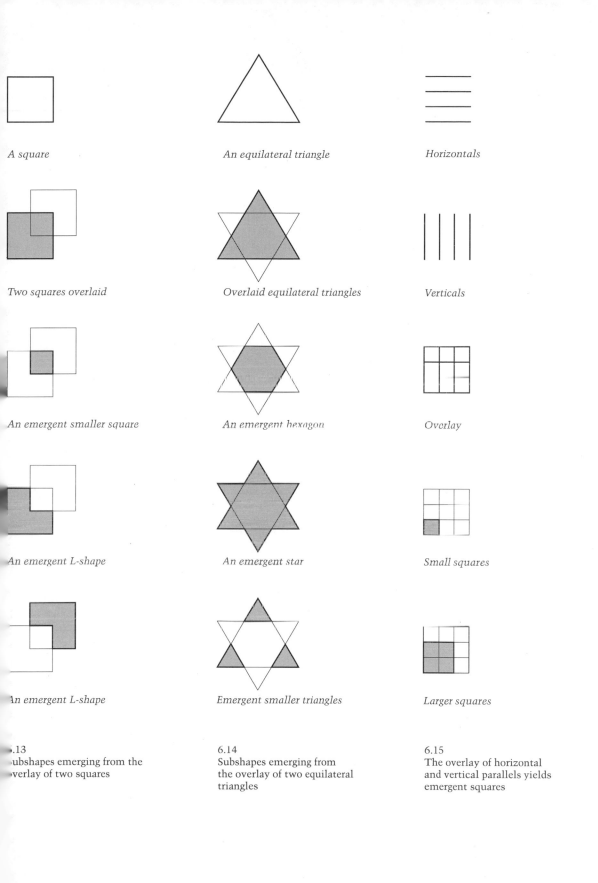

A square

An equilateral triangle

Horizontals

Two squares overlaid

Overlaid equilateral triangles

Verticals

An emergent smaller square

An emergent hexagon

Overlay

An emergent L-shape

An emergent star

Small squares

An emergent L-shape

Emergent smaller triangles

Larger squares

6.13
Subshapes emerging from the
overlay of two squares

6.14
Subshapes emerging from
the overlay of two equilateral
triangles

6.15
The overlay of horizontal
and vertical parallels yields
emergent squares

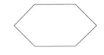

6.16
A "hidden" figure (after Gottschaldt, 1926)

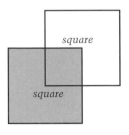

a. ∀ **Square** (large (**Square**))

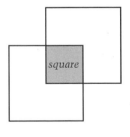

b. ∃ **Square** (not large (**Square**))

6.17
Recognition of different figures leads to different assertions about a drawing

tion to only some finite, small subset of these at any one time. As we saw in chapter 1, some are treated as "figures" and others as part of the "ground." More formally, we might say that those subshapes that have been labeled by the application of recognition rules are the figures currently available for further interpretation, and any others are excluded from consideration. In other words, the quantifier in a statement such as:

∀**Square** (large (**Square**))

is understood to pick out the shapes that are *actually* labeled as squares, not all the shapes that *could* be labeled as squares. It refers to the *set* of subshapes to which we are actually giving attention, not to the indefinite collection to which we *might* give attention. Thus the statement is true of a drawing labeled as shown in figure 6.17a, but false of the same drawing labeled as shown in figure 6.17b.

Let us now consider a simple case of the interpretation of subshapes as depictions of parts of physical elements.[13] Imagine a construction world populated by instances of rectangular blocks and a design world in which compositions of rectangular blocks are specified by making axonometric line drawings. Under the usual conventions, straight lines stand for edges of blocks. When we recognize an instance of a straight line, we can interpret it in any one of four possible ways (figure 6.18): as a convex edge, as a concave edge, as an outer edge seen against the background, or as an outer edge seen against the face of another block. A little further analysis shows that only four types of junctions of straight lines can occur in consistent depictions of the block world: L-shapes, T-shapes, Y-shapes, and arrow-shapes (figure 6.19). Under the usual conventions we interpret all of these as junctions of faces. A Y-shape, for example, might be interpreted as a convex junction or a concave junction (figure 6.20). Since all straight-line, L-shape, T-shape, Y-shape, and arrow-shape instances have several possible interpretations, there will, in general, be many possible combinations of subshape interpretations for a drawing. However, not all of these will be consistent with the axioms of the construction world. The interpretations of the lines in figure 6.21, for example, are not consistent with a world of rectangular blocks. Thus we read drawings by searching for combinations of subshape interpretations that are consistent with the axioms of the construction world.

Drawings are ambiguous when several combinations of subshape interpretations are consistent with the axioms of the construction world. Under the conventions of wire frame axonometric projection and the axioms of a construc-

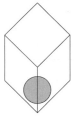
Convex

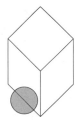
Against ground

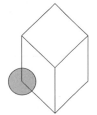
L-shape

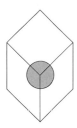
Y shape

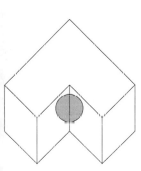
Concave

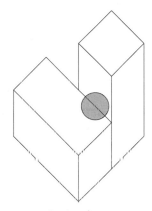
Against face

Arrow-shape

6.18
Different types of edges

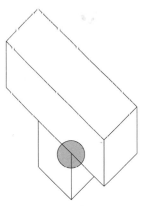
T-shape

6.19
Different types of junctions of
straight lines

TYPES AND VOCABULARIES

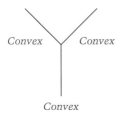

Convex   Convex

Convex

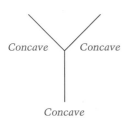

Concave   Concave

Concave

6.20
Consistent interpretations of a
Y-shape as convex vertex and as
a concave vertex

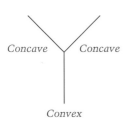

Concave   Concave

Convex

6.21
An impossible junction

tion world of plane-faced solids, for example, the shape shown in figure 6.22 may be consistently interpreted either as a cube seen from above or as a cube seen from below. Figure 6.23 shows a well-known example of a wire-frame drawing that has several consistent interpretations in a world of plane-faced solids. Some wire frames have many different interpretations as polyhedral objects.[14]

Not only different combinations of subshape interpretations, but also different breakdowns of drawings into recognized subshapes can lead to alternative interpretations. Figure 6.24, for example, has two consistent interpretations in a world of cubic blocks. In each of these there are repeating subshapes which we recognize and interpret as cubes. In one, the three dots lie on a single cube, but in the other the three dots lie on three different cubes.[15]

The famous rabbit/duck drawing[16] (figure 6.25) clearly illustrates the interaction of subshape recognition and domain knowledge in interpolation of a depiction. The discrete, central subshape is immediately, and fairly unambiguously, recognizable as a depiction of an eye. Thus we might have a front elevation of an asymmetrical Cyclops or a side elevation of some two-eyed animal. If we dismiss the former conjecture as highly implausible, we can use our general knowledge of the features of animal profiles to suggest conjectures that the left part of the outline must depict either long ears or a bill, and that the right part of the outline must depict either a face looking right or the back of a head. There are four possible combinations of part labels, and we can use considerations of consistency (again drawn from our general knowledge of animals) to eliminate some from further consideration. One combination (bill/back) is consistent with the whole being a duck, a second (ears/front) is consistent with the whole being a rabbit, and the other two lead nowhere: there are no animals with ears growing out from the fronts of their faces or bills growing out from the backs of their heads. Now we can inherit and use knowledge about rabbits and ducks in an effort to sort out the remaining ambiguity. Isn't the neck a bit too thick to be that of a duck? Aren't the protuberances a bit too crisply defined to be floppy rabbit ears? The more details we know about rabbits and ducks the more likely it is that we will find evidence to confirm one or another of the readings.

Architectural sketches—particularly those made at an early stage in a design exploration—can often, like the rabbit/duck drawing, be seen as different things. The various possible readings evoke different knowledge and thus suggest different ways to sharpen and complete the design

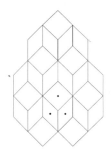

6.24
A figure that can be seen as
two different stacks of cubes

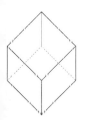

Ambiguous vertex

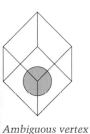

Vertex seen as in front

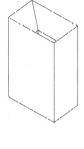

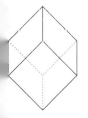

Vertex seen as in back

6.22
A vertex plays different roles
in different interpretations

6.23
A wire-frame figure seen as
several different solids

TYPES AND VOCABULARIES

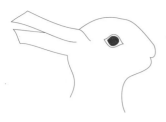

Experienced designers are often highly skilled at using rough sketches as evocative instruments in this way. Finished architectural working drawings, however, play a quite different role: they should unambiguously specify a state of the construction world and contain sufficient information to allow verification that this state satisfies the design requirements.

SUMMARY

The idea of a shape token, which was earlier used in an informal intuitive way, has now been made more precise. A design world is populated by shape tokens from some graphic vocabulary, and a construction world is populated by tokens from some architectural vocabulary. Conventions of depiction establish a mapping between the tokens in the two worlds and enable us to read drawings. From the viewpoint of the critical language, type definitions establish the meanings of common nouns and provide a useful way to structure knowledge. The relations between common nouns (verbal tokens) used in critical assertions, shape tokens used in depictions, and architectural vocabulary elements used in constructing buildings are summarized in figure 6.26.

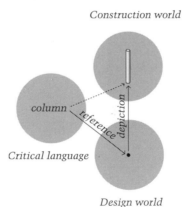

6.26
Relationship of tokens

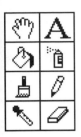

7.1
Icons depicting the shape-manipulation "tools" provided by a computer-aided design system

7.2
A design operator is a function that evaluates to a new state of the design world

OPERATORS

A design operator is a tool for manipulating shapes in a design world. In a design world populated by cardboard polygons, the basic operators might be a matte knife for shaping polygons, hands for translating and rotating polygons, and a glue gun for joining polygons together. In a design world of straight lines and arcs on paper, the basic operators might be a pencil, a straightedge, compasses, and an eraser. And in a computer-aided design system, the operators are programs that manipulate the data structure: these are often invoked by clicking on icons that depict more traditional tools (figure 7.1).

More formally, an operator is a function that evaluates to a new state of the design world (figure 7.2). Operators can thus be described by sentences of the form:

*operatorx (**State1**) = **State2***

State1 and **State2** are variables. By specifying the range of **State1** (the argument of the operator), we can establish the circumstances under which the operator can properly be applied. And by specifying how to compute **State2** for any value of **State1**, we can define the effect of the operator. An operation (instance of the operator) is performed whenever the operator is applied to a particular state in the range of **State1**.

If we can specify an initial state of a design world, plus a set of operators characterized in this way, we have established the state-action tree for that world. Its branches are all the branches that can be constructed by recursive application of the set of operators to the initial state.

The meaning of a design operation is its entailment—the set of facts that become true as a result of it and the set of facts that become false. Thus design operators can, in principle, be characterized semantically in terms of the predicates that survive their application. But this is usually a very formidable task, since alterations to a design may propagate long and complex chains of logical consequences.[1] So designers usually content themselves with very rough and incomplete semantic characterizations of operators, apply operators speculatively, and then explore the consequences through critical discourse.

A practical strategy for developing incomplete but useful characterizations of design operators is to assume that operators apply to shapes and to specify their immediate geometric effects. Less direct effects can then be traced by combining knowledge of geometric effects with facts and rules about the construction world to draw further inferences. For example, enlarging a shape depicting a structural member will have structural performance implications. In this chapter, then, I shall characterize the operators commonly used by designers for creating, deleting, transforming, and combining shapes in design worlds, and I shall show how architectural composition may be understood as a process of applying these operators to shapes.

INSTANTIATION OF SHAPE PRIMITIVES

Instantiation of shapes is the most basic of design actions. The effect of an instantiation operator is to insert a shape token (that is, an instance of a specified shape type) into the design world.

Designers often proceed by instantiation of shape primitives: straight lines, arcs, splines, circles, polygons, and so on. By adding imperatives to the critical language, we can gain a way to specify instantiation operations (to a draftsperson or to a computer). For example, a command to insert a straight line might be written:

instantiate line

more concisely, we might just say:

line

But this is incomplete: it does not specify how long the line is to be, or where it is to be located. The deficiency can be remedied by adding parameters, thus:

line (X, Y, Theta, Length)

The values bound to the variables **X**, **Y**, **Theta**, and **Length** fully specify the particular instance that we want (figure 7.3).

Parameterized commands can be executed in several different ways. In a manual design process a draftsperson might draw the appropriate line with ruler and straightedge. In a Pascal program the command

line (X, Y, Theta, Length);

might be an invocation of a procedure to draw a line on the screen or add a record representing a line to a data structure. A computer-aided design system might interpret a command of similar form by displaying an appropriate line on the

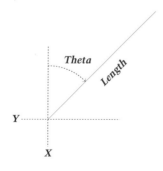

7.3
The parameters of a line

screen. We can also think of the statement as an assertion that the line which concerns us has specified values of **X**, **Y**, **Theta**, and **Length**, and we can make the assertion true (satisfy it) by drawing the line appropriately.

The inverse of instantiation is deletion from the design world. This may be accomplished, for example, by erasing a line on paper, removing a cardboard polygon from a physical model, or deleting a record from a data structure.

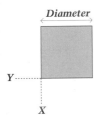

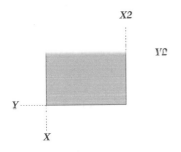

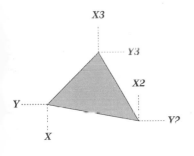

7.4
Some parameterized shapes

INSTANTIATION OF ABSTRACT SHAPE TYPES

Combinations of shape primitives may qualify as instances of abstract shape types. For example, combinations of straight lines may qualify as instances of squares, rectangles, or triangles. Often it is more efficient for a designer to compose by direct instantiation of such combinations than by building them up in primitive-by-primitive fashion.

In order to specify instantiation of abstract shape types, corresponding parameterized commands are needed in the critical language, for example (figure 7.4):

*square (**X**, **Y**, **Diameter**)*
*rectangle (**X**, **Y**, **X2**, **Y2**)*
*triangle (**X**, **Y**, **X2**, **Y2**, **X3**, **Y3**)*

Specified instances might be produced manually by using appropriate templates or rubber stamps. In a computer-aided design system they would be produced by executing corresponding procedures.[2]

Notice that, in these commands, it is not necessary to specify any of the essential properties that characterize the type—for example, that opposite sides of a rectangle are equal. We assume that knowledge of these essential properties is somehow embodied in the production mechanism (a template, procedure, frame, or whatever) and that the essential properties will thus be propagated to all instances. In other words, knowledge of type definitions allows the executor of an instantiation command to "fill in" information that is not explicitly given in the command.[3]

INSTANTIATION OF LABELED OBJECTS

Where a designer works under established conventions of depiction, it is often necessary to instantiate abstract shape types that will serve as depictions of instances of architectural vocabulary elements in the construction world. If circles depict columns in plan, for example, the command

*column (**X**, **Y**, **Diameter**)*

DESIGN OPERATIONS

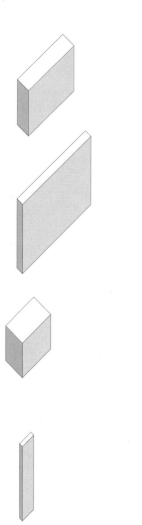

should result in instantiation of an appropriate circle. Similarly, if cuboids stand for walls in plan, the command

*wall (**X**, **Y**, **Length**, **Thickness**, **Height**)*

should result in instantiation of appropriate cuboids (figure 7.5). And the command

*chair (**X**, **Y**, **Rotation**)*

might produce a result something like that shown in figure 7.6. Here we rely on the production mechanism not only to fill in "missing" information, but also to follow the conventions of depiction correctly.

Specialized computer-aided design systems (as opposed to general-purpose drawing or geometric modeling systems) often provide for composition with a pre-defined architectural vocabulary through use of such commands. Typically there are commands to instantiate various types of structural elements (columns, walls, etc.), openings (doors and windows), furniture, and fixtures. Systems for other purposes provide other vocabularies: a pipe layout system provides a vocabulary of pipes, joints, and fixtures; an electronic design system provides a vocabulary of electronic components; and so on.

It should be clear, then, that the reading of a design drawing (or scale model) can be established in two different ways. If the drawing was built up from graphic primitives and abstract shape types, then recognition rules must be applied to produce an interpretation as an arrangement of architectural vocabulary elements in the construction world. But, if the drawing was built up by instantiating labeled objects, then the interpretation of shapes as vocabulary elements in the construction world is given a priori.

7.5
Cuboids instantiated to represent walls of various dimensions and proportions

TRANSFORMATION

Once we have an instance of some type of thing we can perform operations that change it in some way. That is, we can transform it.

As we commonly understand the word, transformations may be either destructive or preservative. A destructive transformation, such as smashing or burning or dismantling, destroys an object. For a well-known architectural example, consider Mies van der Rohe's Barcelona Pavilion of 1929. It was dismantled only a few months after construction, and the pieces were dispersed. Although the material from which it was constructed still exists, it no longer constitutes a pavilion. We would all surely agree that the essence of being a pavilion did not survive this transformation. Under a

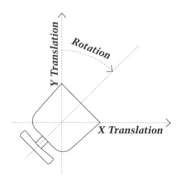

7.6
The parameters of a type of drafting chair

preservative transformation, though, an object is merely modified and remains a thing of its kind. It is still an instance of the same type. If the Barcelona Pavilion had been left in place and painted purple, it would remain a pavilion. If we change the engine in an automobile, we certainly still have an automobile. If we heat a steel beam, it remains (up to a certain point) a steel beam. If we translate or rotate in the plane a rectangular concrete floor slab, it remains a rectangular concrete floor slab. In all these cases, the essential properties of the object remain unaltered, while various accidental properties change. That is, preservative transformations do not alter an object's type.

Another more technical way to put this is to say that a type may have an associated set of transformations which are closed in the type, and, when applied to an instance of that type, always produce new instances of the same type: these transformations alter only accidental properties. But an unclosed transformation may produce an object that does not qualify as an instance of the type. That is, it may change some essential property: it may be destructive rather than preservative. The transformation of scaling, for example, is closed in instances of equilateral triangles (figure 7.7). Whenever we scale an instance of an equilateral triangle up or down, the result is another equilateral triangle. But the transformation of stretching is not closed in this type: if we stretch an instance of an equilateral triangle unequally in the horizontal and vertical directions, then we violate the essential requirement that all sides are of equal length and obtain something that is not an equilateral triangle. Stretching is closed, though, in triangles in general.

The concepts of type, equivalence, and closure are inseparable. We recognize objects as equivalent when we see that there is a transformation that would change one into the other. We say that they are equivalent under this particular transformation. And the transformation is closed within some type of which the objects are both instances.

Transformations of shapes in design worlds represent transformations of corresponding physical objects in construction worlds. However, transformation of a shape may yield a drawing or model that no longer has a consistent interpretation in the construction world or that no longer specifies a feasible arrangement. So it is useful to classify common transformations according to the properties that they preserve, and thus the architectural implications of their execution.

An equilateral triangle

Scaled

Stretched

7.7
Scaling and stretching an equilateral triangle

DESIGN OPERATIONS

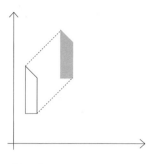

Translation

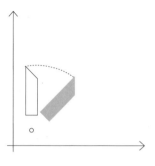

Rotation

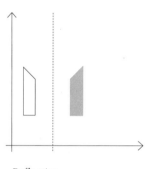

Reflection

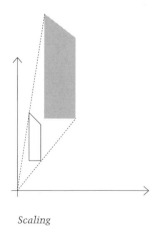

Scaling

7.8
Transformations of a plane shape

The most familiar transformations are translation and rotation, either in the plane or in three-dimensional space (figure 7.8). These preserve shape and size, but alter position. Together with the identity transformation (which leaves an object completely unaltered, and is introduced for technical mathematical reasons), they constitute the proper isometric transformations. Composition often becomes a game of translating and rotating shapes to vary their spatial relations. A designer might do this by moving around cardboard cutouts in plan or by using the translation and rotation operators provided by a computer-aided design system. Since construction components, furniture items, and so on are often rigid objects, whose positions and orientations can be varied relative to each other, it is not surprising that the proper isometric transformations are very commonly used for manipulating shapes in design worlds.

If a designer turns over a cardboard cutout, then reflection is introduced as an additional design operator: the property of handedness is varied. When reflection is added to the proper isometric transformations, in this way, the designer is working with the isometric (or rigid) transformations.

Many architectural elements come in both right-handed and left-handed versions. Bilaterally symmetrical compositions can, for example, be decomposed into right and left halves, which are equivalent under the reflection transformation (figure 7.9). Similarly, doors may swing to the right or to the left (figure 7.10). But consider a type of cupboard that is made only with the door swinging one way: reflection of a shape depicting an instance of this type of cupboard would produce an unrealizable design. Thus reflection of three-dimensional shapes must be used with caution.

The transformation of scaling keeps shape constant, but varies size. Appending scaling to the isometric transformations yields the similarity transformations: differently scaled instances are said to be similar to each other. Scaling of abstract shapes, such as squares and circles, is very common in design. But many architectural vocabulary elements do not scale: they take different proportions as they become larger or smaller. Galileo noted, for example, that corresponding bones of large and small animals have very different proportions (figure 7.11), and, similarly, columns and beams should have proportions appropriate to their lengths.

Sometimes stretch and shear transformations (figure 7.12) are also introduced as operators applicable to shapes in a design world. Dürer employed them in highly systematic fashion to generate wide ranges of variants on the forms of the human face (figures 7.13, 7.14). And architects have

7.9
Right and left halves of the entrance to
Palladio's S. Giorgio Maggiore, Venice,
are equivalent under reflection

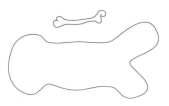

7.11
Proportions of bones of large and
small animals (after Galileo's
*Dialogues Concerning Two New
Sciences*, 1632)

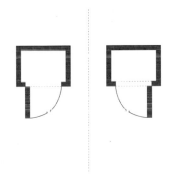

7.10
Cupboards with left-handed and
right-handed doors are reflections of
each other

7.12
Stretch and shear transformations
of a square

DESIGN OPERATIONS

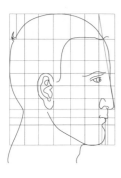

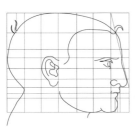

7.13
Dürer's use of stretch transformations to generate images of human faces (after *Four Books of Human Proportion*, 1528)

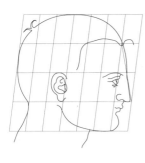

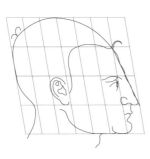

7.14
Dürer's use of shear transformations

sometimes sheared standard elements to fit them to parallelogram-shaped panels along stairs or ramps (figure 7.15). Shear and stretch transformations distort the shapes of objects but always preserve the geometric property of parallelism. Together with similarity transformations, they constitute the affine transformations.

Yet another distorting transformation is the perspective transformation. This results, for example, when a slide of a two-dimensional figure is projected obliquely onto the screen (figure 7.16). Parallels now converge, but a geometric property technically known as cross-ratio is preserved. Perspective transformations are occasionally used by architects to fit orthogonal plans to skewed sites or to create spatial illusions (figure 7.17). Perspective and affine transformations together constitute the linear transformations.

Now imagine that a prototype figure is drawn on an infinitely flexible rubber sheet and that transformed instances may be produced by stretching and twisting the sheet in every conceivable way, provided that it is never broken and rejoined. In his celebrated book *On Growth and Form* (1942) the biologist D'Arcy Thompson used such "rubber sheet" transformations to show how widely divergent organic forms might be regarded as instances of the same broad type (figure 7.18).[4] These transformations, which encompass all those previously discussed, in general preserve only the geometric property of connectedness, and they are known technically as continuous transformations.

Dürer employed nonlinear continuous transformations in a similar way in his *Four Books of Human Proportion* (1528). Figure 7.19 shows a human profile with horizontal construction lines. By varying the intervals between these lines, Dürer subjected the profile to nonlinear distortions to produce grotesque caricatures.

Floor plans of buildings are equivalent under nonlinear continuous transformations when the shapes of corresponding rooms differ but adjacencies between rooms remain the same. Since room adjacencies are often determined by practical imperatives, but an architect may have considerable freedom to vary shape, we can often find this sort of equivalence among plans for the same type of building. Figure 7.20, for example, shows an adjacency diagram, and figure 7.21 shows several Frank Lloyd Wright house plans that realize it. By virtue of this they are all equivalent under nonlinear continuous transformations.

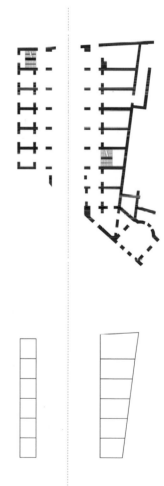

7.15
A sheared version of the Corinthian capital (after Guarini's *Architettura Civile*, 1737)

7.16
Dürer's use of two-dimensional perspective transformations

7.17
Trajan's Market, Rome: the right side becomes a perspective transformation of the left

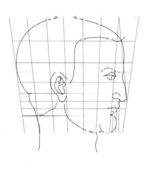

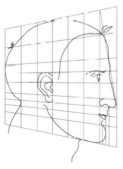

DESIGN OPERATIONS

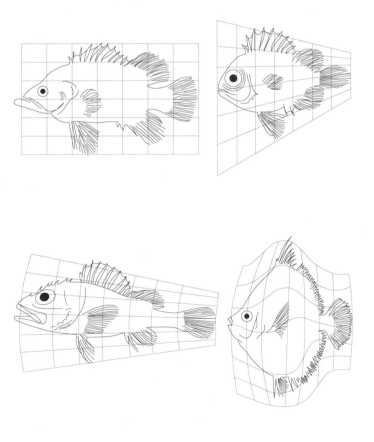

7.18
D'Arcy Thompson's use of continuous
deformations to generate a series of
fishes (after *On Growth and Form*,
1942)

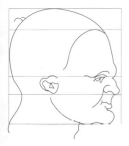

7.19
Dürer's use of nonlinear continuous transformations

7.20
An adjacency diagram: circles represent spaces and lines represent important adjacencies

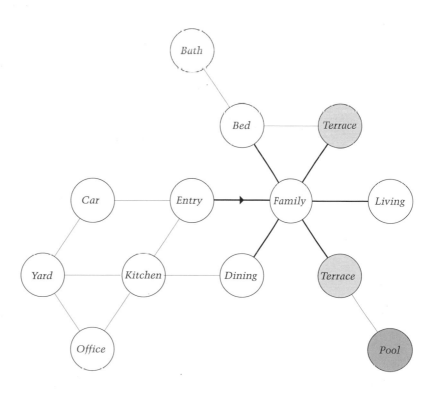

DESIGN OPERATIONS

7.21
Some Frank Lloyd Wright house plans
that have the adjacency diagram
shown earlier and are equivalent under
nonlinear continuous transformations

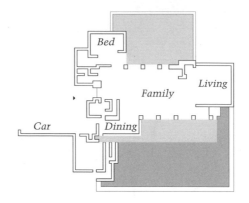

Life House, 1938

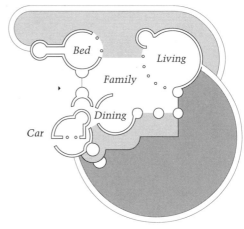

Jester House, 1938

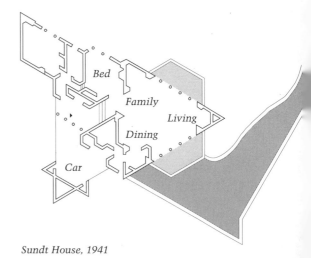

Sundt House, 1941

THE LOGIC OF ARCHITECTURE

Gaudi provides yet another example of the use of nonlinear continuous transformations. For design of vaulting shapes, he frequently employed flexible wires hung with weights. By shifting the suspension points, and varying the numbers, positions, and masses of weights, he could transform a funicular shape. This, when inverted, defined the profile for a similarly loaded arch or vault.

The relations between these various classes of geometric transformations are summarized by figure 7.22, in which each class includes all those below. A universe of design possibilities can be specified by choosing a vocabulary of shape types and some class of transformations to employ as design operators. For a given vocabulary, choosing successively more general classes of transformations will yield nested, successively more extensive universes.

This hierarchy of geometric transformations also provides us with a useful vocabulary for describing spatial relations between shapes in a composition. Where *shape1* and *shape2* are shapes, we can write assertions such as:

translation (shape1) = shape2
rotation (shape1) = shape2
reflection (shape1) = shape2
isometrictransformation (shape1) = shape2
lineartransformation (shape1) = shape2
continuousdeformation (shape1) = shape2

7.22
A taxonomy of geometric transformations

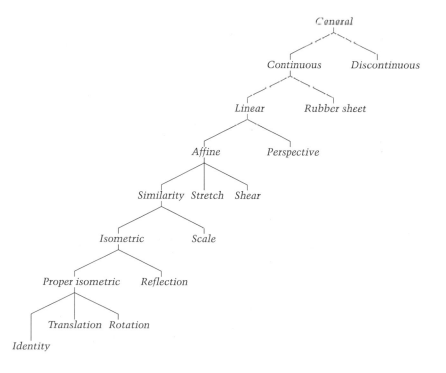

DESIGN OPERATIONS

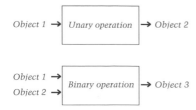

7.23
The arity of an operation

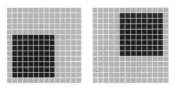

Shape A   *Shape B*

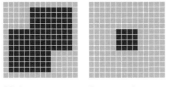

Union   *Intersection*

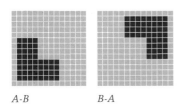

A-B   *B-A*

7.24
Boolean operations on pixel shapes

In other words, we specify that *shape1* is mapped into *shape2* by the given operator. Furthermore, to specify the relation more precisely, we can add transformation parameters, for example:

*translation (shape1, **Xdistance**, **Ydistance**) = shape2*
*rotation (shape1, **Theta**) = shape2*

Such vocabulary can be used to express different sorts of formal analyses of the Frank Lloyd Wright plans shown in figure 7.21. First, we can find isometries among the piers and columns—square ones in the Life house and circular ones in the Jester and Sundt houses. (Repetition of standard construction elements makes practical sense.) Second, there are similarities between the circular rooms in the Jester house, similarities between the triangular rooms in the Sundt house, and affinities between the rectangular rooms in the Life house: this provides each house with formal coherence but allows rooms to vary in size according to function. The essential equivalence of the three plans under continuous deformations is not immediately evident—indeed, it is surprising—because the shapes of corresponding rooms in the three houses, and of the building footprints, are *not* similar.

COMBINATION

A transformation is, technically, a unary operation: execution of a transformation turns one thing into another. Designers also need to perform binary operations, by which two things are combined to produce a third (figure 7.23). Addition and multiplication, for example, are binary operations in the integer numbers.

In a bitmap, union and intersection are useful binary operations. Let us say that a shape is any set of true (black) pixels (figure 7.24). One shape is a subshape of another whenever every pixel of the first is also a pixel of the second. The union of two shapes is the shape consisting of all the pixels in the first shape or the second shape. The intersection of two shapes is the shape consisting of just those pixels in both the first shape and the second shape. We can also define a shape difference (the second shape subtracted from the first) as the shape consisting of just those pixels in the first shape that are not also in the second. And, if we subtract the first shape from the second, we obtain a shape consisting of just those pixels in the second shape that are not also in the first. The set of all subshapes of the complete bitmap grid, and the operations of shape union, intersection, and subtraction, form a Boolean algebra.

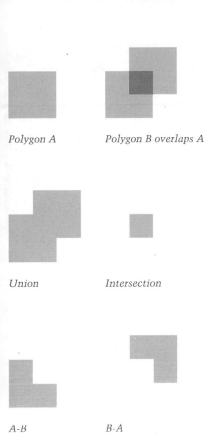

Polygon A   Polygon B overlaps A

Union   Intersection

A-B   B-A

7.25
Boolean operations on plane
polygons

The operations of union, intersection, and subtraction can be defined, in a directly analogous way, for a world of closed polygonal shapes (figure 7.25).[5] Thus if we take a small vocabulary of elementary shapes, the transformations of translation, rotation, reflection and scaling, and Boolean operations, we can establish a rich and extensive universe of polygonal compositions for exploration (figure 7.26).

The Boolean operations can also be defined for a world of closed solids (figure 7.27). Solid modeling systems are computer-aided design systems built around this idea.[6] They usually provide vocabularies of elementary parameterized solids, the similarity transformations, and the Boolean operations. This establishes a universe of three-dimensional compositions of solids.

To avoid some technical problems it is convenient to define binary operations in line worlds in a similar, but subtly different way.[7] Let us say that one straight-line segment is included in a second straight-line segment if the slopes and intercepts of the two lines are the same and if the endpoints of the second line lie between the endpoints of the first (figure 7.28). This definition is straightforwardly extended to other types of lines, such as arcs and splines. A shape, then, is a collection of lines, and a shape is a subshape of another whenever every line of the first shape is also a line of the second shape (figure 7.29). The addition of two shapes, then, is the shape consisting of all the lines in the first shape or the second shape, or produced by combining lines in the first shape or the second shape (figure 7.30). And the subtraction is the shape consisting of just those lines in the first shape that are not in the shape subtracted.

Some interesting universes of compositions can be established with the line addition and subtraction operations. If we can instantiate horizontal and vertical straight lines of any length (for example, by using pencil, parallel rule, and right-angle square), and add and subtract lines, we can explore a universe of all possible shapes composed of horizontal and vertical lines. If we introduce rotation of lines as an additional parameter (for example, by adding an adjustable square to our kit of drafting instruments), the universe expands to include all possible straight-line compositions. At the limits of this universe are the empty shape and the universal shape. The empty shape has no lines and is a subshape of every shape. The universal shape consists of all possible straight lines and has every shape as a subshape.

The derivation of complex shapes from simple ones by means of binary operations can be depicted by a binary tree, as shown in figure 7.31. If we record for each node in the

7.27
Boolean operations on closed solids

Vocabulary of polygons

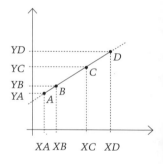

7.28
Line BC is included in line AD

Some shapes in the universe

7.26
A universe of shapes that contains a unit square and a half-square triangle and is closed under orthogonal translations, scaling, and Boolean operations

THE LOGIC OF ARCHITECTURE

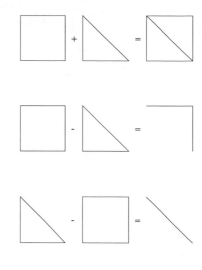

7.30
Addition and subtraction of line shapes

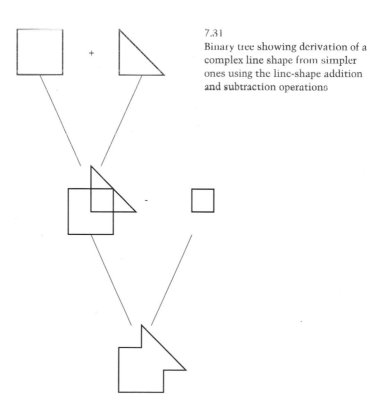

7.31
Binary tree showing derivation of a complex line shape from simpler ones using the line-shape addition and subtraction operations

7.29
A line shape and some of its infinitely many subshapes

DESIGN OPERATIONS

A   B   A ∩ B

7.32
Intersection is not closed in the plane
polygons with interiors

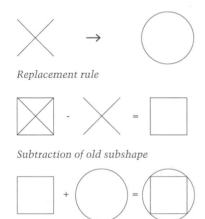

Replacement rule

Subtraction of old subshape

Addition of new subshape

7.33
Replacement of a subshape

tree the transformation parameters of the operand shapes,
and the operator that was applied, we obtain a procedure for
reconstructing the shape—in effect, a concise description of
it. This technique for encoding descriptions of complex
shapes finds practical application in computer-aided design:
the constructive solid geometry (CSG) method of shape
description that is commonly used in solid modelers, for
example, is based on application of Boolean operators to elementary closed solids (Requicha, 1980; Kemper and Wallrath,
1987).

It is usually convenient to define binary operations in
such a way that they are closed in some shape type that particularly interests us. For example, the addition and substrac-
tion operations are closed in line shapes: they can never produce something that is not a line shape. But the Boolean
operations are *not* closed in the plane polygons.[8] Consider,
for example, two squares coincident at an edge, as shown in
figure 7.32. Their intersection is *not* a closed shape with an
interior, but a one-dimensional straight line.

REPLACEMENT

Anybody who has worked with a word processor is familiar
with the operation of replacing one character string with
another. Similarly, a designer may need to replace a shape of
one type with a shape of another. Replacement might be
local (replace *that* X by a circle) or it might be global (replace
all Xs by circles). We can specify replacements by means of
rules, as shown in figure 7.33, in which the subshape to be
replaced appears on the left side and its replacement appears
on the right side. In a line world replacement amounts to
subtraction of the old shape followed by addition of the new
one. Draftsmen do this by erasing then redrawing. In a computer-aided design system, information describing the old
shape is deleted from the data structure and replaced by
information describing the new shape.

The same replacement operation may produce different
results when it is applied in different ways. Consider, for
example, the simple line shape shown in figure 7.34a.
Parallel replacement of squares by circles produces the result
shown in figure 7.34b, but serial replacement of squares by
circles produces the sorts of results shown in figure 7.34c.

The way that a replacement operation works may also depend on the way that emergent shapes in a composition have
been recognized and labeled. This is illustrated in figure 7.35:
different applications of a rule for recognizing and labeling
squares induce different replacements of squares by circles.

a. An arrangement of squares

b. Parallel replacement

c. Sequential replacement

7.34
Replacement of squares by circles

7.35
Recognition controls replacement

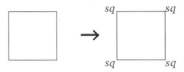

A recognition rule

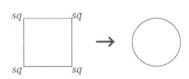

A replacement rule

An unlabeled shape

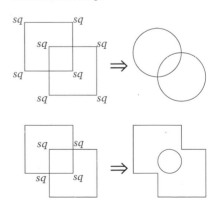

Different applications of the recognition rule induce different replacements

DESIGN OPERATIONS

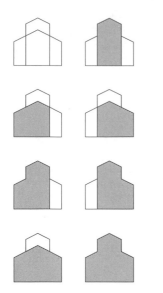

7.36
Disambiguating an elevation drawing
by replacing transparent polygons
with opaque ones

7.37
Elevation diagram of Palladio's S.
Francesco della Vigna, Venice (after
Wittkower, 1962)

Designers often begin with states of design worlds that have ambiguous interpretations as proposals for three-dimensional buildings and, through erasure and replacement, sharpen them into less ambiguous representations. Figure 7.36, for example, shows how a wire-frame elevation sketch may be resolved, in various ways, into an unambiguous layering of planes by erasure of verticals and gables and substitution of shaded polygons for empty ones. It seems very likely that Palladio proceeded in much this way in his explorations of overlaid temple fronts applied to church facades (figure 7.37).

ALGEBRAS

A designer, then, creates a composition (a state of the design world) by instantiating, transforming, and combining shapes. Compositional alternatives can be produced by choosing different shape vocabulary elements for instantiation and by performing different sequences of transformation and combination operations. Thus the designer's compositional universe is bounded and structured by the shape vocabulary available for instantiation and by the repertoire of shape transformation and combination operators provided by the design world.

Technically, the design world models an algebra—a set of things (the carrier set of the algebra) together with operators defined on those things and closed in the set. In this case, the things are states of the design world, and the operators provide the designer with a way to get around from one state to another; they are the means of exploration. More formally, a design algebra is a triple $\langle V, T, C \rangle$ where V is a vocabulary of shapes available for instantiation in the design world, T is a repertoire of shape transformation operators, and C is a repertoire of shape combination operators. The carrier set of the algebra, denoted $V^\star$, consists of all those shapes that can be produced by instantiating vocabulary elements, transforming shapes, and combining shapes. Each element of $V^\star$ is a state of the design world, and the operators in T and C are closed in $V^\star$.

A designer should be concerned, first of all, that $V^\star$ contains shapes relevant to the task at hand. If, for example, $V^\star$ contains only straight-line shapes and the design context calls for curves, then the designer is exploring the wrong terrain. Secondly, the instantiation, transformation, and combination operators should conveniently structure the process of exploring $V^\star$: they should allow the shapes of interest to be constructed and varied in quick and elegant ways. Finally, the efficiency of the model—that is, the speed with which operations are executed—is also important. A computer-aided design system, for example, may model a given design algebra much more efficiently than pencil, paper, and traditional drafting instruments.

A standard computer-drafting system clearly exemplifies the specification and implementation of a design algebra appropriate for use in architecture. Such a system provides for instantiation of straight lines, arcs, circles, and usually a few more complicated shapes such as rectangles. It provides a shape addition operator for "grouping" primitives into more complex shapes and a shape subtraction operator for deleting unwanted shapes. The usual shape transformation operators are translation, rotation, reflection, and scaling.

A solid-modeling system implements a rather different kind of algebra. The vocabulary typically consists of parametric boxes, cylinders, spheres, cones, and prisms. The shape combination operations are union, intersection, and subtraction of solids. These can be applied not only to pairs of instances of the solid primitives, but also to pairs of solids that have themselves resulted from combination operations, so that complex solids can be built from simple primitives through recursive combination. Translation and rotation operators are usually provided for positioning solids in three-dimensional space. Reflection and scaling are sometimes provided as well, but these may be avoided since they can have disconcerting effects when applied to three-dimensional solids.

SUMMARY

A design world is fundamentally characterized by its shape vocabulary and operators. These establish, for exploration, a set of shape possibilities that includes the vocabulary and is closed under application of all of the operators.

8

LANGUAGES OF ARCHITECTURAL FORM

GRAMMATICAL COMBINATION

The trouble with algebras, as universes of design possibilities, is that they usually contain too much. They tend to contain vast numbers of possibilities that have no architectural meaning whatsoever, plus possibilities that are meaningful but irrelevant or uninteresting. The state-action trees that they establish contain numerous branches that are not worth exploring. We need some way to curb promiscuous combination of shapes, to tighten up the rules of the game.

One powerful way to do this is to introduce the idea of grammatical combination of parts. We can, if we so choose, specify in the type definition of an architectural vocabulary element that it is only instantiated in certain kinds of combinations with other elements. That is, we specify certain external relations in the type definition. The analogy here with parts of speech is close; it is essential to being an English noun that it is only instantiated in English sentences in certain kinds of combinations with other words, as given by the rules of English grammar. Thus not every string of English words is an English sentence: only strings that comply with the rules of English grammar count as sentences. A clear and simple illustration of this kind of thing in architecture is provided by Alberti's handling of columns, piers, entablatures, and arches (figure 8.1), as analyzed by Rudolf Wittkower (1962):

In his religious buildings Alberti consistently avoided the combination of arch and column. When he used columns he did, in fact, give them a straight entablature, while when he introduced arches, he made them rest on pillars with or without half-columns set against them as decoration. Alberti found the models for both forms in Roman architecture. But whereas the first motif is Greek, the Romans playing the role of mediators, the second is Roman. The first motif is based on the functional meaning of the column, the second on the cohesion and unity of the wall. To explain this latter point: in the Colosseum the arched pillars may be interpreted as residues of a pierced wall, with the half-columns, which carry the straight entablature, placed against them as ornament. In practice, therefore, Alberti's conception of the column is essentially Greek, while his conception of the arch is essentially Roman.

Critics sometimes suggest that certain usages violate rules of grammatical combination. Vitruvius warned that Ionic capitals should not be combined with Doric entablatures,

8.1
Albertian usage (following Roman
precedent) of columns, entablatures,
piers, and arches

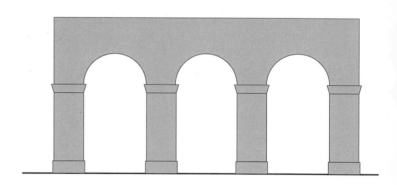

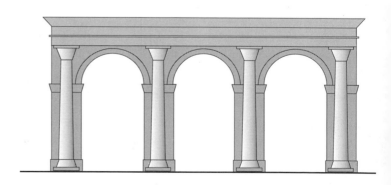

"the usage of each class having been fixed long ago." Augustus Welby Pugin, in *The True Principles of Pointed or Christian Architecture* (1841), noted a difficulty that arose when English architects proposed to apply Greek porticos to churches (figure 8.2):

Christian churches require bells, by the sound of which the faithful may be called to their devotions. The bells, to be distinctly heard, must be suspended in a tower or belfry, and these are features utterly unknown in Greek architecture. A tower composed of a number of small porticos, set over one another, and placed in front of a mock temple, is a most glaring absurdity; nor is a tower of this description, starting out of nothing at the top of a portico, any better.

He was no better pleased by the application of Greek porticos to houses (figure 8.3).

Neither are they better adapted for domestic purposes; for it is still more absurd to see two or three tiers of windows introduced in the shell of a Greek temple, the roof of which is broken by numerous stacks of vainly disguised chimneys.

In biological thought, very similar ideas about restrictions on ranges of combinatorial possibility were formulated by Cuvier. In his *Leçons d'anatomie comparée* (1800) he noted (as Aristotle had done) that each kind of organ may take many forms, and that, if any form could coexist with any other form, a huge combinatorial universe would result. However, he argued, combinations must meet certain conditions, and only the combinations that meet these conditions actually exist in nature.

8.2
"A most glaring absurdity": application of a Greek portico to a church, as depicted by Pugin in *The True Principles of Pointed or Christian Architecture*, 1841

8.3
"A Grecian temple outraged in all its proportions and character": Pugin's depiction of the combination, in a house, of the Greek temple with windows and chimneys

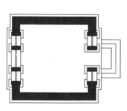

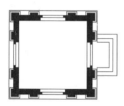

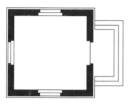

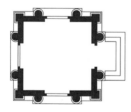

8.4
Substitution of alternative wall
and entrance treatments for a
square plan (after Gibbs's *A Book
of Architecture*, 1728)

SIMPLE PRESCRIPTIVE RULES

The grammatical rules of a language of architectural form, like those of a spoken language, may be specified in a variety of formats. The simplest approach, as employed, for example, by Pugin, is to display various exemplars of "correct" and "incorrect" practice. This technique has very commonly been employed by architectural theorists, from Vitruvius to the present day.

A more sophisticated approach is to state generalized prescriptive rules, as in elementary language textbooks. The Renaissance architectural theorists were particularly fond of doing this. In his Four Books of Architecture (1570) Palladio, for example, introduced rules of composition as follows:

And altho' variety and things new may please every one, yet they ought not to be done contrary to the precepts of art, and contrary to that which reason dictates; whence one sees, that altho' the ancients did vary, yet they never departed from the universal and necessary rules of art, as shall be seen in my book of antiquities.

Typical of the prescriptive rules given by Palladio for villa designs are:

The rooms ought to be distributed on each side of the entry and hall; and it is to be observed, that those on the right correspond with those on the left, that so the fabrick may be the same in one place as in the other. . . .

The windows on the right hand ought to correspond to those on the left, and those above directly over them that are below; and the doors likewise ought to be directly over one another, that the void may be over the void, and the solid upon the solid, and all face one another, so that standing at one end of the house one may see to the other, which affords both beauty and cool air in summer, besides other conveniences.

REPLACEMENT RULES

Yet another approach is to specify replacement rules. Grammarians of spoken language, for example, often set out sentence schemata like:

The_____ is green.

Then they specify the type of word substitutable for the blank, in this case a noun. Thus the schema might be expressed:

*The **Noun** is green.*

Noun is a variable ranging over all the English nouns: substitution of any instance of an English noun, such as *grass*, yields a grammatical English sentence.

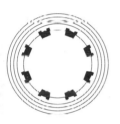

Architectural theorists have occasionally established schemata and demonstrated substitutions in much the same way. James Gibbs (1728), for example, produced diagrams showing how various wall and entrance treatments could be substituted for each other in square and circular pavilions (figures 8.4, 8.5). In his *Encyclopaedia of Architecture* (1846), J. C. Loudon took a bare cube as the schema for a cottage, then showed how different exterior treatments might be substituted as appropriate to the owner's status. More recently, Bernard Tschumi has programmatically employed substitution of architectural elements from a chosen lexicon within the framework of a gridded ten-meter cube to generate a set of pavilions for the Park of La Villette in Paris.

RECURSIVE REPLACEMENT

Replacement rules become particularly interesting if they are applied recursively. Figure 8.6 shows how the recursive application of a simple replacement rule to an initial square yields plans for increasingly elaborate fourfold Islamic gardens, such as that of the Taj Mahal, which was originally subdivided by paths and canals into sixty-four smaller squares. Notice that the rule can be applied an unlimited number of times. Thus a very simple rule system specifies a countably infinite set of design possibilities for exploration.

Elaboration of this principle leads to a powerful technique for specifying universes of similarly-structured objects. Let us assume, for example, that we are concerned with a type of object known as a sentence, and that a sentence always consists of a noun phrase followed by a verb phrase. This can be expressed by the replacement rule[1]:

Sentence → NounPhrase VerbPhrase

The rule tells us that, whenever we see the string of symbols on the left-hand side, we can replace it by the string of symbols on the right-hand side. A second rule establishes the essential properties of a noun phrase:

NounPhrase → Article Noun

And a third rule establishes the essential properties of a verb phrase:

VerbPhrase → Verb NounPhrase

Finally, there are rules establishing the ranges of the variables **Article**, **Noun**, and **Verb**:

Article → a, the
Noun → column, beam
Verb → supports, loads

8.5
Substitution of alternative wall and entrance treatments for a circular plan (after Gibbs, 1728)

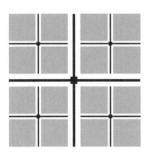

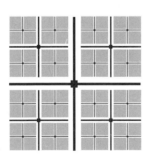

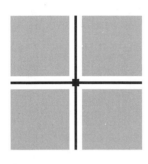

8.6
The Islamic garden rule, as used in the garden of the Taj Mahal

(The comma indicates an alternative.) These rules are known as productions, and the set constitutes a production system, as follows:

Rule 1   ***Sentence → NounPhrase VerbPhrase***
Rule 2   ***NounPhrase → Article Noun***
Rule 3   ***VerbPhrase → Verb NounPhrase***
Rule 4   ***Article*** *→ a, the*
Rule 5   ***Noun*** *→ column, beam*
Rule 6   ***Verb*** *→ supports, loads*

These six replacement rules, together with the starting symbol **Sentence**, constitute a phrase-structure grammar that generates a simple language.[2] Sentences in the language are generated by recursive application of the production system to the starting symbol to generate a sequence of symbol strings. A rule applies, and can be executed, whenever a sub-string of the current symbol string is matched by the left-hand side of a rule. We say that a new symbol string is *derived* from the current symbol string by application of that rule. A derivation is a sequence of such rule applications. Derivations terminate when no further matches can be found. Here, then, is an example of a derivation:

Starting symbol   ***Sentence***
By rule 1   ***NounPhrase VerbPhrase***
By rule 2   ***Article Noun VerbPhrase***
By rule 3   ***Article Noun Verb NounPhrase***
By rule 2   ***Article Noun Verb Article Noun***
By rule 4   *a **Noun Verb Article Noun***
By rule 4   *a **Noun Verb** the **Noun***
By rule 5   *a column **Verb** the beam*
By rule 6   *a column supports the beam*
Termination

This derivation is depicted graphically by the tree diagram in figure 8.7. Steps in derivations are often denoted as follows:

By rule 6   *a column **Verb** the beam* ⇒
                  a column supports the beam

The symbol ⇒ is read "derives."

    Sometimes, in a derivation process, several different substitutions are allowable. For example, the intermediate string

Article Noun Verb Article Noun

consists of five variables, each with two possible values, so $2^5 = 32$ different sentences can be produced from it. Thus a concise grammar can specify a large (in some cases countably infinite) set of sentences. Alternative derivations can be rep-

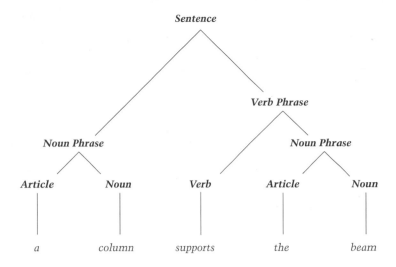

resented by a state-action tree in which the root is the starting symbol **Sentence**, branches represent applicable rules, internal nodes are "incomplete" sentences (strings that still contain variables), and "complete" sentences in the language (strings with no variables) are at terminal nodes.

Now let us assume that, for every production in the grammar there is a corresponding inverse, or recognition rule, as follows:

Reduction 1	**NounPhrase VerbPhrase → Sentence**
Reduction 2	**Article Noun → NounPhrase**
Reduction 3	**Verb NounPhrase → VerbPhrase**
Reduction 4	*a, the* → **Article**
Reduction 5	*column, beam* → **Noun**
Reduction 6	*supports, loads* → **Verb**

These recognition rules can be applied recursively to a string of words to determine whether the string is a sentence in the language; that is, whether it complies with the grammatical rules. If the string can be reduced to the starting symbol **Sentence**, then it is a sentence: it has been shown to satisfy the predicate *sentence (**String**)*. Here is an example of a successful reduction:

Given string	*the beam loads a column*
By reduction 4	**Article** *beam loads a column*
By reduction 4	**Article** *beam loads* **Article** *column*
By reduction 5	**Article Noun** *loads* **Article** *column*
By reduction 2	**NounPhrase** *loads* **Article** *column*
By reduction 5	**NounPhrase** *loads* **Article Noun**
By reduction 2	**NounPhrase** *loads* **NounPhrase**
By reduction 6	**NounPhrase Verb NounPhrase**
By reduction 3	**NounPhrase VerbPhrase**
By reduction 1	**Sentence**
Termination	

Compilers perform such reductions when they check the syntax of programs in computer languages, and language students do so when they diagram sentences.[3]

In summary, a grammar concisely encodes a type definition. If it is executed in generative mode it produces instances of the type, and if it is executed in recognition mode it determines whether or not a given object is an instance. Furthermore, the grammar assigns a syntactic structure to instances: it specifies a way (or perhaps alternative ways) of decomposing instances into parts of various recognizable types, such as noun phrases, verb phrases, and so on.

Technically, the language L specified by a grammar is a subset of the carrier set V^* of an algebra established by the vocabulary V and combination operators (figure 8.8). The vocabulary is divided into nonterminal elements (variables) and terminal elements (constants). In our example, the nonterminal vocabulary consists of the symbols **Sentence**, **NounPhrase**, **VerbPhrase**, **Article**, **Noun**, and **Verb**. The terminal vocabulary consists of six English words: *a, the, column, beam, supports, loads*. The concatenation operator applied to the terminal vocabulary yields an infinite number of strings, such as:

the the the
a the beam column
supports loads a

Even if we specify that a string must be exactly five words long, there will still be $6^5 = 7,776$ strings. But we admit as sentences only those strings of terminals that are derived from the starting symbol **Sentence** by application of the rules. Thus our grammar specifies that only thirty-two of these five-word strings are sentences in the language.

8.8
The language L specified by a grammar is a subset of the carrier set V^* of an algebra

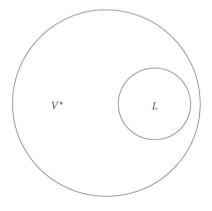

THE LOGIC OF ARCHITECTURE

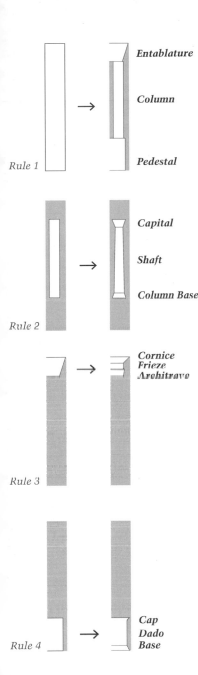

Entablature

Column

Pedestal

Rule 1

Capital

Shaft

Column Base

Rule 2

Cornice
Frieze
Architrave

Rule 3

Cap
Dado
Base

Rule 4

8.9
The rules of a simple grammar
that generates schematic designs
for classical columns

If we want to use a grammar to restrict the possible states of a design world, we must formulate the rules in terms of the types of shapes, labels, and relations populating that world. This can be done in many different ways. Let us begin with a simple example.

Parallels of the classical orders usually specify that an order consists of three parts: pedestal, column, and entablature. This might be expressed verbally by the replacement rule:

Order → Pedestal Column Entablature

Then further rules of trichotomous subdivision might be added:

Pedestal → Base Dado Cap
Column → ColumnBase Shaft Capital
Entablature → Architrave Frieze Cornice

The same rules may be expressed graphically, as shown in figure 8.9.

So far this is not a very interesting grammar, since it merely specifies a single object subdivided into nine parts. But it begins to specify a more interesting language if we introduce rules that provide for alternative substitutions, such as:

Capital → Doric, Ionic, Corinthian

Furthermore, we can introduce rules that tell how to detail the various parts. For example, a Doric capital is detailed as follows:

Capital → Necking *echinus* **Abacus**
Abacus → *plinth cymation fillet*
Necking → *cincture astragal fillets*

Figure 8.10 shows graphic versions of these rules and figure 8.11 illustrates their application to derive a complete Doric capital. It is easy to see how a complete parallel of the orders might be encoded by such rules.

When run in generative mode these rules tell how to compose the parts of a classical column correctly: they encode knowledge of how instances of this type of artifact are put together. When run in recognition mode they tell how to parse a classical column into a hierarchy of labeled parts (figure 8.12). (These rules parse any classical column in a unique way, but in general grammars may parse objects in multiple ways.) Figure 8.13 illustrates the step-by-step reduction process by which an object is recognized and labeled as a classical column.

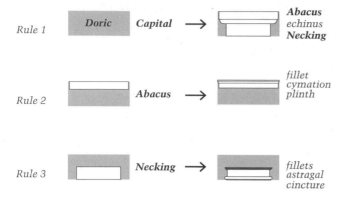

Rule 1   **Doric** **Capital** → **Abacus**
echinus
Necking

Rule 2   **Abacus** → fillet
cymation
plinth

Rule 3   **Necking** → fillets
astragal
cincture

8.10
Rules for detailing a Doric capital

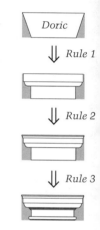

Doric
⇓ *Rule 1*

⇓ *Rule 2*

⇓ *Rule 3*

8.11
Top-down refinement of the
design of a Doric capital

8.12
A tree diagram depicting the
derivation and structure of a
schematic classical order

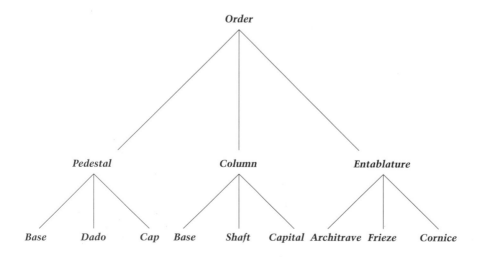

THE LOGIC OF ARCHITECTURE

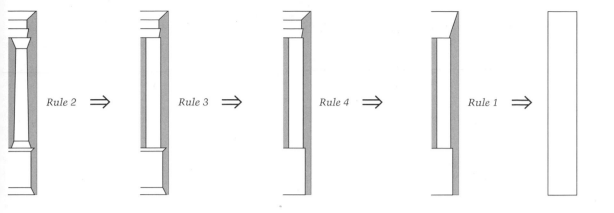

Rule 2 ⟹   Rule 3 ⟹   Rule 4 ⟹   Rule 1 ⟹

8.13
Reduction of a classical order

Notice how the classical rules, as I have expressed them here, structure a top-down design process: the designer begins with a very abstract definition and recursively refines it into a detailed drawing of an instance of the type. The design strategy is to accomplish the final goal of producing a complete, detailed drawing via solution of a sequence of sub-problems. The subgoal, at each stage, is to appropriately refine the current design to the next level of detail.

Conversely, the classical rules structure a bottom-up recognition process. We first look for classical vocabulary elements such as astragals and cinctures, then check to see that these are correctly combined into higher-level components such as Doric capitals. Then we check that these higher-level components are correctly combined, and so on recursively until we can show that the whole composition not only has the correct classical parts, but is also correctly put together.

All this works because a classical order is, like a sentence, a linear sequence of elements (running bottom to top instead of left to right). Thus we can embed a grammar in an algebra in which the sole operation is concatenation of sequences of elements. But in general, if we want to specify languages of two-dimensional and three-dimensional form, we must embed grammars in algebras that have wider repertoires of operations. One way to do this is to parameterize all the vocabulary elements, as shown in figure 8.14. Assignments of values to parameters then specify geometric transformations of instances, and required spatial relationships of elements in compositions can be expressed by writing predicates of the parameters. So we can more completely express the rule governing relationships of pedestal, column, and entablature in an order by writing:

Parameterized parts of a classical
column and their relationships

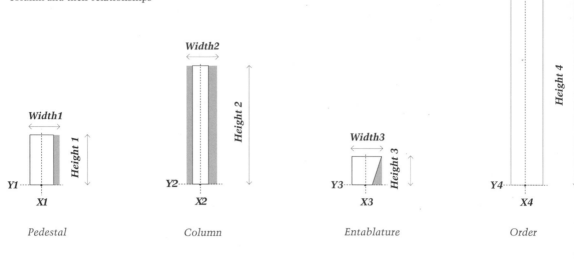

Pedestal   Column   Entablature   Order

8.15
Correctly proportioned classical
column (according to the rules
given by Vignola)

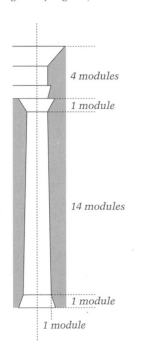

4 modules

1 module

14 modules

1 module

1 module

Order (X4, Y4, Height4, Width4) →
    Pedestal (X1, Y1, Height1, Width1)
    Column (X2, Y2, Height2, Width2)
    Entablature (X3, Y3, Height3, Width3)
such that
equal (X4, X1)
equal (Y4, Y1)
equal (Width4, Width1)
equal (X1, X2)
equal ((Y1 + Height1), Y2)
equal (Width1, Width2)
equal ((Y2 + Height2), Y3)
equal (Width2, Width3)
equal (Height4, (Height1 + Height2 + Height3))

This rule could be elaborated to specify the correct classical
ratio of column diameter to height, and so on (figure 8.15).

    The designer's first task, in producing a design within this
language, is to choose a value of **Height4** such that the order
fits correctly into its context. This decomposes into subtasks of dimensioning and correctly relating pedestal, column, and entablature. The goal, in each of these subtasks, is
to choose values for the variables such that the specified
predicates are satisfied. Each of these subtasks then decomposes into still lower-level subtasks, and so on until values
have been chosen for all the variables, predicates at every
level have been satisfied, and the order has been designed
down to the smallest detail.

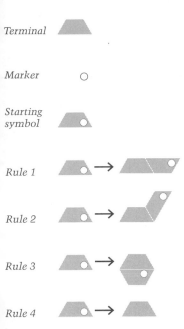

Terminal

Marker

Starting symbol

Rule 1

Rule 2

Rule 3

Rule 4

8.16
The rules of the half-hexagon table grammar

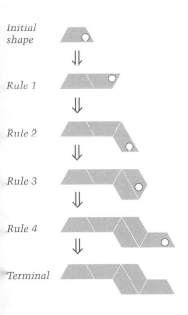

Initial shape

⇓

Rule 1

⇓

Rule 2

⇓

Rule 3

⇓

Rule 4

⇓

Terminal

8.17
Derivation of a design in the half-hexagon table grammar

Figure 8.16 illustrates another example of a grammar defined in a two-dimensional world of closed shapes. There is one terminal vocabulary element—a half-hexagon of fixed dimension—and one marker element—a white circle. (Markers function like construction lines: they guide the development of compositions but do not appear in completed compositions.) The game defined by this grammar is conveniently played with cardboard cutouts and coins. There is no explicit parameterization of vocabulary elements. We assume, instead, that the isometric transformations (identity, translation, rotation, and reflection) may be applied to any half-hexagon or circle. Let us also assume that the half-hexagons depict tables in a furniture layout.

The positions of the markers define attachment points for new tables. The starting symbol is a single table with a single attachment point on one edge. There are three rules for attachment of new tables in different ways, and a fourth rule simply removes the attachment point to terminate the attachment process. A rule applies when its left-hand side can be brought into coincidence with a subshape by some isometric transformation. Recursive application of the rules derives sequences of arrangements such as that shown in figure 8.17. Some completed designs in the language are illustrated in figure 8.18.

Now let us introduce two additional rules, as illustrated in figure 8.19. One recognizes and labels a type of arrangement called a circle, and the other recognizes and labels a type called a triad. We can now formulate problems such as "Construct an arrangement that includes two circles and a triad." Figure 8.20 illustrates a solution.

In this case the rules of the grammar structure a bottom-up design process. Fully-detailed components (the half-hexagon tables) are given at the outset, and the designer must assemble these (much as in a jigsaw puzzle) in such a way that specified qualities emerge. A small part of the infinite state-action tree that must be searched for a solution is shown in figure 8.21.

This tree may be searched systematically in either depth-first or breadth-first fashion. In depth-first search the designer picks an alternative from among the several available at each node, and so follows a branch deeply into the tree until a solution is found or until it becomes clear that the branch will not lead to a solution. If the branch does not lead to a solution, the designer backtracks then follows another branch, and so on. In breadth-first search, instead of diving

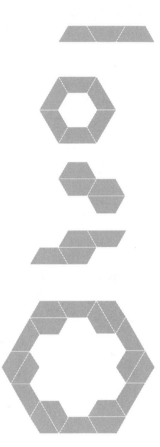

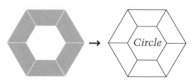

Rule 5

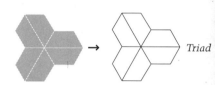

Rule 6

8.19
Recognition and labeling rules

8.18
Some plan arrangements in the
language specified by the half-
hexagon table grammar

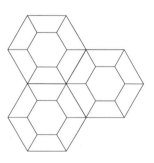

8.20
A solution to the problem
"Construct an arrangement that
includes three circles and a triad"

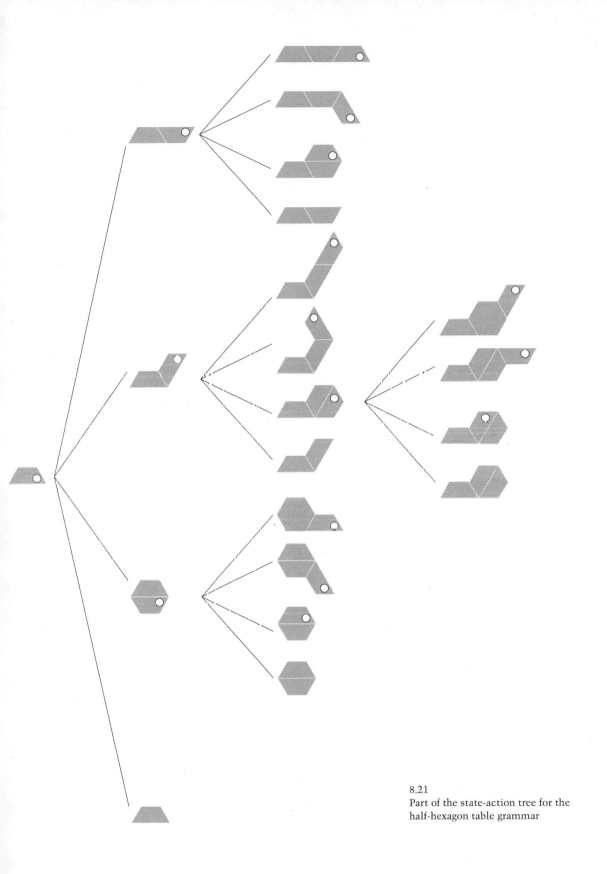

8.21
Part of the state-action tree for the
half-hexagon table grammar

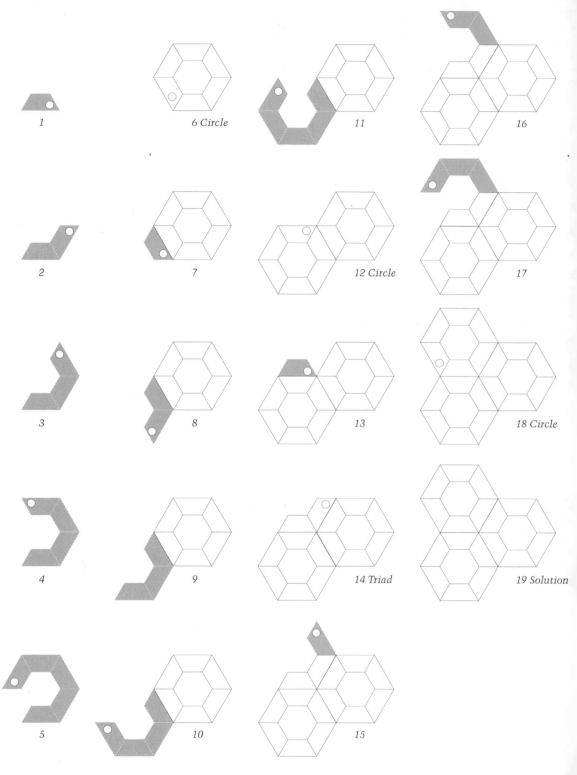

8.22
Approaching the solution via a
sequence of subgoals

THE LOGIC OF ARCHITECTURE

deeply into the tree, the designer pushes uniformly into it, level by level. All of the nodes at the first level are examined, then all of the nodes at the second level are developed and examined, and so on.

Both of these strategies become much more efficient if the designer has some good way of deciding which branches look most promising and exploring those first. In this case, the most obvious strategy is to accomplish the final goal via a sequence of subgoals of fitting individual pieces appropriately in place. The overall goal can be decomposed into subgoals of forming circles and triads. These subgoals, in turn, can be decomposed into lower-level subgoals of choosing correctly among rules one, two, and three (which fit tables against their predecessors in different ways) at each stage. If the current intermediate subgoal is to form a circle, for example, it is appropriate to choose rule two (which constructs a fragment of a circle). And if the current intermediate subgoal is to form a triad, it is appropriate to choose rule three (which constructs a fragment of a triad). By intelligently relating means to ends in this way, a designer can rapidly construct a solution (figure 8.22).

GRAMMARS WITH SCALING

In the half-hexagon table grammar, shape equivalence is defined under isometric transformations. But we can, if we wish, define equivalence under broader classes of transformations. Figure 8.23, for example, shows a simple grammar that generates compositions of right triangles. In this case, a rule applies when its left-hand side can be brought into coincidence with a subshape by some similarity transformation.

If we think of grammars purely as abstract systems, we can define shape equivalence in any way we like. But if we want to relate a grammar to a particular construction world, it is more useful to define shape equivalence in a way that reflects the properties of that world. If real half-hexagon tables are made in just one size, for example, it makes sense to think of them as equivalent under rigid transformations, but it is *not* useful to broaden the definition of equivalence to provide for scaling. But if rooms can be made any size, we might find it useful in a floor-plan grammar to define shape equivalence under similarity or affine transformations. Figure 8.24 shows a grammar for Le Corbusier's spiral museum. Here room shapes that can be brought into coincidence by translation, right-angle rotation, and unequal scaling are taken to be equivalent.

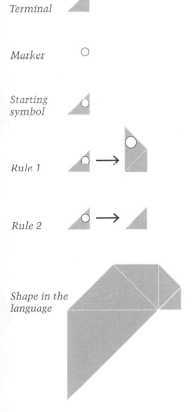

8.23
A simple grammar with scaling

Terminal

Marker

Starting symbol

Rule 1

Rule 2

Shape in the language

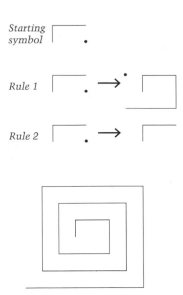

Starting symbol

Rule 1

Rule 2

A design in the language

8.24
A grammar for Le Corbusier's spiral museum

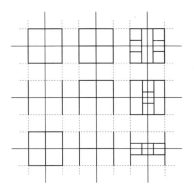

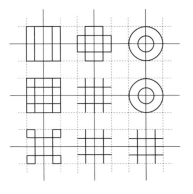

8.25
Skeletons of plan construction lines
(after Durand's *Partie graphique des cours d'architecture à l'Ecole Royale Polytechnique*, 1821)

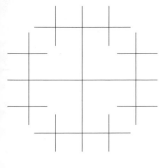

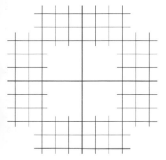

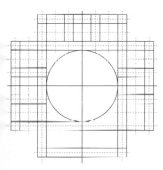

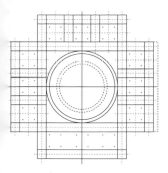

Purely top-down and purely bottom-up design processes, as illustrated by these examples, are limiting cases that we rarely encounter in practice. Instead, the rules of grammars usually establish complex domains in which exploration of possibilities may proceed in both top-down and bottom-up directions. J. N. L. Durand's *Précis des leçons d'architecture* (1802–5) and *Partie graphique des cours d'architecture* (1821) clearly illustrate this.[4]

Durand's text and diagrams constitute a compendium of neoclassical design rules. Cross-axes, grids, squares and circles are taken as primitive shapes, and a diagram (figure 8.25) shows how to assemble these, in bottom-up fashion, into symmetrical skeletons of construction lines. Another key plate (figures 8.26, 8.27) illustrates the top-down process of recursively refining a skeleton into a fully detailed floor plan. Numerous additional plates illustrate a lexicon of alternative substitutions (figure 8.28) and examples of syntactically correct combinations of elements (figure 8.29). Durand's rules do not quite provide a complete, consistent specification of a classical architectural language, but it is straightforward to develop them into a grammar that does.

If you try to design within the framework of Durand's rules, it soon becomes evident that the strengths and weaknesses of top-down and bottom-up strategies are complementary. In top-down design the subproblems are ones of choosing and adapting elements to fit within a framework that has been established at a higher level. At a certain point it may prove impossible to substitute or to adapt any of the available elements to fit as required. This necessitates moving back to a higher level of abstraction and adjusting the overall framework so that the lower-level problems are redefined. Conversely, in bottom-up design, the subproblems are ones of assembling known pieces to achieve specified emergent properties. At a certain point it may prove impossible to find a combination of the pieces at hand that achieves the desired result. This necessitates moving back to a lower level of abstraction and redesigning the components so that they can be put together in different ways—thus redefining the higher-level problems.

8.26
Steps in the top-down process of refining a skeleton into a fully detailed plan (after Durand's *Précis des leçons d'architecture*, 1802–5)

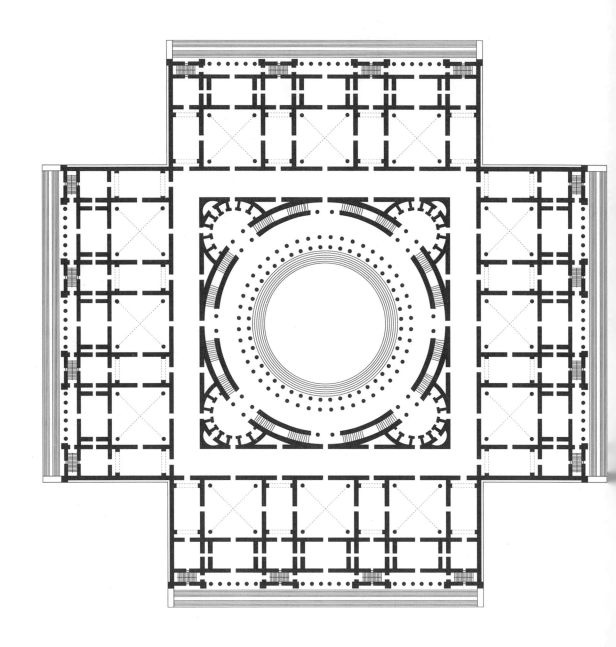

8.27
The final plan, after shapes
representing architectural elements
from the classical lexicon have been
substituted and all construction
lines have been removed

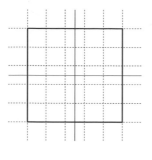

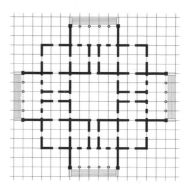

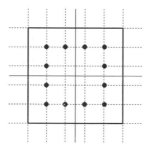

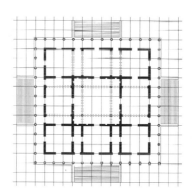

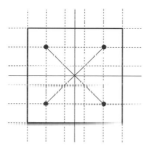

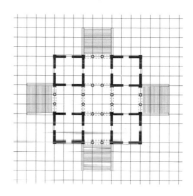

8.29
Examples of syntactically correct
compositions (after Durand's *Partie
graphique des cours d'architecture*)

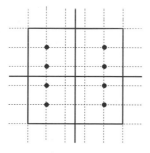

8.28
Alternative substitutions from the
classical architectural lexicon (after
Durand's *Partie graphique des cours
d'architecture*)

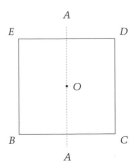

8.30
Association of labels with points
and with ends of line segments

For a final example, let us consider a fairly sophisticated grammar to generate villa floor plans in the style of Palladio. Since Palladio was one of the first architects to explore plan ideas by sketching numerous variants, it is appropriate to define this grammar in a two-dimensional world of lines. It will suffice to take as the starting point the algebra of straight-line shapes under shape addition and subtraction that was introduced in chapter 4. Where L^* is the universe of two-dimensional straight-line shapes, then, the Palladian grammar specifies a subset P of L^*.

Stiny (1980) has defined, for this sort of world, a powerful type of grammar known as a parametric shape grammar.[5] Shapes, under Stiny's definition, consist of points, lines, and labels. Labels are alphabetic characters or character strings and may be associated with points and lines as illustrated in figure 8.30. Rules specify how subshapes of a composition in progress may be replaced by other shapes. A rule applies if there is a similarity transformation that will bring the shape on the left-hand side into coincidence with a subshape of the composition in progress such that there is a one-to-one match of labels. Shapes have proportion parameters, and the values of these can be left unassigned by the grammar so that dimensionless plan schemata, which can be proportioned in different ways, are produced. (When rules are applied it is assumed that assignments to the parameters of the matching shapes are the same.) Labels are used to control application of rules and to define termination conditions.

Notice that, in this formalism for defining grammars, the sharp distinction made earlier between terminal shapes (which appear in completed designs in a language) and marker shapes ("construction lines," which do not appear in completed designs) is abandoned. A derivation terminates when labels (not markers) have been eliminated. The importance of this becomes evident when we consider the roles of shape in depictions. Where there is a sharp distinction between terminals and markers, we assume that terminals depict physical components and assemblies in the construction world, while markers are just organizing abstractions that do not depict physical objects in the construction world. Thus in the earlier example, half-hexagons depict tables in the construction world, but the circular markers do not depict anything in the construction world. But in a language specified by a parametric shape grammar, as now defined, shapes may have more or less precise meanings in the construction world. This allows for a design to evolve smoothly from a

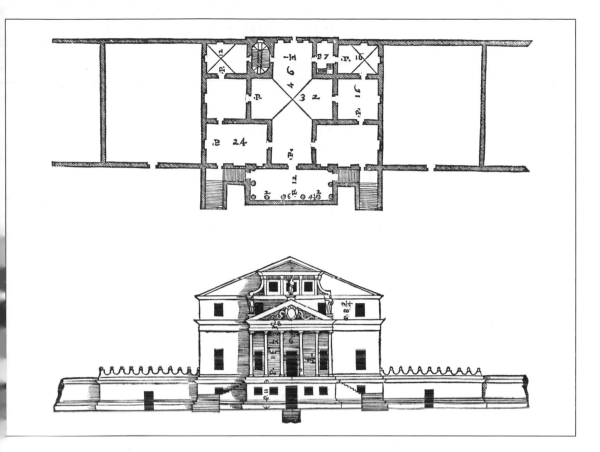

initial vague sketch to final working drawings that precisely specify the sizes, shapes, materials, and locations of physical components.

The Palladian grammar given here is formulated as a parametric shape grammar.[6] It is a slight modification of a grammar published by Stiny and Mitchell in 1978. I will discuss the vocabulary and rules of the language and illustrate them through a step-by-step derivation of the plan of the Villa Malcontenta (figure 8.31).

The grammar derives plans in top-down fashion, working from the footprint and an organizing grid down to the details of walls, columns, doors, and windows. Thus it fairly closely follows Durand's method. Derivations are organized into eight main stages, as follows:

1. grid definition
2. exterior-wall definition
3. room layout
4. interior-wall realignment
5. principal entrances—porticos and exterior wall inflections
6. exterior ornamentation—columns
7. windows and doors
8. termination.

(0,0) • A

8.32
The initial shape from which all villa
plans are generated: an axis through
a labeled point

The initial shape, from which all plans are generated,
establishes a point labeled A at the origin of the coordinate
system (figure 8.32). Tartan grids are generated around this
point using the rules specified in figure 8.33. Figure 8.34
shows how these rules are applied to generate a small tartan
grid. The grid required for layout of the Villa Malcontenta
(and derived using these rules) is shown in figure 8.35. The
dimensioning lines (with arrowhead) indicate the parameters
controlling grid dimensions. We will leave values unassigned here and simply assume that any assignment of values
complies with Palladio's well-known rules of proportion and
maintains bilateral symmetry about the central axis.

Once a grid is generated, it is circumscribed by a rectangle
to define an exterior wall. This operation is performed by
the rule specified in figure 8.36. The effect of applying this
rule to the grid of the Villa Malcontenta is shown in figure
8.37. For clarity, the wall positions have been shaded.
Meanings of shapes are now becoming less ambiguous. We
can see that some of them specify locations for solid construction elements and others specify locations for habitable
voids.

The rules specified in figure 8.38 provide for formation of
rectangular, I-shaped, T-shaped and +-shaped central rooms.
Application of rules 13, 12, and 18 to the Villa Malcontenta's
wall pattern produces the result illustrated in figure 8.39.
Notice how the meanings of lines have shifted as the design
has evolved. They began as abstract gridlines, then were
seen as possible boundaries between solids and voids, and are
now seen as room boundaries. Similarly, the interior polygons are now seen as rooms.

Interior wall realignment is a subtlety occasionally introduced to allow achievement of appropriate dimensions and
proportions. The rules of this are specified in figure 8.40.
They are not applied in derivation of the Villa Malcontenta
plan.

The rules for handling principal entrances are specified in
figure 8.41. Palladio drew on an extensive lexicon of entrance
treatments (probably in response to the varying status of his
clients, and the exigencies of site and budget), so quite a few
rules are needed. The Villa Malcontenta's treatment is illustrated in figure 8.42.

The addition of columns to a portico can be handled in
many different ways: it becomes the occasion for an uncon-
strained ornamental flourish. Palladio's numerous variation

8.33
Rules for the generation of bilaterally
symmetrical tartan grids

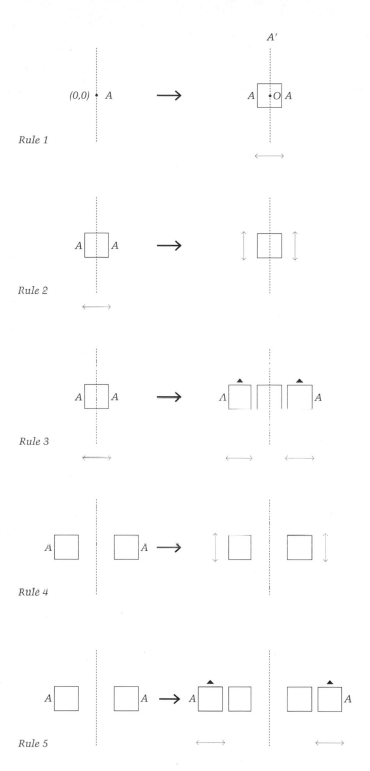

Rule 1

Rule 2

Rule 3

Rule 4

Rule 5

8.33 (cont.)

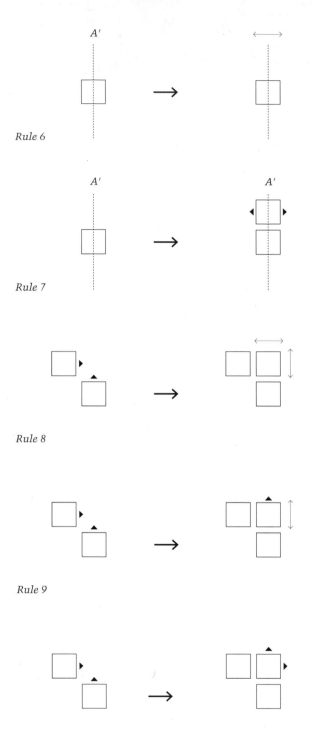

Rule 6

Rule 7

Rule 8

Rule 9

Rule 10

8.34
Application of the rules to generate
a small tartan grid

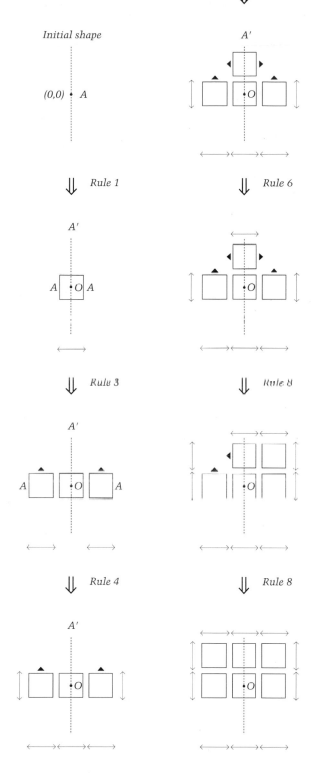

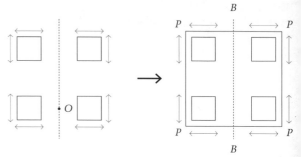

Rule 11

8.36
Rule for inscribing an outer rectangle
to define exterior wall surfaces

8.35
The tartan grid generated for the
Villa Malcontenta

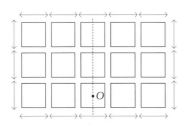

Undimensioned layout

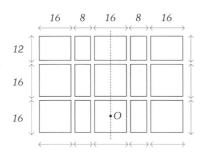

*Layout with correct Palladian values
assigned to dimensioning variables*

8.37
The underlying wall pattern of the
Villa Malcontenta

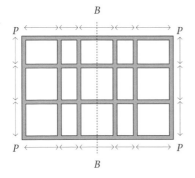

8.38
Rules for concatenation of cells to
produce larger and more complex
rooms

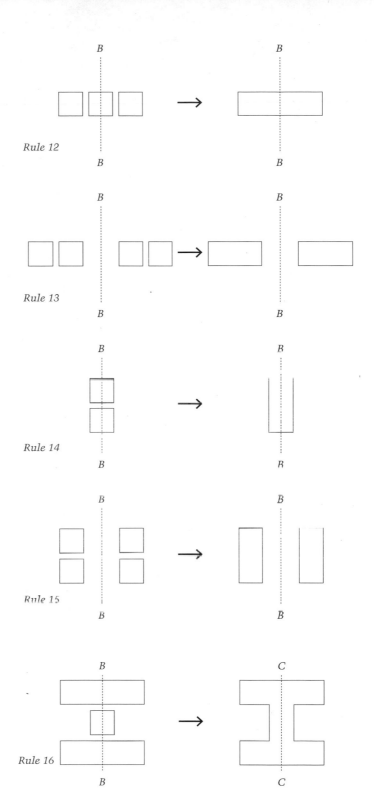

Rule 12

Rule 13

Rule 14

Rule 15

Rule 16

8.38 (cont.)

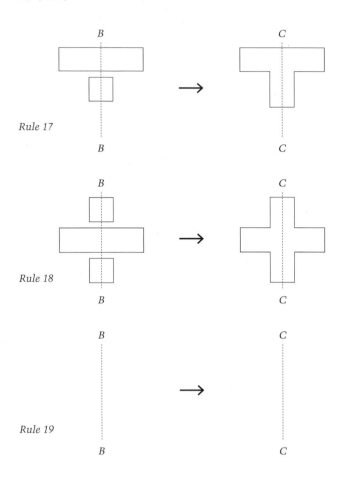

Rule 17

Rule 18

Rule 19

8.39
Derivation of the room layout of the
Villa Malcontenta

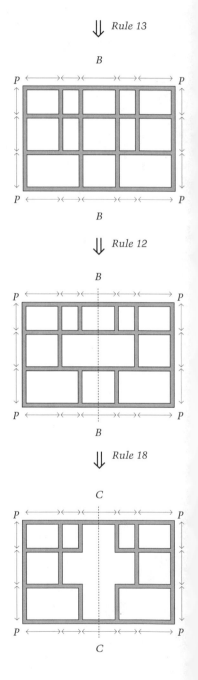

⇓ *Rule 13*

⇓ *Rule 12*

⇓ *Rule 18*

8.40
Rules for interior wall realignment

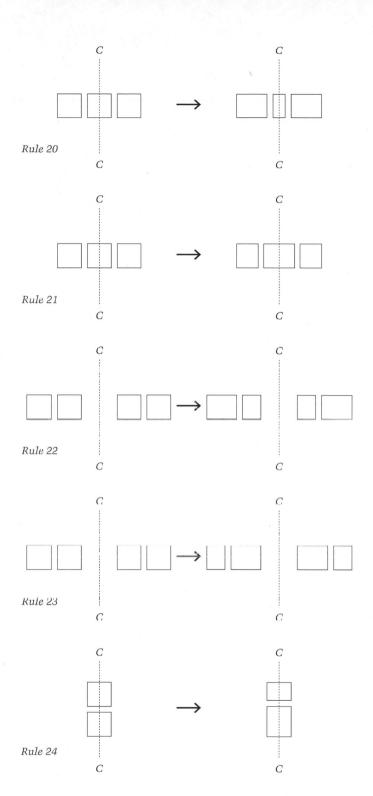

Rule 20

Rule 21

Rule 22

Rule 23

Rule 24

8.40 (cont.)

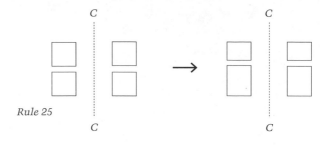

Rule 25

8.41
Lexical insertion rules providing for a
wide variety of entrance treatments

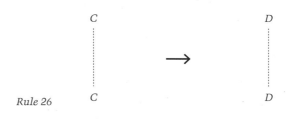

Rule 26

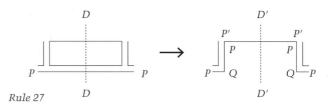

Rule 27

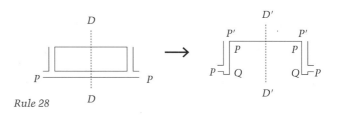

Rule 28

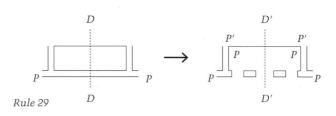

Rule 29

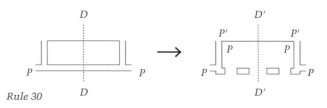

Rule 30

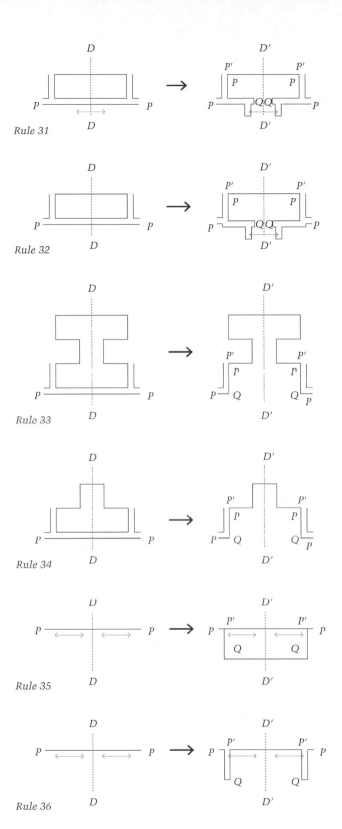

Rule 31

Rule 32

Rule 33

Rule 34

Rule 35

Rule 36

8.41 (cont.)

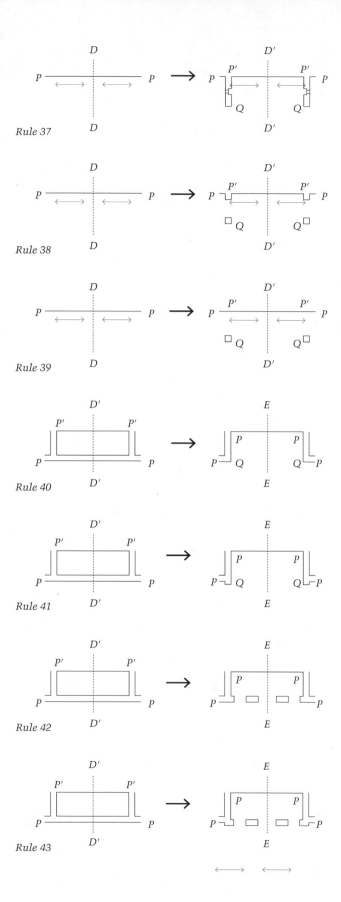

Rule 37

Rule 38

Rule 39

Rule 40

Rule 41

Rule 42

Rule 43

THE LOGIC OF ARCHITECTURE

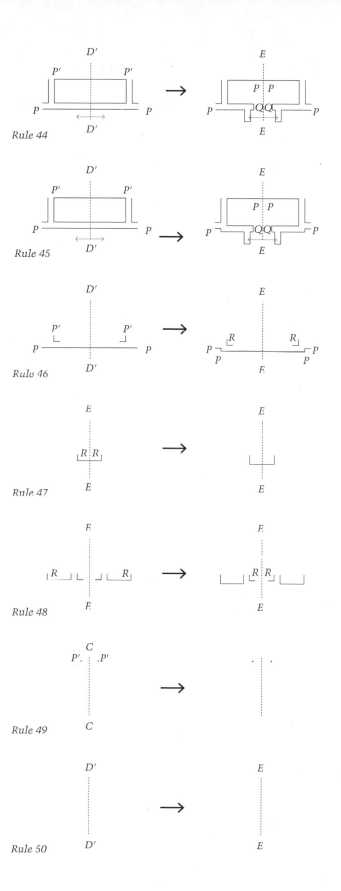

Rule 44

Rule 45

Rule 46

Rule 47

Rule 48

Rule 49

Rule 50

8.42
Addition of the front entrance and
inflection of the back wall of the
Villa Malcontenta

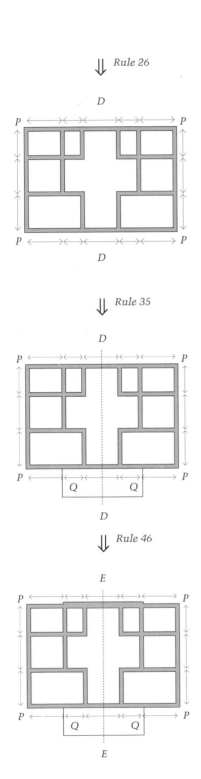

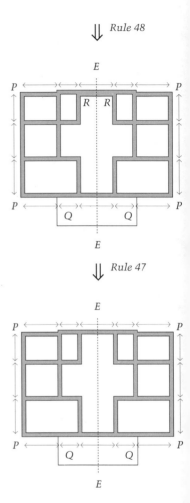

on the theme of portico columns are enumerated by the rules specified in figure 8.43, and figure 8.44 shows how the Villa Malcontenta columns are inserted.

The distinction that arises here between construction and enumeration of possibilities is an important one. We can encode Palladio's principles of room layout in a few simple rules, then construct layouts as required by recursive application of these rules: we do not need an exhaustive catalogue of Palladian room layouts. But it is hard to make useful generalizations about entrance treatments, so we must resort to enumerating the possibilities one by one.

By contrast, there *are* a few, strict, general principles for placement of doors and windows. These are expressed by the rules in figure 8.45, and application to the Villa Malcontenta is shown in figure 8.46.

Finally, termination rules are specified in figure 8.47. For the most part these provide for erasing the construction lines and labels that were used to guide the plan generation process. When the termination rules are applied in the Villa Malcontenta derivation, the final plan shown in figure 8.48 is produced. At this stage, the mappings of shapes to construction world elements are completely unambiguous: shapes stand for rooms, walls, columns, doors, and windows. You could build from this drawing.

This grammar generates all the uniaxial' villa plans published in Palladio's *Four Books of Architecture* (figure 8.49), together with many plans sketched elsewhere by Palladio, and a rich catalogue of original plans in a convincing Palladian manner. Since the grid construction rules can be applied indefinitely, to generate grids of increasing size, this grammar specifies a countably infinite universe of villa designs for exploration. However, the number of room layouts possible within a grid of specified size is finite. Figure 8.50, for example, shows the twenty possibilities within a 3 by 3 grid. Notice that the Villa Angarano appears in this catalogue as number four.

With a 5 by 3 grid the number of possible room layouts grows to 210. It is convenient to classify these according to the shapes of the central rooms. Figure 8.51 shows the complete catalogue of 119 5 by 3 layouts with rectangular central rooms. Five of the layouts from the *Four Books of Architecture* appear here: Villa Badoer, Villa Zeno, Villa Emo, Villa Ragona, and Villa Poiana.

There are only five 5 by 3 layouts with I-shaped central rooms, as shown in figure 8.52. The Villa Pisani (the only such layout to appear in the *Four Books of Architecture*) is the first of these. The other four are obvious variants on the Villa Pisani theme.

Lexical insertion rules providing for
a variety of ways to add columns
flanking the front entrance

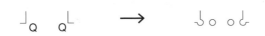

Rule 51

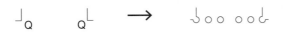

Rule 52

Rule 53

Rule 54

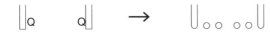

Rule 55

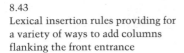

Rule 56

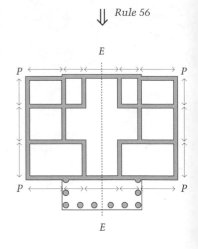

Rule 57

⇓ *Rule 56*

8.44
Addition of front columns to the Villa
Malcontenta

8.45
Rules for placement of doors and
windows

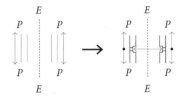

Rule 58

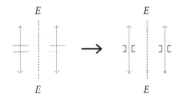

Rule 59

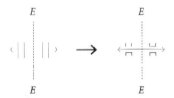

Rule 60

Rule 61

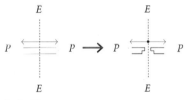

Rule 62

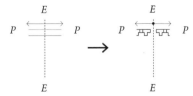

Rule 63

8.46
Derivation of the Villa Malcontenta's
pattern of openings

⇓ *Rule 58*

⇓ *Rule 61*

⇓ *Rule 59*

⇓ *Rule 62*

⇓ *Rule 60*

⇓ *Rule 63*

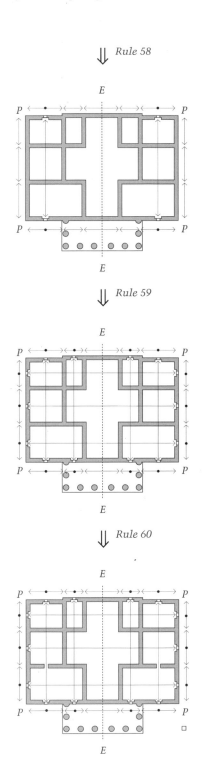

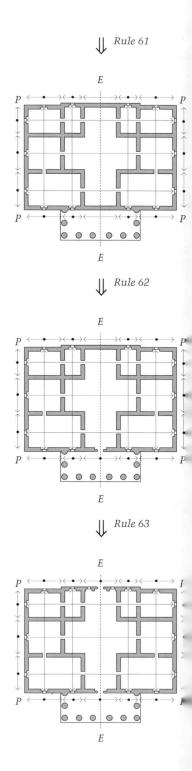

THE LOGIC OF ARCHITECTURE

Rule 67

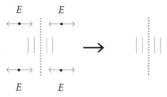

Rule 68

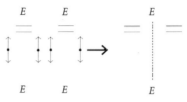

Rule 69

Rule 70

P →

Rule 71

E →

Rule 72

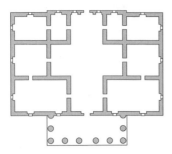

8.48
The final plan of the Villa
Malcontenta, after application of
termination rules to remove
remaining construction lines and
labels

8.49
Schematic plans of the uniaxial
villas published in Palladio's
Four Books of Architecture and
generated by the grammar

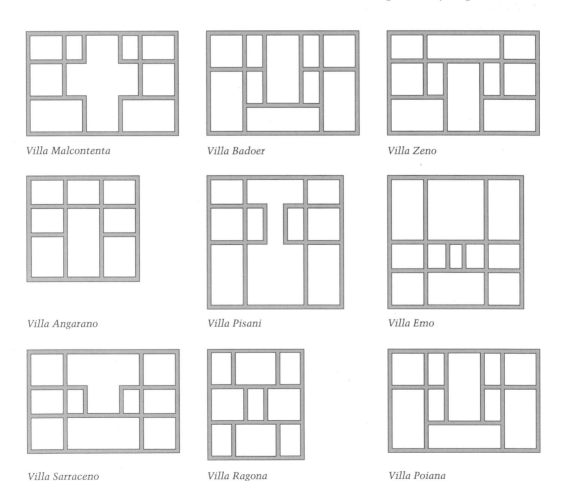

Villa Malcontenta

Villa Badoer

Villa Zeno

Villa Angarano

Villa Pisani

Villa Emo

Villa Sarraceno

Villa Ragona

Villa Poiana

THE LOGIC OF ARCHITECTURE

8.50
Complete enumeration of designs
in the language generated by the
Palladian grammar: all the 3 by 3
schematic plan layouts produced
by rules 1 to 19

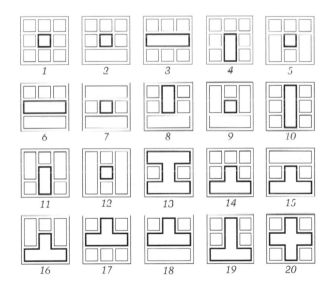

8.51
All the 5 by 3 schematic plan layouts
with rectangular central rooms in the
Palladian language

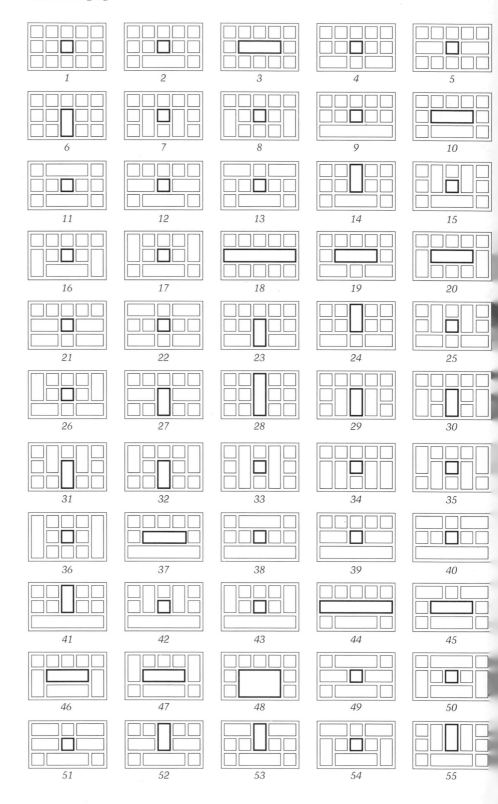

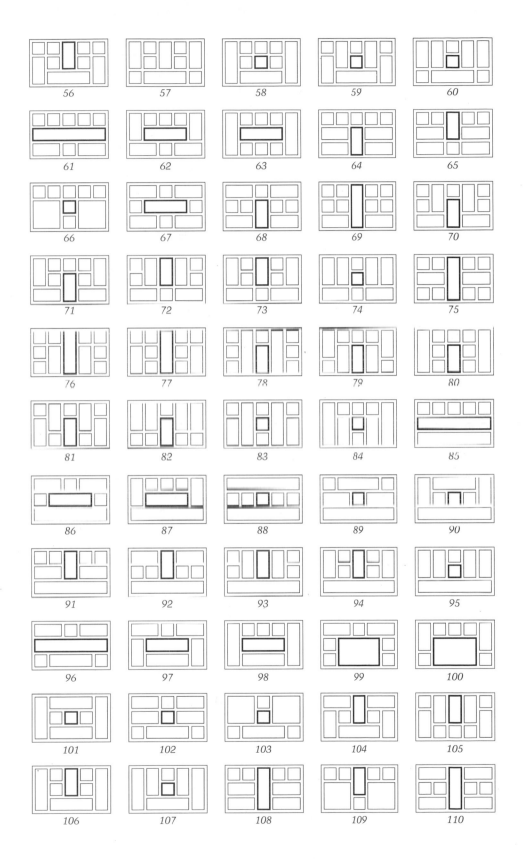

LANGUAGES OF ARCHITECTURAL FORM

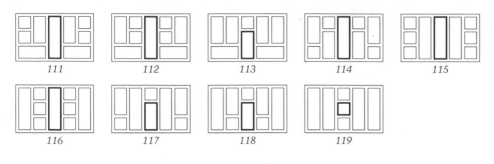

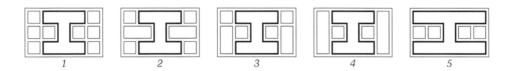

8.51 (cont.)

8.52
All the 5 by 3 schematic plan layouts
with I-shaped central rooms in the
Palladian language

A T-shaped central room allows considerably more freedom in organization of the auxillary rooms than does an I-shaped central room. The catalogue shows 78 variants on the theme of the Villa Sarraceno (figure 8.53).

Finally, there are eight possible 5 by 3 layouts with +-shaped central rooms (figure 8.54). The Villa Malcontenta is number two, and there are five more straightforward variants on the theme of the Villa Malcontenta. The catalogue is completed by two layouts in which both arms of the cross completely span the plan.

As noted in chapter 2, Palladio thought that only a few ratios of small whole numbers were suitable for the proportions of room plans. If we assume that any room in a layout can be proportioned in any of these ratios (subject to the requirement of bilateral symmetry), and that we know at least one room dimension, the combinations of possible room proportions yield systems of simultaneous, linear, integer equations which we can attempt to solve for values of all the dimensioning parameters. In general, some of these systems will have positive solutions (the values that we seek) and some will not (meaning that the corresponding combination of room proportions cannot be realized in the given layout). Thus any layout can be developed into fully

8.53

All the 5 by 3 schematic plan layouts
with T-shaped central rooms in the
Palladian language

LANGUAGES OF ARCHITECTURAL FORM

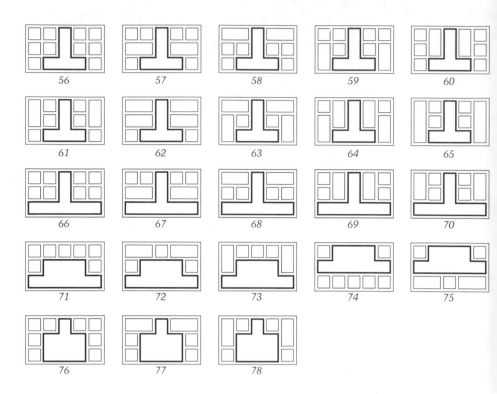

8.53 (cont.)

8.54
All the 5 by 3 schematic plan layouts with
+-shaped central rooms in the Palladian
language

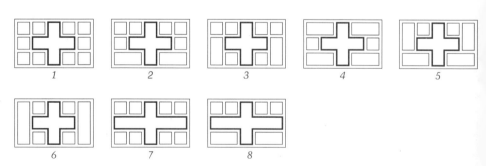

THE LOGIC OF ARCHITECTURE

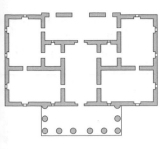

Villa Hollywood

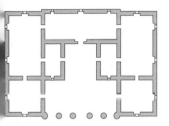

Villa Vine

8.55
Some original, fully developed
"Palladian" villas generated by
the grammar

dimensioned plans with correct Palladian proportions. Finally, any schematic plan can be detailed in numerous ways by application of rules governing selection and placement of doors, windows, and entrance features. Figure 8.55 shows some examples of original, fully developed villa plans in the language specified by the grammar.

In essence, the grammar concisely encodes knowledge of how to put together Palladian villa plans—the kind of knowledge traditionally acquired by perusal of the *Four Books* and through apprenticeship in the studio. If we consider the corresponding reductions, it also provides a way to recognize villa plans as Palladian—by successfully reducing them back to points labeled A.

DESIGN AS COMPUTATION

The view of design that has been developing through this discussion can now be made more precise. We have seen that a design world provides shape tokens which depict architectural elements. The rules of a grammar specify the ways in which these tokens may be manipulated. A design process is a computation of specified predicates according to these rules; that is, a sequence of operations on the shape tokens undertaken in an effort to satisfy predicates asserted about the design world.

To put this in another way, we can say that the syntactic rules governing a design world establish an architectural type (such as that known as the Palladian villa), and predicates expressed in a critical language establish the requirements of a particular moment and context.[8] The goal of the designer's computation is to instantiate the type in a way appropriate to that moment and context.

A basic structure is given to the design world by the initial vocabulary of shapes, the operators that can be applied to them, and the algebra that results. But knowledge of the type, as expressed in rules for recognition, refinement, and assembly of parts, provides much more structure.

The process of finding a solution to a design problem is a trial-and-error one of applying rules to generate candidate solutions, then computing predicates to determine whether candidate solutions are acceptable solutions.[9] The basic structure of this process is illustrated in figure 8.56. It is known, technically, as a generate-and-test process taking place in a search space.

A computational device to execute such a process needs a generation mechanism, a test mechanism, and a control strategy (rules for determining what alternative to try next).

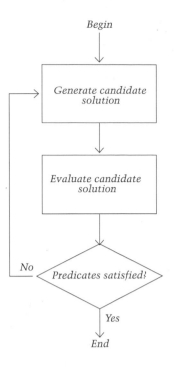

Begin

Generate candidate
solution

Evaluate candidate
solution

No

Predicates satisfied?

Yes

End

8.56
The basic trial-and-error structure of
a design process

Design intelligence may be located either in the generation mechanism or in the test mechanism. In the former case, the rules of the grammar assure with high probability (or perhaps even guarantee) that an acceptable solution will be quickly produced: the evaluation mechanism has little or nothing to do. In the latter case, the generation mechanism indiscriminately produces alternatives, and it is up to the evaluation mechanism to sort out the acceptable ones by bringing a knowledge base to bear, drawing inferences, and exploring the entailments of alternatives. In other words, you can get acceptable results by combining smart designers with dumb critics, or by teaming smart critics with dumb but energetic designers. You may prefer God (a smart designer with no need for a critic) or evolution (indiscriminate generation but deadly effective criticism).

Given a generation mechanism and a test mechanism, the efficiency with which a solution can be found will depend on the control strategy that is used. Depending on the structure of the problem, either depth-first or breadth-first search may prove to be the more efficient. And efficiency can usually be enhanced by choosing appropriate subgoals, developing more promising alternatives before less promising ones, and abandoning branches as soon as it becomes clear that they are unlikely to lead to a solution.

Different types of computational devices may be used to generate proposals, test them, and apply control strategies. For example, a computer can be used to generate alternatives by mechanically applying the rules of a shape grammar, with a human critic inspecting and testing the machine's proposals. Or a human designer might generate alternatives which are then evaluated by analysis programs or knowledge-based computer systems. In a completely manual design process all the generation and testing is performed by a human designer, or the tasks are divided among members of a design team. And in a fully automated design process the computer both generates and tests.

This formulation seems uncomfortably mechanistic and reductionist if we assume that a designer works in a closed world of fixed rules, limited knowledge, and predefined goals. This may, indeed, be the case in some specialized areas of design, but an architect usually works with a complex structure of facts, rules, and goals that can grow and change as a design process unfolds. The task is not just to solve a well-defined problem but to discover interesting possibilities and relate them, through critical discourse, to our knowledge and experience. Design elucidates *both* what we can have *and* what we want.

SUMMARY

As a foundation for designing, we need a theory of what
types of shapes among the indefinitely many emergent subshapes in an evolving design should receive our attention.
We have now seen that the left-hand sides of shape rules
specify the shape types of interest, and that available recognition mechanisms (computer implemented, or in the human
perceptual system) provide a way to find instances of these.
We also need to know what to *do* with these shapes when we
find them; the right-hand sides of shape rules establish
potential directions for further development of the design,
and the available operators (for instantiation, transformation,
and combination of shapes) provide the means to carry out
that development.

Ideally, the rules of an architectural grammar should provide a well-formed representation of a class of buildings in a
construction world. In other words, the language specified
by the grammar should include a depiction of every possible
building in the class, and every design in the language should
be for a possible building in that class. Of course there can
be differences of opinion about the extension of a class of
possible buildings, and hence about whether or not a grammar provides a well-formed representation. Some may think,
for example, that the Palladian grammar specifies too many
possibilities, and some may think that it specifies too few. It
depends on what you understand by "Palladian villa."

I do not want to suggest that designers necessarily follow
explicit grammatical rules (though they sometimes do). Nor
do I want to speculate (as an orthodox, functionalist, cognitive scientist might) that a designer's mental states are states
of an abstract computational device and that design is the
mental derivation of shapes. The essential points are that
design exploration is rarely indiscriminate trial-and-error but
is more usually guided by the designer's knowledge of how to
efficiently put various types of compositions together and
that such knowledge can often be *made* explicit, in a concise
and uniform format, by writing down shape rules.

9

FUNCTION

FUNCTIONAL DESCRIPTIONS

In *De Anima* Aristotle pointed out that we can describe a physical object not only by specifying its form and materials, but also by specifying its functions.[1] While "the physicist" would describe a house as "stones, bricks, and timbers," Aristotle suggested, "the essence of a house is assigned in such a formula as 'a shelter against destruction by wind, rain, and heat.'" There is some evidence to suggest that the distinction drawn here between formal and functional descriptions is actually grounded in a difference of brain mechanisms for perceiving form and function. For example, Warrington and Taylor (1973), in studies of brain-damaged patients, found that damage to the left parietal lobe can impair ability to recognize the function of an object, while leaving intact the ability to perceive its three-dimensional shape. Conversely, damage to the right parietal lobe produces the opposite effect. Be this as it may, the distinction is certainly of fundamental importance to us here: if we do not want to treat architectural design as a purely formal game, we must introduce into our critical language predicates specifying functions. We need, for example, to be able to specify as a design objective the provision of shelter against destruction by wind, rain, and heat. In this chapter I shall consider how to do so.

ACTIONS

Essentially a description of form tells what an object *is*, while a functional description tells what it *accomplishes*. That is, it specifies actions with effects that interest us. Thus we might functionally describe a knife by saying that it cuts or a glass by saying that it holds wine or a traffic light by saying that it controls traffic. So we normally use verbs in describing function, by contrast with our use of adjectives in describing physical properties and our use of prepositions and comparatives in describing physical relations. Very often, too, the name that we give to a physical object is a condensed functional description formed from a verb. Consider for example "eraser," "computer," "bathroom," "air-conditioner," and even "shelter."

Another way to describe an action (and hence a function) is as an input/output pair (figure 9.1). For example, the function of a toaster might be described by:

9.1
Description of a function in terms of
inputs and outputs

toaster (bread) = toast

This illustrates the relation between the logical and everyday senses of "function": formally speaking, the toaster executes a function mapping from bread to toast. It also maps from raw muffins to toasted muffins, and so on. We can use variables to provide for this, and write:

*toaster (**X**) = **Y***

where the range of **X** consists of all the sorts of things that we might want to toast, and the range of **Y** consists of all the sorts of things that we can get when we do so. The function "toaster" is then a subset of ordered pairs in the Cartesian product of **X** and **Y**, as specified by the following rules:

toaster (bread) = toast
toaster (muffin) = toasted muffin
toaster (bagel) = toasted bagel
toaster (cheese) = melted cheese

Notice that it transforms bread into toast and muffins into toasted muffins, but not bread into toasted muffins: you would need a device that executed another (rather more unusual) function to accomplish that.

Sometimes it is convenient to use numerical variables, as for example in:

*lightbulb (**Electricity**) = (**Light**)*

This specifies that *lightbulb* is a function mapping some input of electricity into some output of light. We might describe the mapping by a set of ordered pairs of numerical values for the two variables or, more concisely, by mathematical formulae linking the two variables. The use of mathematical formulae to describe physical functions in this way has become a cornerstone of modern engineering.

AFFORDANCES, FUNCTIONS, AND SIDE EFFECTS

A functional description does not specify just any action that happens to be performed by an object. We are much more restrictive about what we admit as functions. Specifically, a functional description tells of the useful actions performed by that object in some particular context. For example, if we say that somebody's heart performs the function of circulating blood, then we specify a useful action that it performs in the context of that person's body. But we would not say that in the context of the body, the heart performs the function of making the sound of heartbeats; this appears to be merely a useless side effect. Further, if the heart were placed in some other context, say a jar of formaldehyde, then its behavio

THE LOGIC OF ARCHITECTURE

Column

Handrail

9.2
Architectural homonyms: different usages of same-shaped elements

would be different. It would no longer circulate blood in the body, so this, obviously, could no longer be its function. But it might then perform some other function, for example the instruction of medical students.

A convenient way of beginning to sort out these complexities is to say that an object may, by virtue of its physical characteristics, afford[2] different functions in different contexts. Thus, by virtue of its weight, a brick affords holding down when placed on top of a pile of papers. By virtue of the friction developed between brick and floor, it also affords the function of doorstop. And, by virtue of its compressive strength, it affords a structural function when used in a wall. Clearly we can see an object as something in one context and use it as something else in another context.

When context is indefinite, then, the function of an object is relatively ill defined. But, if we consider an object to be an element of an architectural language, the syntactic rules of that language will specify the contexts in which it can appear. We can then consider the object's roles in those contexts and so produce a relatively well-defined (if potentially complex) functional description. For example, a long, thin, hollow, metal cylinder might have very many different uses. But, in a particular architectural language, it can be used as a column if the grammar allows it to be placed under a beam, it can be used as a handrail if the grammar allows it to be placed beside a stair, and it can be used as a pipe if the grammar allows it to be placed end-to-end with other pipes (figure 9.2).

DIRECTION TOWARD GOALS

In a given context, then, we sort the effects of the various actions performed by an object into useful ones and irrelevant or pernicious side effects. We regard actions with useful effects as goal-directed, and therefore classify them as functions.

Such classification is relative to a state of knowledge and a point of view. We regard circulation of blood as a function because we know that this supports life, and we take this to be good. But we cannot see any good following from the production of the sound of heartbeats. If medical research were to reveal some hitherto unknown effect of the sound of heartbeats that we recognized as valuable, then we would reinterpret production of the sound of heartbeats as a function of the heart. Or, consider the production of heat by a lighting system. Usually this is regarded as an undesirable side effect. But a clever engineer might capture this heat and use it to reduce the building's energy consumption. So the production of heat now becomes a function. Yet again, a computer program might have a bug; but this might be relabeled as a feature if somebody finds that its effect is somehow useful.

In general, actions afforded by an object become functions when we discover how to make use of them—when we can direct them toward the achievement of some goal. To describe a function fully, then, we should specify not only the action of interest, but also the goal toward which that action is directed. We might describe the hour hand of a clock, for example, by saying that it rotates *in order* to indicate the time (Bobrow, 1985).

FUNCTIONAL CONNECTIONS

A claim that an action is useful invites a question about the viewpoint from which usefulness is defined. What is useful to the landlord of a building may not be useful to the tenant, and a biological feature that is useful for the survival of a species may not be useful to an individual organism in some specific context. Must we take the Aristotelean position (as developed, for example, in *Nichomachean Ethics*) that the concepts of function (*ergon*) and good are inextricably interrelated, and so consider functions as contributions to some ultimate good? Does this require us to consider the purposes of God?

A reasonable way to avoid these complexities is to say, simply, that an action of an object is a function if its effect is to provide something that another object requires in order to perform its functions. Thus we define function in an indirect, recursive way. We must ask, of course, how the recursion eventually terminates—but I will come back to that.

Two physical objects are functionally connected whenever a function of one is to provide something that the other requires. A power outlet and a light fixture are functionally connected, for example, when the outlet provides the fixture with the electricity required to illuminate a room. In other words, the function of the outlet is to supply electricity, or:

outlet (supply) = electricity

And the function of the light fixture is:

fixture (electricity) = light

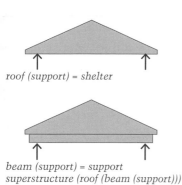

roof (support) = shelter

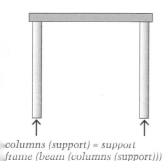

beam (support) = support
superstructure (roof (beam (support)))

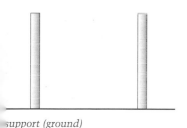

columns (support) = support
frame (beam (columns (support)))

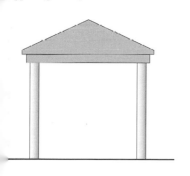

support (ground)

ut (roof (beam (columns (ground))))
r
ut (superstructure (columns (ground)))
r
ut (roof (frame (ground)))

Thus the functional connection by which electricity is supplied to produce light is described by:

fixture (outlet (supply)) = light

In general, functional connections are established by spatial relationships: plugging a fixture *into* an outlet enables the outlet to provide electricity, placing a column *under* a beam enables it to provide support, and so on. This is because the required physical action will take place only when the spatial relationship of the objects satisfies certain requirements. When an object is an element of an architectural language, then, the syntactic rules of that language specify how to form functional connections by locating the object in the right place.

PHYSICAL SYSTEMS

A physical system[3] may now be defined, provisionally, as a collection of functionally interconnected physical objects. Thus, for example, an automobile engine is a physical system of mechanical parts, the human body is a physical system of organs, a structural frame is a physical system of columns and beams, a beam is a physical system of web and flanges, and a house is a physical system of rooms and circulation spaces. A physical system's chains of functional connection—that is, its chains of causality leading to useful results—are what particularly interest us.

Consider, for example, a "primitive hut" much like the one described by Langier (figure 9.3). A roof provided with support gives shelter. A beam provides support to the roof, columns provide support to the beam, and the ground provides support to the columns. We can identify two overlapping subsystems: the superstructure, which provides shelter and requires support from columns, and the frame, which provides support to the roof and requires support from the ground. Identification and naming of subsystems in this way is an act of reification—addition of objects to the universe of discourse (just as we did, earlier, in developing formal descriptions). A thing that provides support to the roof in the context of a hut is called a frame. Frames might take many different forms, but to know what a frame *is* is to know how to use things made from columns and a beam to support the roof of a hut. A hut, taken as a whole, is a system of roof, frame, and ground (alternatively, superstructure, columns, and ground) organized to provide shelter. More concisely, from a functional viewpoint, it *is* a shelter against destruction by wind, rain, and heat (figure 9.4).

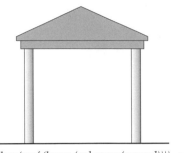

hut (roof (beam (columns (ground)))) →

hut (roof (beam (support))) →

hut (roof (support)) →

hut (shelter)

9.4
The primitive hut: a physical system
that provides shelter to the interior
and requires support from the ground

Within a physical system, the functions of most of the components are consumed in internal functional interconnections: they provide what other components require. The functions provided by the system as a whole are those *not* consumed in internal functional interconnections. Similarly, the functions required by the system as a whole are those not provided internally. Thus functions are defined relative to some system boundary, beyond which we choose not to pursue chains of cause and effect. This boundary may be drawn arbitrarily but, in order to avoid infinite regress, it must be drawn somewhere.

Often there are natural places to draw a system boundary. In consideration of the physical functions of organs, for example, it is natural to draw a boundary around the individual organism and define functions relative to the goal of individual survival. In architecture we usually take the individual building as the system, and in urban design we take the individual settlement.

We can also draw a boundary anywhere within a system to define a subsystem. The functions provided by the subsystem are those not consumed in internal functional interconnections, and the functions required are those not provided internally. The interface of the subsystem to its context is defined by the functional connections that cross the subsystem boundary.

It is usually most convenient to draw subsystem boundaries such that there are relatively dense functional interconnections within the subsystem and relatively few crossing the subsystem boundary (figure 9.5).[4] This allows us to understand a complete system as an organization of semi-independent subsystems interacting in well-defined ways across their interfaces. Thus we think of the human body, for example, as an organization of a skeletal system, a muscular system, a circulation system, a nervous system, and so on. Similarly, we usually divide a building into support system, enclosure system, ventilation system, heating system, lighting system, plumbing system, electrical supply system, mechanical circulation systems, safety systems, communication systems, and control systems.

When we have segmented a system in this fashion we can describe the way that it works by specifying the functions of each subsystem and the functional connections that are made.[5] This could be done in the logical notation introduced earlier, but the task can become a lengthy and tedious one. It will be more convenient, for our purposes here, to use an equivalent graphic notation introduced by Freeman an

9.5
Subsystem boundaries are drawn to minimize functional connections across boundaries

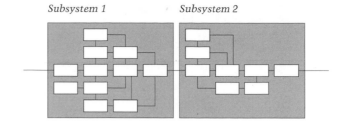

9.6
The Freeman and Newell notation depicts functional connection by head-to-tail connection of output and input arrows, and nesting of subsystems by nesting of boxes

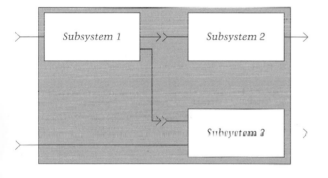

Newell (1971). In this notation, a subsystem is represented by a labeled box (figure 9.6). Functions provided by a subsystem are represented by outward-pointing arrows, and functions required are represented by inward-pointing arrows. Thus a functional connection, in which one subsystem provides a function required by another, is depicted by a head-to-tail connection of arrows. Systems consisting of several functionally interconnected subsystems are depicted by nesting boxes within boxes.

Now let us consider a complex system described in the Freeman and Newell notation (figure 9.7). If we are interested only in the functions of the system as a whole, we can treat the whole thing as an opaque "black box" and consider only the input and output arrows. If we want to know roughly how the system works, we can look at the highest-level subsystems and their functional interconnections. If we want to know how these subsystems work internally, we can go down another level, and so on recursively.

The functions of each subsystem might simply be described verbally. Alternatively, they might be described quantitatively by writing procedures that convert values of input variables into values of output variables. In this way, a computer model that simulates the functioning of the system can be produced.

Notice how our ability to produce an intelligible functional description depends on our knowledge of how to parse a system into elements and subsystems in some appropriate way. Imagine, for example, trying to produce a functional description of a building by dividing it into inch-thick vertical slices, specifying the functions provided and required by each, and tracing the functional connections. The recognition rules of a grammar usually tell how to decompose a building in a more "natural" and useful way, but they do not necessarily parse it into discrete, nested subsystems (figure 9.8a): they may identify overlapping subsystems (figure 9.8b). Recognition of different subsystems leads to development of different functional descriptions. Often, a complex system must be understood not as a simple hierarchy, but as a structure of overlapping and interlocking subsystems.[6]

A more refined definition of a physical system can now be given. I shall take it that a physical system is any physical object with a useful ability that can be explained by specifying its parts (functional components) and describing their functional connections. To design a physical system is to select functional components that will perform as required and specify an arrangement of these parts that will allow them to interact as required.

9.7
Depiction of functional organization
at different levels of abstraction

System as a whole

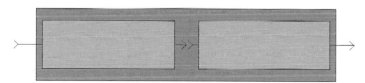

High-level functional organization

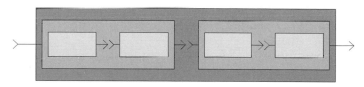

Lower-level functional organization

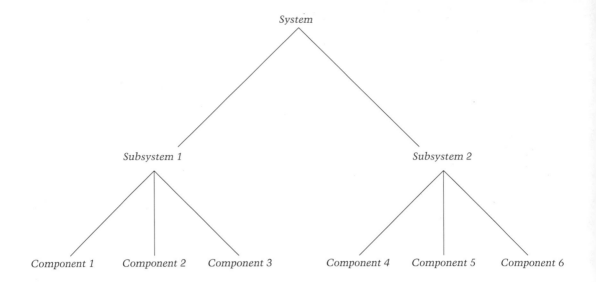

a. Discrete subsystems

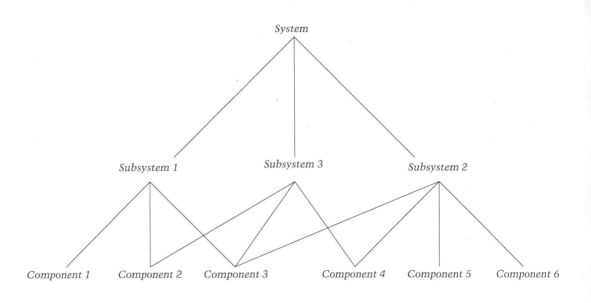

b. Overlapping subsystems

9.8
Different ways to decompose a
system

A building might make money for a developer or represent the dwelling of a god. Clearly these are important functions, but not (at least in any direct sense) physical ones, so some generalization of the definition of function as role in a physical system seems necessary. This can be accomplished by introducing the idea of a human society composed of individuals and of groups such as families, communities, and so on. If we want to understand and describe how a society works, we will at least need to consider patterns of human movement and assembly; that is, the physical activity system that operates within a society. Further, if we focus upon economic transactions between individuals and groups, we can describe the economic system associated with the society. And, if we focus upon acts of communication, we can describe the cultural system. Then we can begin to consider the roles that artifacts (including buildings) play within such systems, in much the same way that we have considered their roles within physical systems.

There is, indeed, a long tradition of functional analysis of activity, cultural, and economic systems within societies.[7] Its roots can be traced back to the works of various nineteenth-century social theorists: Comte, Spencer, and Marx, in particular. In its modern form, it was pioneered by the sociologist Emile Durkheim and by the anthropologists Bronislaw Malinowski and A. R. Radcliffe-Brown. Durkheim's (1933) most essential contribution was to insist that, in attempting to understand and explain a social phenomenon, "we must seek separately the efficient cause which produces it and the function it fulfills." Malinowski (1936) proposed that, "in every type of civilization, every custom, material object, idea and belief fulfills some vital function, has some task to accomplish, represents an indispensable part within a working whole." He developed a close analogy between the workings of a living organism, and this led him to suggest that the functions of institutions, customs, and so on could be defined in terms of their contributions to maintaining stability and survival of the system as a whole. Radcliffe-Brown (1952) emphasized processes of adaptation and adjustment which have the effect of maintaining the integrity and continuity of the system.

However, the functional analysis of ongoing activity, cultural, and economic systems is much less straightforward than the functional analysis of artificial physical systems, or even that of living systems. Generally it is not so easy to draw the boundaries of the system of interest. Within the system there are entities, structures, and actions that are difficult to identify and describe with precision: institutions, norms, conventions, customs, laws, recurrent activities, patterns of beliefs and ideas, and the like. And questions of value enter in subtle and complex ways. Is it adequate to define function, ultimately, in terms of contribution to stability, integrity, and survival of the system as a whole, as functionalist social scientists have tended to do? What actions and effects are valued, and by what individuals and groups? Might a function from the viewpoint of some particular group within the society be a dysfunction from the viewpoint of another? If the system as a whole malfunctions in some way, might not generation of social change be more important than maintenance of stability?

Functionalist social science clearly has its limitations, then, and its larger claims should be treated with considerable caution. But its suggestion that functions can be defined in relation to human activity systems, economic systems, and cultural systems, as well as in relation to physical systems, remains fundamentally useful.

Specifically, we usually take it that the essential function of a building is to shelter the space required for some human activity. This has often led theorists to classify buildings according to the activities that they accommodate. Vitruvius, for example, first discussed temples. Then, in Book V, he undertook to "treat of the laying out of public places." Under this head fell the forum, treasury, prison, senate house, theater, colonnades and walks, baths, palaestra, harbors, breakwaters, and shipyards. Finally, in Book VI, he dealt with private houses, with the farmhouse and the Greek house as subclasses.

Alberti developed a much more detailed and systematic functional classification, explicitly based upon a theory of social roles and organization. In Book IV of his *Ten Books* he spoke of "the several divisions of human conditions, whence arises the diversity of buildings," and elaborated:

Yet when we take a view of the great plenty and variety of buildings all about us, we easily perceive that . . . this great variety and difference among them, are owing principally to the variety there is among mankind. So that, if according to our method we would make a careful enquiry into their sorts and parts, it is here that we must begin our disquisition, namely, from the nature of mankind, and wherein they differ from one another; since upon their account it is that buildings are erected, and for their uses varied: so that having thoroughly considered these things, we may treat of them more clearly.

His functional classification incorporated such fine distinctions as that between a castle for a tyrant and a palace for a king, and included elaborate enumerations of variants, for example:

Of the commissaries, chamberlains, public receivers and the like magistrates, whose business is to supply and preside over the public granaries, chambers of accounts, arsenals, markets, docks and stables; as also of the three sorts of prisons . . .

Reflecting the context of eighteenth-century French society, Jacques-François Blondel's *Cours d'architecture* (1771–77) established a functional classification that included theaters, dance halls, vauxhalls, cemeteries, colleges, hospitals, charnel houses, hotels, exchanges, libraries, academies, factories, fountains, baths, markets, fairs, slaughterhouses, barracks, town halls, prisons, arsenals and lighthouses.

Following the foundation of the Ecole Polytechnique in Paris at the end of the eighteenth century, the school's first professor, J. N. L. Durand, published his systematically comprehensive text *Précis des leçons d'architecture données à l'Ecole Polytechnique* in two volumes in 1802–5. Earlier we considered the grammar of architectural composition that was established in the first volume. The second volume set out the functional classification of buildings in a Napoleonic city. Henry Russell Hitchcock (1958) has summarized it as follows:

First he deals with urbanistic features, including not only bridges, streets, and squares, but also such supposedly essential elements of the ideal classicizing city as triumphal arches and tombs. A second section considers temples (not churches, it is amusing to note), palaces, treasuries, law courts, town halls, colleges, libraries, museums, observatories, lighthouses, markets, exchanges, custom houses, exhibition buildings, theatres, baths, hospitals, prisons, and barracks. Here were all the individual structures of the model Napoleonic city.

From ancient times it is possible to trace a general tendency toward greater articulation and diversity in these functional classifications, reflecting increasing complexity of social organization and functioning. Nikolaus Pevsner explored this, in some detail, in his *A History of Building Types* (1976). For example he identified a line of development, beginning in the Middle Ages, when,

. . . the market hall may break away from the town hall, and may itself split up into a corn hall and a cloth hall, and when the law courts as well as the exchange begin to require extra buildings. Then in the later sixteenth century, government offices first received a building of their own: the Uffizi. But the top storey of the Uffizi became the Medici art gallery, and special museum buildings began to be segregated from the palaces of which they and also the major libraries had formed part. . . . That museums and libraries became public is one aspect of the rise of the middle class into prosperity.

Through the nineteenth century, with the Industrial Revolution and rapid urbanization, many new functional classes—the railway station, exhibition building, and department store, for example—were to emerge. And the pace has continued to accelerate through the twentieth century, with the development of new classes ranging from motels, gas stations, and airports to suburban shopping centers, video arcades, and laundromats.

An ecological analogy can be useful here (provided that we do not push it too far). In an ecosystem, the phenomenon of coevolution may be observed. As an ecosystem as a whole evolves, a range of ecological niches emerges, and niches are occupied by appropriately adapted species of organisms. Individual species adapt in the direction of more closely fitting their niches, and this in turn affects the pattern of the whole. The overall result may be that the system evolves in the direction of greater diversity of species, or reduced diversity, or that the system stabilizes at some level. Many scholars, perhaps most notably Robert Park (1925), have drawn a close analogy between social systems and ecosystems. From this viewpoint, we should expect to find that processes of social transformation and evolution generate niches which are filled by appropriately adapted "species" of buildings and rooms, and that different societies (like different ecosystems) will evolve different levels of species diversity.

ARCHITECTURAL PROGRAMS

A document that enumerates the activities to be accommodated in a building and specifies how this should be done is known as an architectural program (or brief, in Britain). Vitruvius, for example, stated the program for a house (figure 9.9) as follows:

We must next consider the principles on which should be constructed those apartments in private houses which are meant for the householders themselves, and those which are to be shared in common with outsiders. The private rooms are those into which nobody has the right to enter without

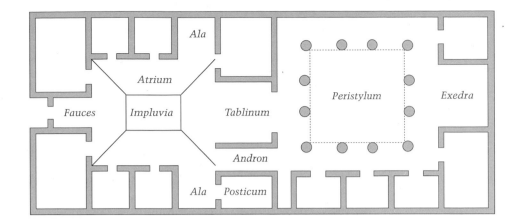

9.9

A typical Roman house, with specialized spaces provided to shelter a variety of the inhabitants' activities

an invitation, such as bedrooms, dining rooms, bathrooms, and all others used for the like purposes. The common are those which any of the people have a perfect right to enter, even without an invitation: that is, entrance courts, cavaedia, peristyles, and all intended for the like purpose. Hence, men of everyday fortune do not need entrance courts, tablina, or atriums built in grand style, because such men are more apt to discharge their social obligations by going round to others than to have others come to them.

Further, he distinguished varieties of programs, according to the station of the owner:

Those who do business in country produce must have stalls and shops in their entrance courts, with crypts, granaries, storerooms, and so forth in their houses, constructed more for the purpose of keeping the produce in good condition than for ornamental beauty.

For capitalists and farmers of the revenue, somewhat comfortable and showy apartments must be constructed, secure against robbery; for advocates and public speakers, handsomer and more roomy, to accommodate meetings; for men of rank who, from holding offices and magistracies, have social obligations to their fellow-citizens, lofty entrance courts in regal style, and most spacious atriums and peristyles, with plantations and walks of some extent in them, appropriate to their dignity. They need also libraries, picture galleries, and basilicas, finished in a style similar to that of great public buildings, since public councils as well as private lawsuits and hearings before arbitrators are very often held in the houses of such men.

Often programs specify not only the types and sizes of spaces, but also the ambient conditions to be provided within them. Vitruvius wrote:

We shall next explain how the special purposes of different rooms require different exposures, suited to convenience and to the quarters of the sky. Winter dining rooms and bathrooms should have a southwestern exposure, for the reason that they need the evening light, and also because the setting sun, facing them in all its splendour but with abated heat, lends a gentler warmth to that quarter in the evening. Bedrooms and libraries ought to have an eastern exposure, because their purposes require the morning light, and also because books in such libraries will not decay. In libraries with southern exposures the books are ruined by worms and dampness, because damp winds come up, which breed and nourish the worms, and destroy the books with mould, by spreading their damp breath over them.

Dining rooms for Spring and Autumn to the east; for when the windows face that quarter, the sun, as he goes on his career from over against them to the west, leaves such rooms at the proper temperature at the time when it is customary to use them. Summer dining rooms to the north, because that quarter is not, like the others, burning with heat during the solstice, for the reason that it is unexposed to the sun's course, and hence it always keeps cool, and makes the use of the rooms both healthy and agreeable. Similarly with picture galleries, embroiderers' work rooms, and painters' studios, in order that the fixed light may permit the colours used in their work to last with qualities unchanged.

Alberti gave even more elaborate environmental requirements, not all of which are convincing. In a stable, for instance, he required that "the moon's beams do not come in at the windows," since they would make the horse "wall-eyed and give him grievous coughs."

Many programs also specify the adjacencies and proximities to be provided. Among the requirements enumerated by Vitruvius were:

Bathrooms . . . should adjoin the kitchen; for in this situation it will not take long to get ready a bath in the country. . . . Let the pressing room, also, be next to the kitchen; for in this situation it will be easy to deal with the fruit of the olive. Adjoining it should be the wine room.

As the explanations suggest, the activities housed in the spaces are functionally connected: one must closely precede the other in time, or closely adjoin it in space, so the corresponding spaces must be closely linked to facilitate adequate performance of the activities.

Alberti was particularly scholarly and systematic in his specification of adjacency and proximity requirements, and carefully related them to activity patterns, customs, and environmental requirements. So, for example, a country house for a gentleman should be organized as follows:

The kitchen ought to be neither just under the noses of the guests, nor at too great a distance; but so that the victuals may be brought in neither too hot nor too cold, and that the noise of the scullions, with the clatter of their pans, dishes and other utensils, may not be troublesome.

The mistress of the family should have an apartment, in which she may easily hear every thing that is done in the house.

The wife's chamber should go into the wardrobe; the husband's into the library.

Their ancient mother, who requires tranquility and repose, should have a warm chamber, well secured against the cold, and out of the way of all noises either from within or without.

If a man is sick, let him make use of a close-stool; but when he is in health, surely such nastiness cannot be too far off.

In the French academic tradition programs became more precise and rigorous. An essential part of this tradition, in the eighteenth and nineteenth centuries, was the Grand Prix de Rome, an annual architectural competition established at the Académie Royale d'Architecture in 1720. In conjunction with the great academic texts, such as those of Blondel, Durand, and later Guadet, the Grand Prix competitions firmly established the idea of a formalized architectural program,[8] against which designs could be checked for compliance. The program for the Grand Prix (which was different each year) specified a building type and described the activities to be accommodated, together with their space requirements. It was a formal document—in the early years simply dictated to competitors, later given in written form. Competitors who failed to follow the requirements of the program were eliminated from competition.

As described by Neil Levine (1982), the program for the Grand Prix normally consisted of three parts: a brief introductory paragraph, known as the *chapeau*; the main text, giving details of requirements; and a final section, giving overall dimensions of the building or site and the number and scale of drawings required. The main section set out requirements in terms of the major spatial elements and was organized hierarchically, beginning with the major rooms and ending with the subsidiary ones.

It is straightforward to formalize even further and express architectural programs as collections of predicates that we want to be satisfied by a design, stated in the language of first-order logic. Here are some examples:

larger (kitchen, 80) and smaller (kitchen, 120)
warmer (kitchen, 65) and colder (kitchen, 75)
ventilated (kitchen)
daylit(kitchen)
adjacent (kitchen, dining)

It becomes part of the critic's task to evaluate these predicates for a given design proposal.

In general, then, an architectural program describes an activity system and enumerates the component activities that are to be provided with shelter by the spaces of a building. It specifies how large the spaces need to be in order to accommodate their activities, the precise qualities of shelter that are desired, and the relationships of spaces that are necessitated by activity relationships. The basic roles of the building's physical subsystems (which the architect must design) are thus to supply the support, enclosure, circulation connections, light, warmth, and other things that the spaces listed in the program require.

Modernism assigned a particularly crucial role to the architectural program. It was assumed that an abstract set of predicates could be formulated prior to the architectural work and independently of it, and that it was then the designer's task to satisfy these predicates as completely and efficiently as possible. This seems a little innocent now, since it conceives of social systems in an unrealistically static way, assumes a logical consistency that may be illusory, and ignores the tendency of buildings to change the very patterns that they were designed to accommodate. But the predicates of the program still provide an important starting point for critical reasoning about architectural possibilities.

MEANING

The theorists and critics of modernism have tended to focus their discourse on the programs of buildings and on the performances of buildings as physical systems, but in recent years there has been renewed interest in a third aspect of function—the roles that buildings and parts of buildings play in symbol systems.[9] The philosopher Nelson Goodman (1985) has gone so far as to claim that "a building is a work of art only insofar as it signifies, means, refers, symbolizes in some way."[10]

Vitruvius clearly recognized that buildings and parts of buildings function as symbols, and he attempted to elucidate the way they do this by telling a series of tales about the invention of the classical orders (figure 9.10). He began with the Doric:

Wishing to set up columns in that temple, but not having rules for their symmetry, and being in search of some way by which they could render them fit to bear a load and also of a satisfactory beauty of appearance, they measured the imprint of a man's foot and compared this with his height. On finding that, in a man, the foot was one sixth of the height, they

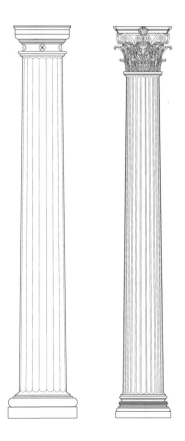

9.10
The strong, masculine Doric column and the slender, feminine Corinthian, as interpreted by Vignola, *Rules of the Five Orders*, 1562

applied the same principle to the column, and reared the shaft, including the capital, to a height six times its thickness at its base. Thus the Doric column, as used in buildings, began to exhibit the proportions, strength, and beauty of the body of a man.

What, exactly, is Vitruvius telling us here? Surely he cannot be saying (as some commentators have thought) that a Doric column depicts or describes a man: if so, it is a curiously imperfect attempt. He appears to be claiming, instead, that a Doric column exemplifies some characteristically masculine properties—particular proportions, an appearance of strength, and lack of adornment.

Goodman (1976, 1984, 1985) has carefully distinguished denotation and exemplification as different varieties of reference.[11] In denotation (which includes naming, description, and depiction), a symbol applies by pointing, in some way, to something. Thus, for example, "Parthenon" denotes a particular building in Athens, as does a picture of the Parthenon. But in exemplification, reference runs in the opposite direction, "from symbol to certain labels that apply to it or to properties possessed by it."[12] The Doric column, then, exemplifies thickness and the strength following from that. The Doric column does not, however, literally possess the property of masculinity: it does so metaphorically, by virtue of its properties of thickness, strength, and plainness. In Goodman's terminology, exemplification of metaphorically possessed properties is "expression": the Doric column expresses masculinity.

Vitruvius next considered the Ionic column:

Just so afterwards, when they desired to construct a temple to Diana in a new style of beauty, they translated these footprints into terms characteristic of the slenderness of women, and thus first made a column the thickness of which was only one eighth of its height, so that it might have a taller look. At the foot they substituted the base in place of a shoe; in the capital they placed the volutes, hanging down at the right and left like curly ringlets, and ornamented its front with cymatia and with festoons of fruit arranged in place of hair, while they brought the flutes down the whole shaft, falling like the folds in the robes worn by the matrons.

He summarized the differences:

Thus in the invention of the two different kinds of columns, they borrowed manly beauty, naked and unadorned, for the one, and for the other the delicacy, adornment, and proportions characteristic of women.

Thus the Ionic column exemplifies slender proportions and delicate adornment, and so expresses femininity.

Next, Vitruvius made a similar analysis of the Corinthian column:

The third order, called Corinthian, is an imitation of the slenderness of a maiden; for the outlines and limbs of maidens, being more slender on account of their tender years, admit of prettier effects in the way of adornment.

Here we have even slenderer proportions, even prettier adornment, and so the expression of maidenliness.

Finally, he traced the chain of reference one step further:

The temples of Minerva, Mars, and Hercules, will be Doric, since the virile strength of these gods makes daintiness entirely inappropriate to their houses. In temples to Venus, Flora, Proserpine, Spring-Water, and the Nymphs, the Corinthian order will be found to have peculiar significance, because these are delicate divinities and so its rather slender outlines, its flowers, leaves, and ornamental volutes will lend propriety where it is due. The construction of temples of the Ionic order to Juno, Diana, Father Bacchus, and the other gods of that kind, will be in keeping with the middle position which they hold; for the building of such will be an appropriate combination of the severity of the Doric with the delicacy of the Corinthian.

Thus, by virtue of the expression of its columns, a temple alludes to the gender of the god to which it is dedicated: propriety demands that this allusion should be appropriate. In Goodman's terminology, this is a case of "mediated reference."

In general, we can consider four basic varieties of reference by buildings and parts of buildings: denotation, exemplification, expression, and mediated reference. Very occasionally buildings may denote, as for example when a seafood restaurant depicts a fish (figure 9.11). Much more frequently they exemplify material properties, proportions, symmetries, and other formal properties, or functional characteristics such as strength or efficiency. Expression may follow from exemplification, and complex chains of mediated reference may develop.

To deal with this, our critical language needs predicate symbols denoting the referential functions of architectural elements and subsystems. We might need to say, for example:

exemplifies (column, strength)
expresses (column, masculinity)
alludes (column, Mars)

9.11
Architectural denotation: a seafood restaurant that depicts a fish

The conditions for correct application of such predicates are not, however, likely to be as stable or straightforward to formulate as those for physical and programmatic predicates. We can assemble explicit facts and rules about how symbols work in a particular culture, and we can draw useful critical conclusions from these, but it would be foolhardy to assume that any set of such conclusions exhausted the meaning of an architectural proposal. In particular, the closed, artificial knowledge bases maintained by computer systems, as opposed to the knowledge bases of human critics who participate in a culture, are likely to provide only crude approximations to architectural meaning.

FUNCTIONAL TYPOLOGY

We have now seen how architectural elements and subsystems may perform a variety of physical, social, and symbolic functions. It follows that we can define types not only in terms of formal characteristics, but also in terms of functional characteristics. That is, we can classify the objects that we manipulate in architectural composition not only according to what they look like, but also according to what they are good for.

There is considerable psychological evidence that functional classification of objects does play an important role in our thought processes. Duncker (1945), for example, noted the phenomenon of "functional fixedness"—the tendency to recognize certain uses of an object immediately, taking these to be characteristic of the object, while ignoring other possible uses unless these are explicitly pointed out. This suggests that we access our knowledge about the uses of things through a functional classification scheme. Krauss (1952) studied children's definitions of nouns and found that they were often functional in character: "A table is to sit at," "a book is to read," and so on. Nelson (1973) presented experimental evidence that a child "forms categories on the basis of function and generalizes to new instances on the basis of form." In their well-known study of concepts, Miller and Johnson-Laird (1976) concluded, on the basis of such evidence, that we tend to classify objects by function rather than by form. Johnson-Laird (1988) has summarized:

When George Miller and I undertook an analysis of concepts, we soon realized that tables, unlike human beings, do not have a canonical shape: they come in a profusion of shapes. Moreover, you can recognize an object as a table even if it has a shape unlike any table you have ever seen. We were forced to conclude that an artifact can be identified as a member of a category, not because of any intrinsic aspect of its three-dimensional shape, but because its form, dimensions and other visible properties, whatever they may be, are perceived as appropriate for a particular function. You can see the possibilities inherent in the artifact. It is a table because it has a surface on which you could rest utensils.

It is easy to see the practical advantages, in everyday life, of classifying objects according to what we can use them for. But, since function may vary with context, we must always be prepared to reclassify—to recognize that "this x will make a good y" if it is placed in some new context. Picasso elegantly demonstrated this when he made a realistic bull's head by juxtaposing the handlebars and saddle of a bicycle (figure 9.12). Later, so the story goes, he speculated that a resourceful mechanic might find it and remark, "This bull's head will make excellent handlebars and a saddle for my bicycle."[13] The artist and the mechanic here deploy different languages that happen to have some vocabulary elements in common. In the artist's language these elements, when appropriately related, serve to depict parts of an animal. But in the mechanic's language these same elements, when related in a quite different way, play roles in a mechanical system.

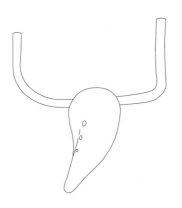

9.12
Picasso's bull's head

FUNCTIONALIST CRITICISM

In chapter 1 we saw how aesthetic value might be defined in terms of form. An alternative, or perhaps complementary, approach is to define it in terms of the concept of function that has now been developed. We can take as our starting point analysis of some sentences that express judgments about physical objects.[14] Consider, for example, sentences such as:

This man is good.

Here *good* is simply employed as a predicate. However, there is another common usage of *good* in English, exemplified by:

This is a good knife.

Here *good* is used not as a predicate, but as an adjunct to a noun. Now moral philosophers have given particular attention to the adjunctive use of *good*, and have pointed out that this is appropriate only under certain circumstances

Specifically, the standard argument goes, *good* can be applied adjunctively only to nouns that denote classes of objects about which we can rationally have expectations, as to what instances will look like, or do, or be used for. *Good* is applied when our expectations are satisfied to a greater than usual degree. Thus a good circle is an unusually well formed one, and a good knife is one that cuts unusually well: where types are characterized by form, *good* denotes well-formedness, and where types are characterized by function, *good* denotes superior performance.

Thus functionalist criticism begins with some system of functional classification of artifacts, then expresses judgments about adequate performance of functions. A building might, for example, be judged a good, bad, or mediocre church. If later used for another purpose it might then be judged a good, bad, or mediocre theater, or warehouse.

The language of functionalist criticism can be elaborated by introducing adjuncts that identify different kinds or dimensions of good performance. Thus we might speak of a sharp knife, a strong beam, or a thermally-efficient heat exchanger, but not (except in very unusual circumstances) of a thermally-efficient knife or a sharp heat exchanger. Modern engineering has introduced the additional refinement of numerical scales to express sharpness, efficiency, strength, and so on.

A further and more doubtful step is to identify beauty with good performance. The tendency to do this can be traced back to Socrates. His views are recorded in Xenophon's *Recollections of Socrates* (*Memorabilia*). In the context of a discussion of the good and the beautiful, Socrates was asked (by Aristippus): "Is a dung basket beautiful then?" And he gave the reply: "Of course, and a golden shield is ugly, if the one is well made for its special work and the other badly." Later, he took up the issue with the armorer Pistias, and asked him: "How then do you make a well-shaped breastplate to fit an ill-shaped body?" Pistias forthrightly answered: "I make it fit; that which fits is well shaped." So Socrates drew the conclusion: "It seems to me then, that you do not speak of [a breastplate's being] well shaped in an absolute sense, but only in regard to its function." Finally, he suggested that architectural beauty may be understood in the same way: "To put it shortly, the house in which the owner can find a pleasant retreat at all seasons is presumably at once the pleasantest and most beautiful."

This kind of attitude entered into modern architectural thought largely through the influence of the eighteenth-century Italian theorist Carlo Lodoli.[15] According to Lodoli, "In architecture only that shall show that has a definite function, and which derives from the strictest necessity." Furthermore, ornament was to be strictly banished as functionally superfluous, and "architecture must conform to the nature of the materials." Thus beauty was taken to be a consequence of honest and direct response to necessity and to material. In our own century the architect/engineer Pier Luigi Nervi (1956) has very closely echoed these sentiments, demanding in buildings "a structural essence, a necessary absence of all decoration, a purity of line and shape" and claiming that "every improvement in the functional and technical efficiency of a product brings about an improvement in its aesthetic quality" (figure 9.13).

Functionalist criticism may be not only evaluative, but also diagnostic. In other words, it may try to explain *why* an element or subsystem performs well or badly. Diagnosis is a matter of identifying relevant differences between the forms of elements or subsystems that perform as expected and those that do not. A room might be bad for some purpose because it is too small, and a beam might be good because it is made of particularly strong material. This requires an understanding of the relationships between form and function—an issue that I shall take up in the final chapter.

9.13
A "structural essence": roof structure by Pier Luigi Nervi with bending moment diagram superimposed to show how shape responds to structural necessity

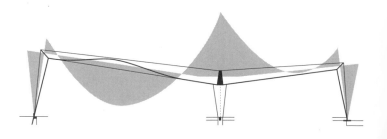

We have now seen how architectural vocabulary elements can be characterized both formally and functionally. Instances of a given vocabulary element have shape and material properties in common. The syntactic rules of a language of architectural form specify where in a composition such instances can occur. In these contexts they can play certain useful roles—their architectural functions.

Functionalist criticism is concerned with how *well* architectural elements and subsystems perform their roles within a building. The function of a building as a whole is established by its program, so the performance of elements and subsystems must be evaluated relative to the program. Good performance is a matter both of adequacy in a role and of economy of means.

In general, functionalist criticism takes an Aristotelian view of architecture: it deals with ends, and with the adequacy of means to those ends. The usual ends are to provide adequate space for specified activities, to achieve adequate performance of the structural system and other physical subsystems, and to exemplify, express, and allude in memorable ways. More concisely, in the famous words of Sir Henry Wotton, the ends of architecture are commodity, firmness, and delight.

FUNCTIONALLY MOTIVATED DESIGN

FUNCTIONAL INTERPRETATION

In order to produce and justify designs that not only have desired formal properties but also satisfy specified practical requirements, a designer must be able to infer the functions of architectural elements and compositions from their formal properties. In other words, the designer must be able to produce functional interpretations of designs and must check these against the functional requirements set out in the problem formulation. The problem of functional interpretation may be stated more precisely as follows: *given* a composition in some language of architectural form *and* a critical language with predicates that ascribe function, *infer* functional descriptions (expressed in the critical language) of elements, subsystems, and the system as a whole.

In everyday life, too, we often need to infer the functions of actual buildings and parts of buildings.[1] In doing so we adopt what the philosopher Daniel Dennett (1987) has called a "design stance": we treat the building as an object designed to fulfill certain functions and try to infer what those functions might be. (This contrasts, in Dennett's terminology, with the "physical stance" that we adopt toward, say, an ocean wave: we treat it as obeying the laws of physics. And it also contrasts with the "intentional stance" that we adopt toward an organism: we treat it as possessing goals, beliefs, and rationality.)

We could scarcely operate in the world if we were not able to recognize that doors are for entering buildings, that light fixtures are for providing illumination, and so on. In the case of familiar objects, we might simply rely on remembered associations of functions with forms, but this would not enable us to understand new and unfamiliar objects. Clearly we need, as well, some way to infer functions from forms.

Derivation of functional inferences requires application of rules that relate observations about forms and locations of architectural elements to conclusions about their functions. These rules must encode knowledge of the conditions that the form of an element or subsystem must satisfy if it is to perform some specified function adequately, together with knowledge of how functional connections must be made. If an object satisfies these conditions, we can legitimately see it as an instance of the functional type in question. If an object is located under a beam, for example, and it is shaped and dimensioned for sufficient strength, we can legitimately see it as a column.

When we have sufficient knowledge of such conditions we can produce functional interpretations of systems in compositional fashion, by considering the possible functions of the elements and the ways that they are related—much as we can establish the meaning of a sentence from the possible senses of its component words and the way they are put together. We can use the same rules to reason about how architectural elements must be shaped, dimensioned, and assembled in order to satisfy functional requirements. The rules enable us to explore the functional implications of form and the formal implications of function.

In this chapter, then, I shall consider conditions of functional adequacy, ways to formulate them precisely, and use of knowledge about them in producing functional readings of designs and in the synthesis of design proposals.

FUNCTIONAL ADEQUACY AND EQUIVALENCE

A component of a system is functionally adequate if and only if its physical characteristics allow it to effectively perform its role within that system. Consider, for example, the story of Thomas Edison's invention of the incandescent light bulb. He first established the role of the filament as one of transforming inputs of electricity into outputs of light. Then he tested numerous candidate filaments until he found one that did not burn out immediately; that is, until he found one that was functionally adequate.

Two components are functionally equivalent when they both adequately perform a specified role. For example, we can replace the wheel of a car by a functionally equivalent spare wheel or the lead in a mechanical pencil by another lead or the blade of a knife by another blade. The use of functionally equivalent interchangeable parts in this way has become one of the cornerstones of modern industrial production.

A conceptually more interesting possibility is that the replacement component, though functionally equivalent, has a different internal functional organization and physical form. Consider, for example, a cooking pot handle consisting of a metal shaft and an insulating grip: it could be replaced by a wooden handle which does not separate the functions of providing leverage and insulation in this way. To take a more complex case, an incandescent lighting fixture plugged into a wall socket and illuminating a room might be replaced by a fluorescent fixture, plugged into the same socket, and providing much the same illumination. Even more strikingly, architects sometimes produce alternative but apparently functionally equivalent proposals in response to the same context and requirements. Figure 10.1, for example, illustrates alternative "gothic" and "classic" proposals made by Schinkel for the Werdersche Kirche in Berlin. Notice that objects may be functionally equivalent in one context but not in another. In other words, they may be good for performance of different but overlapping ranges of actions. I can, for instance, use both a screwdriver and a kitchen knife to open a jam jar, but I cannot use the screwdriver to carve roast beef.

10.1
Architectural synonyms: plans of Schinkel's functionally equivalent proposals for the Werdersche Kirche in Berlin

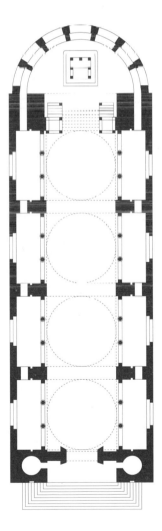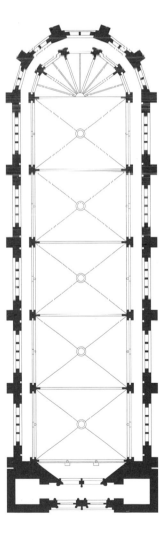

To claim that form follows function is to claim that some formal feature or quality of an object is necessary for functional adequacy: if the feature or quality is not present, then the object cannot perform the function we have in mind. For example, the ancient physician Galen claimed that the characteristic formal features of the human hand were necessary if it were to perform its functions adequately. In his treatise *On the Usefulness of the Parts of the Body*[2] he first considered the necessity of the cleft shape:

One and indeed the chief characteristic of a prehensile instrument constructed in the best manner is the ability to grasp readily anything of whatever size or shape that man would naturally want to move. For this purpose, then, which was better—for the hand to be cleft into many divisions or to remain wholly undivided? Or does this need any discussion other than the statement that if the hand remained undivided, it would lay hold only on the things in contact with it that were of the same size as it happened to be itself, whereas, being subdivided into many members, it could easily grasp masses much larger than itself, and fasten accurately upon the smallest objects? For larger masses, the hand is extended, grasping them with the fingers spread apart, but the hand as a whole does not try to grasp the smallest objects, for they would escape if it did; the tips of two fingers are enough to use for them. Thus the hand is most excellently constituted for a firm grasp of things both larger and smaller than itself. Furthermore, if it was to be able to lay hold on objects of many different shapes, it was best for it to be divided into many differing members, as it now is, and for this purpose the hand is obviously adapted best of all prehensile instruments. Indeed, it can curve itself around a spherical body, laying hold of and encircling it from all sides; it surrounds firmly objects with straight or concave sides; and if this be true, then it will also clasp objects of all shapes, for they are all made up of three kinds of lines, convex, concave, and straight.

Next, he argued that two opposing hands are necessary for grasping large and heavy objects:

Since, however, there are many bodies whose mass is too great for one hand alone to grasp, Nature made each the ally of the other so that both together, grasping such a body on opposite sides, are in no way inferior to one very large hand. For this reason, then, they face toward one another, since each was made for the sake of the other, and they have been formed equal to one another in every respect, a provision suitable for instruments which are to share the same action.

Finally, he observed the necessity of variation in the sizes of fingers and of possession of an opposing thumb:

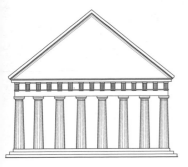

Too steep: tiles slide off

Correct

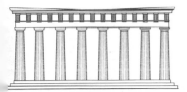

Too flat: does not drain

10.2
Choisy's analysis of the classical temple roof

Now when you have considered the largest objects that man can handle with both hands, such as a log or rock, then give heed, pray, to the smallest, such as a millet seed, a very slender thorn, or a hair, and then, when you have considered besides how very many bodies there are that range in size from the largest to the smallest, think of all this and you will find that man handles them all as well as if his hands had been made for the sake of each one of them alone. He takes hold of very small objects with the tips of two fingers, the thumb and forefinger, and slightly larger objects with the same two fingers, but not with just the tips; those still larger he grasps with three fingers, the thumb, forefinger, and middle finger, and if there are any larger yet, with four, and next, with five. After that the whole hand is used, and for still larger objects the other hand is brought up. The hand could act in none of these ways if it were not divided into fingers differently formed; for it was not enough in itself for the hand merely to be divided. What if there had been no finger opposing the four, as there is now, but all five of them had been produced side by side in one straight line? Is it not very clear that mere number would be useless, since an object to be held firmly must be either encircled from all sides or at least laid hold of from two opposite points? The ability to hold an object firmly would be destroyed if all the fingers had been produced side by side in one straight line, but as it is, with one finger set opposite the rest, this ability is nicely preserved; for this one finger has such a position and motion that by turning very slightly it acts with each of the four set opposite to it.

Such analyses can be carried out not only of components in natural systems, but also of components of designed artificial systems. In *Physics* (Book II, Chapter IX), for example, Aristotle asked: "Why is a saw like this?" He then answered:

In order that it may have the essential character of a saw and serve for sawing. This purpose, however, could not be served if it were not made of iron. So if it is to be a saw, and to do its work, it must necessarily be made of iron.

The positivist architectural theorists and historians of the nineteenth century were fond of analyzing architectural form in similar fashion. Consider, for example, a classical temple roof (figure 10.2). In a famous analysis, Auguste Choisy (1899) suggested that such a roof could fail to provide shelter in two ways: if the pitch were too flat, then the water would not drain away; but if the pitch were too steep, then the tiles would slide off. Therefore, he suggested, the physical property of pitch "is ruled by this double condition."

These authors are all claiming, in effect, that the characteristic formal features and qualities of system components can be explained in terms of functions. But is this logically justified?

Essentially, we are asked to accept that a given fact and two rules allow us to prove a second fact. The given fact is that, at a certain time t, a component c functions adequately in a system s. More concisely, we can write:

Given fact   *functions (c)*

The first rule asserts that, in the particular type of artifact under consideration, the action that yields a useful result depends on satisfaction of a particular condition—of sufficient hardness, for example. If the artifact functions adequately, we can conclude that the condition must be satisfied. More formally, we can write:

Rule 1   *functions (c) → quality (c)*

Note that *quality (c)* is not necessarily the only condition that must be satisfied: there might be an indefinite number of such conditions. A saw blade might need to satisfy conditions of sufficient hardness, sufficient sharpness, sufficient length, and so on. Furthermore, since different actions can yield the same result, different types of artifacts with the same function may need to satisfy different conditions: a welder's torch cuts by virtue of sufficient hotness rather than sufficient hardness.

The second rule specifies a way to satisfy the condition *quality (c)*. It asserts that, if formal feature f is present in component c at time t, then, as an effect, the predicate *quality (c)* is satisfied. We can write:

Rule 2   *feature (c, f) → quality (c)*

Hence, it is claimed, we can conclude that, at time t, the formal feature f is present in component c. Thus:

Conclusion   *feature (c, f)*

So we might, for example, paraphrase Aristotle's argument about the saw as follows:

Fact   *cuts (saw)*
Rule 1   *cuts (saw) → hard (saw)*
Rule 2   *material (saw, iron) → hard (saw)*
Conclusion   *material (saw, iron)*

Similarly, we might paraphrase Choisy's argument about the temple roof:

Fact	*shelters (roof)*
Rule 1	*shelters (roof) →*
	drains (roof) and
	not unstable (roof)
Rule 2	*pitch (roof, classicalangle)→*
	drains (roof) and
	not unstable (roof)
Conclusion	*pitch (roof, classicalangle)*

When we lay them out this way, it is easy to see that the arguments are invalid: they involve the fallacy of affirming the consequent. But if we were to alter the second rule to a biconditional, in each case, the logical problems would disappear. Aristotle's argument would become:

Fact	*cuts (saw)*
Rule 1	*cuts (saw) → hard (saw)*
Rule 2	*material (saw, iron) ↔ hard (saw)*
Conclusion	*material (saw, iron)*

Rule 2 now asserts that saying the saw is hard is equivalent to saying that the saw is made of iron. But rule 2 is now empirically false: we know that not only iron but many hard metals would satisfy the condition of sufficient hardness. Similarly, with Choisy, it would be implausible to maintain that *only* the classical angle provided stability and drainage.

RELATING FORM VARIABLES TO FUNCTION

This difficulty can be overcome by introducing appropriate variables to describe formal features. We might, for example, assume a variable **Metal** ranging over the hard metals available to Greek saw makers—bronze, iron, and so on. We claim that, as far as a Greek saw maker was concerned, saying that a saw was hard was equivalent to saying that it was made of metal: it could *only* be made of metal. We can now reformulate Aristotle's argument thus:

Fact	*cuts (saw)*
Rule 1	*cuts (saw) → hard (saw)*
Rule 2	*material (saw, **Metal**) ↔ hard (saw)*
Conclusion	*material (saw, iron)*
	or
	material (saw, bronze)
	etc.

The conclusion (a valid one) is a disjunction formed by the values of **Metal**.

The rule on which we rely here expresses knowledge of a particular construction world—that of Greek saw makers. It

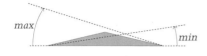

10.3
Constraints on roof pitch

specifies available ways to satisfy a condition of sufficient hardness in that construction world. The construction world of modern saw makers is quite different, encompassing many more ways to satisfy a condition of sufficient hardness. If we were to refer to *this* construction world instead, the range of **Metal** and the conclusion of the argument would be different. Modern saw makers have more ways to accomplish their purpose than their Greek counterparts: for them, form follows function less closely.

Choisy's argument can be reformulated in the same way by introducing a numerical variable **Angle** ranging from 0° to 90°, and two numerical constants *min* and *max* (figure 10.3). The argument is now written:

Fact	*shelters (roof)*
Rule 1	*shelters (roof)* → *drains (roof)*
Rule 2	*greater (**Angle**, min)* ↔ *drains (roof)*
Conclusion	*greater (**Angle**, min)*

We can also argue:

Fact	*shelters (roof)*
Rule 1	*shelters (roof)* → *not unstable (roof)*
Rule 2	*less (**Angle**, max* ↔ *not unstable (roof)*
Conclusion	*less (**Angle**, max)*

So we can validly conclude that the value of **Angle** must lie somewhere between *min* and *max*. These two constants are constraints on the value of the design variable **Angle**. Once again we have relied on knowledge of a particular construction world. A modern architect has available roofing materials that are more waterproof and more stable than Greek tiles, so roof angles are less constrained: they can range from flat to very steep.

So far we have identified two ways in which a Greek temple roof could fail to perform its sheltering function: it might leak or the tiles might slide off. Further, we have identified conditions that must be satisfied in order *not* to fail in these ways and available means of satisfying these conditions. We could continue this line of investigation by considering other modes of failure and corresponding constraints. For example, the roof would collapse if the span were too great, so we must impose a constraint (again, relative to a particular construction world) on the variable **Span**. Eventually we could identify all the variables that make a difference to the functioning of the roof and associate appropriate constraints with each one. We could then claim that satisfaction of these constraints is practically sufficient to guarantee that a roof will be functionally adequate. In other words, if the constraints are satisfied, we have no reason to believe that the roof will fail. Of course our knowledge might be incomplete, and the roof might fail anyway in some unexpected way, but we cannot do better than draw conclusions from the best knowledge that we have.

Now it is possible to state some general principles governing the relationship of form and function within a particular architectural language. Generally, an architectural language establishes a repertoire of forms (the vocabulary) that an architect can use, and the syntactic rules of that language specify possible contexts of use. An architect needs to understand the useful roles of vocabulary elements in their possible contexts: a waterproof triangular prism provides shelter when placed over an interior, a cylinder of strong material provides support when placed under a beam, and so on. For each vocabulary element, possible context, and role in that context, there are conditions of functional adequacy that can be expressed as constraints on the values of form variables. Thus full characterization of a vocabulary element requires specification not only of essential formal properties, but also of possible contexts of use, roles in those contexts, and conditions of functional adequacy that must be satisfied. The classical roof type, for example, is characterized by its symmetrical, triangular, prismatic form, by its location above an interior, by its role in that location of providing shelter, and by constraints on pitch and span.

Constraints may be more or less difficult and expensive to satisfy. A vocabulary element is appropriate for a particular role when the constraints can be satisfied more easily and inexpensively than the constraints applying to other vocabulary elements in that role. A vertical rectangle is a more appropriate form for the section of a wooden beam than a horizontal rectangle because the vertical rectangle will satisfy the condition of adequate strength with use of appreciably less material. Similarly, a symmetrical form is more appropriate for an axially loaded freestanding column than an asymmetrical one. The syntactic rules of an architectural language usually encode knowledge of appropriateness by restricting usage of vocabulary elements to contexts in which they efficiently serve practical purposes. Thus in most architectural languages, wooden rectangular prisms that are not too long and not too shallow serve as beams, and concrete cylinders that are not too thin serve as columns.

a. Vase

b. Ambiguous

c. Cup

d. Ambiguous

e. Bowl

10.4
Types of containers characterized by their ratios of width to height (after Labov, 1973)

In effect, constraints expressing conditions of functional adequacy establish limits on the adaptability of a vocabulary element to fit different contexts within a building. That is, they limit the extension of the type. A beam cannot be made too shallow to fit and play its role in the space available or it will fail to provide support, and a classical roof cannot span too great a distance to shelter a large space underneath.

Sometimes constraints of this nature establish distinctions between subtypes of artifacts. Consider, for example, the containers shown in figure 10.4. They vary in their ratios of width to height. Vases need to be narrow in order to hold flowers upright, so people tend to classify 10.4a as a vase. Cups need to be short for comfortable holding in the hand, so people tend to classify 10.4c as a cup. And bowls need to be wide to present the surfaces of their contents, so people tend to classify 10.4e as a bowl. The ratios in 10.4b and 10.4d do not clearly exemplify narrowness or shortness or wideness, so these containers do not clearly express their functions, and people find them difficult to classify. Similarly, functionally expressive architecture develops when elements are fashioned to not only satisfy conditions of functional adequacy, but also to do so in a way that clearly exemplifies the qualities on which adequacy depends. A building with cylindrical columns and rectangular beams is more functionally expressive than a building with rectangular columns and cylindrical beams, though both may be functionally adequate.

In their book *Language and Perception* Miller and Johnson-Laird (1976) suggest that joint use of formal and functional criteria is generally characteristic of human mechanisms of object classification and recognition. They consider, for example, a dictionary definition of "table":

An article of furniture supported by one or more vertical legs and having a flat horizontal surface on which objects can be placed.

They note that this has two parts: "one having to do with the conventional function of tables, the other with their perceptual appearance." If we consider only the formal side, an object **X** must meet the following conditions for being an instance of a table:

X is an object.
X is movable, connected, and rigid.
X has a flat surface.
There are parts of **X** that extend out from the side opposite to the flat surface.

The functional side may be elaborated:

X is a table

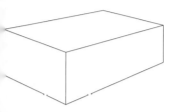

X serves as a table

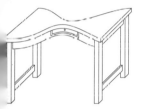

X is a poor table

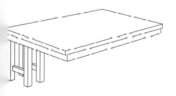

X is a structurally inadequate table

10.5

Instances of tables (the last two after Harelman, 1971)

A table is used for working or eating or playing games; the top is used to support various smaller objects required in the course of those activities.

Conditions of functional adequacy weld the two sides together:

A table should have a worktop, a surface that is horizontal so that objects will not roll or slide off and flat so that objects can stand on it. Moreover, the surface would be useless if it were not firm and at a convenient height from the floor (not horizontal upside down), so rigid legs are required to support it.

They conclude that "the schemata of many artifacts weld together form and function. . . . It would be a mistake to rely wholly on one or the other."

In an elaboration of this account, Miller (1977) has proposed that tables might be characterized in the following way:

*table (**X**) if formoftable (**X**)*
        and
    *functionoftable (**X**) is possible*

where the definition of *formoftable* is in terms of formal characteristics, and the definition of *functionoftable* is in terms of functional characteristics. Note the introduction of the modal operator *possible*: for object **X** to be a table it is necessary for it to have the specified form, but it need not actually function as a table. Such functioning must merely be possible. (This accords with the view of function that I developed earlier.) You know that *functionoftable (**X**)* is possible, relative to the given circumstances, if you can see how to use **X** as a table. Conversely, you know that *functionoftable (**X**)* is not possible if you can see a reason why **X** cannot be used as a table. In the context of design, the knowledge that is invoked to determine whether *functionoftable (**X**)* is possible will be knowledge of conditions of functional adequacy in the assumed construction world. The instances of tables shown in figure 10.5 illustrate this definition. The first is unquestionably a table. The second is formally a stone slab, but it provides a flat surface to support small objects and therefore serves as a table. The third is formally a table, but one that is unlikely to function very effectively: we might say that it is not a good table. The fourth is formally and functionally a table, but in any reasonable construction world it would fail by falling over.

The surrealist "crisis of the object" that André Breton identified in *La Surréalisme et la Peinture* (1927) was generated by subverting artifact classifications formed in this way.

Mêret Oppenheim's furry teacup and spoon took the shapes of familiar household items and suggested a use, but flaunted failure to satisfy an obvious condition of functional adequacy. Maurice Henry swathed a violin in bandages to make it conspicuously unplayable and called the piece *Homage to Paganini*. Marcel Duchamp signed a urinal to satisfy a necessary condition for that object to be a work of art and challenged viewers to consider whether that condition might also be sufficient. Magritte depicted a typical pipe and inscribed the definition "This is not a pipe." Architects can play similar games by using elements that exemplify certain shape or material properties to suggest a function while in other respects exhibiting denial of that function: at Williams College, Charles Moore made Ionic capitals that are suspended from a cantilevered balcony and that float above shafts that stop a few inches short.

ELEMENT SELECTION PROBLEMS

In general, then, architectural vocabulary elements are characterized in terms of their essential formal features, their possible contexts, their functions in those contexts, and the conditions that they must satisfy in order to function adequately. Formal essences are established by a designer's commitment to particular formal qualities (e.g. symmetry) and by knowledge of the formal possibilities inherent in the materials and processes available in the relevant construction world. If lathes are available for turning wood or metal for example, then various solids of revolution can become part of an architectural vocabulary. Functional essences are established by the capacities of elements to perform action and the designer's understanding of those actions as means to serve architectural ends. Possible contexts, as expressed in syntactic rules, follow from conceptions of appropriate use and possibilities of physical fit. And conditions of functional adequacy can be established by observation and experiment.

Where there are severe technological restrictions, as in ancient Greek society, architectural vocabularies tend to be relatively small and stable. But where construction worlds are technologically advanced, it becomes possible for architectural vocabularies to grow large. The industrial revolution, in particular, brought about an enormous expansion of architectural vocabulary as new materials and processes became available. Large vocabularies typically contain functionally equivalent elements that differ in form (much as spoken language has synonyms) and formally equivalent elements that function differently (as a spoken language has

THE LOGIC OF ARCHITECTUR

homonyms). A column supporting a beam might be round or square (synonym); a vertical duct might be visually indistinguishable from a column (homonym).

When a purpose can be served by choice of different forms, and when equivalent forms can serve different purposes, a designer must choose a particular way of relating form and function in much the same fashion that a poet must choose a particular way of relating sound and sense. An architect, like a poet, can make choices that yield desired formal qualities such as rhythm and symmetry. Furthermore, since functional equivalence (like synonyms) are never exact, these choices produce subtle but important inflections of functionality and expression. They can be made with rhetorical intent, to produce emphasis, irony, and so on.

Considered more broadly, this is an issue of appropriate architectural diction—one that was of great concern to the architectural theorists of the nineteenth century, who were faced with the enormous vocabulary expansion resulting from the industrial revolution. Viollet-le-Duc adopted the stance of a language reformer, advocating a new diction of vivid structural expression, boldly expressed cast iron, and dramatic diagonals (Summerson, 1963). Louis Sullivan, in *Kindergarten Chats* (1918), railed against what he saw as the chaotic diction of his contemporaries:

Imagine for instance:
    Horse-eagles.
    Pumpkin-bearing frogs.
    Frog-bearing pea vines.
    Tarantula-potatoes.
Sparrows in the form of whales, picking up crumbs in the street.
    If these combinations seem incongruous and weird, I assure you in all seriousness that they are not a whit more so than the curiosities encountered with such frequency by the student of what nowadays passes for architecture.

ELEMENT DESIGN PROBLEMS

Element design problems arise when an architect wants to use an instance of a particular type of element to play a particular role in a particular context within a composition. The task is to choose values for the form parameters such that the conditions of functional adequacy in that role are satisfied and a fit to the context is achieved. The square wheel and the square peg in the round hole both fail as solutions to element design problems, but for different reasons: the square wheel does not work (violates a condition of functional adequacy), and the square peg does not fit.

An element design problem is formulated by establishing the form parameters for which values must be chosen in order to specify an instance together with the conditions that the chosen values must satisfy. For example, the Greek sawmaker's blade design problem might be stated:

choose **Material**

such that hard (**Material**)

Similarly, the temple roof design problem might be stated, in more mathematical format:

choose **Angle**

such that min < **Angle** < max

The designer of a rectangular beam of given material, to carry a given load over a given span, must choose values for section **Depth** and **Width** such that maximum allowable tensile, compressive, and shear stresses in the material are not exceeded.

An element design problem is solved when it can be demonstrated that chosen values for the form parameters satisfy the specified conditions. The demonstration might be accomplished by prototype testing—trying out saw blades on a block of wood or loading a beam to destruction, for example. More often it is accomplished by reasoning: facts and rules in the knowledge base about the construction world are used to prove the assertion that the chosen values satisfy the requirements. In practice, the knowledge base may or may not provide the means necessary to derive this proof, and the actual derivation may be a trivial or a complex process.

Different types of elements may perform the same function but, by virtue of their essential internal structure, have different kinds and levels of adaptability to context. Consider, for example, the two classical types of arched openings shown in figure 10.6. The Colosseum motif has one degree of dimensional freedom and is best adapted to vertical bays. It can vary in overall size, but it cannot vary much in proportion unless the springing-points of the arch are also allowed to shift vertically, thus changing the character of the opening and possibly disrupting horizontal alignments in a composition. By contrast, the Palladian motif (as used in the Basilica at Vicenza) has two degrees of dimensional freedom and is equally well adapted to horizontal or vertical bays. Variations in proportion can be accomplished by adjusting the widths of the side bays, while leaving the central arched opening unchanged.

10.6
The adaptability of motifs

The Colosseum motif: one degree of freedom

The Palladian motif: two degrees of freedom

FUNCTIONALLY MOTIVATED DESIGN

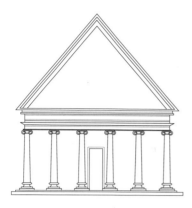

10.7
Pugin's vision of a "classical" temple adapted to the damp English climate (after *The True Principles of Pointed or Christian Architecture*, 1841)

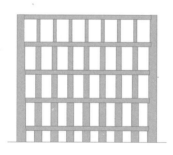

10.8
Economy of means: the brick piers in the elevation of Louis Kahn's Phillips Exeter Academy Library are no thicker than they have to be

Sometimes the interrelationships of design variables established by the type definition, together with the requirements of fit to context and functional adequacy, overconstrain an element design problem, so that no solution is possible. Pugin (1841) argued, for example, that the classical temple roof type could not be adapted to the damp English climate, since the minimum angle needed for drainage in this context would produce a form that would no longer count as classical (figure 10.7). Either the formal or the functional essence of the type would have to be violated. Similarly, engineers often face situations where the span and loading of a beam are given, but the available space is not sufficiently deep to accommodate a beam that would be functionally adequate. The problem must be redefined by lightening the load, shortening the span, increasing the available depth, or choosing a different type of beam section that is better adapted to the given conditions.

Occasionally the requirements will so constrain the problem that just one solution is possible. In this case, in a strong sense, form follows function. More often there will be many feasible solutions, and we need some way to choose between them. Since resources needed to realize a design, such as steel, land, and money, are usually scarce relative to our potential uses for them, it makes sense to apply the principle of economy of means: a designer usually seeks the solution that minimizes use of some scarce resource (figure 10.8). Hannes Meyer forcefully phrased this principle at the opening of his manifesto "Building" (1928). "All things in this world," he wrote, "are a product of the formula: (function times economy)." Design, then, became a matter of organizing building materials into "a constructive whole based on economic principles." This was not an "aesthetic" but a "biological" process: "Thus the individual shape, the body of the structure, the colour of the material and the surface texture evolve by themselves and are determined by life."

Meyer's vision of an inexorable logical process leading to one "best" solution has been realized, in limited contexts, by computer programs that search the whole universe of potential solutions for those that satisfy feasibility requirements and minimize some objective function defined on the design variables.[4] It is often possible to use such programs, for example, to minimize the amount of material in a structural member or the total floor area of a plan or the total thermal load of a building envelope. Techniques of differential calculus, linear and nonlinear programming, and dynamic programming are typically used to produce optimal solutions.

Meyer maintained that it was an absurdity to talk about this kind of design in terms of aesthetics at all: "If a building provides adequately, completely, and without compromise for its purpose it is a good building, regardless of its appearance" (Mumford, 1952). But other advocates of optimal design have argued that strict attention to economy of means will automatically yield beauty. The nineteenth-century functionalist theoretician Horatio Greenough, for example, wrote[5]:

If we compare the form of a newly invented machine with the perfected type of the same instrument, we observe, as we trace it through the phases of improvement, how weight is shaken off where strength is less needed, how functions are made to approach without impeding each other, how straight becomes curve, and curve is straightened, till the straggling and cumbersome machine becomes the compact, effective, and beautiful engine.

With deft irony, though, Thorstein Veblen suggested that Greenough's principle might be inverted. In *The Theory of the Leisure Class* (1899) he proposed that "articles are to an extent preferred for use on account of their being conspicuously wasteful; they are felt to be serviceable somewhat in proportion as they are wasteful and ill adapted to their ostensible use." He went on to explain that (at least in some social contexts) conspicuous waste may be an effective way to establish heightened social status, and hence may be taken as a design objective.

However the objective is defined, the task of element design is to specialize a general concept appropriately to a given physical context and role within a system. The values chosen for design variables must at least satisfy known feasibility constraints. And, where there are multiple feasible solutions, additional criteria may be adduced to distinguish between better and worse ones. The designer's task then becomes one of refining and perfecting, either by trial-and-error or through use of formal optimization techniques.

MULTIFUNCTIONALITY

Elements are often used, in architectural compositions, to play several different roles simultaneously. Windows, for example, are usually expected both to provide light to an interior and to prevent heat loss from an interior. If they are large they tend to provide good lighting at the expense of thermal efficiency, but if they are small they tend to achieve thermal efficiency at the expense of lighting quality. The designer's task, then, is not just to specify form parameters that result in optimal lighting, nor is it just to specify form parameters that result in optimal thermal performance, but to find a solution that responds to *both* objectives.

One common approach to multi-objective element design problems is to establish rules for trading one objective off against another, then to seek an optimal balance. A second approach is to establish thresholds of acceptability, so that all the objectives except one are converted into constraints. Thus a designer might seek optimal lighting subject to maintaining some acceptable level of thermal performance, or, conversely, the objective might be optimal thermal performance subject to maintaining some acceptable level of lighting. Tradeoff ratios and constraints may shift according to conditions prevailing in the construction world. In cold climates where heating fuel is scarce, it is likely that windows will be made small to minimize heat loss, and poor lighting conditions will be accepted. But in temperate climates, where little heating is required, window sizes are less constrained.

A more subtle approach than either of these is to look for ways to vary parameters such that performance in one respect is improved without corresponding degradation in other respects—in other words, to explore sets of Pareto-optimal[6] solutions.

FUNCTIONAL ARTICULATION

Instead of using a single multifunctional element to play a variety of roles, a designer may decide to let several different elements play these roles individually. A window shutter for example, might be replaced by the combination of a blind to provide visual privacy and an air conditioner to provide ventilation. Where there is a high level of articulation into distinct components, there is greater opportunity for optimally specialized form to emerge. In *Parts of Animals*, for example, Aristotle noted that in some insects the proboscis functions both as a tongue and a sting, while in others these functions are articulated. He commented:

It is better, when it is possible, that one and the same organ should not be put to dissimilar uses; that is, there should be an organ of defence which is very sharp, and another organ to act as a tongue, which should be spongy and able to draw up nourishment. And thus, whenever it is possible to employ two organs for two pieces of work without their getting in each other's way, Nature provides and employs two. He habits are not those of the coppersmith who for cheapness sake makes you a spit-and-lampstand combination. Still where two are impossible, Nature employs the same organ to perform several pieces of work.

10.9
Evolution and functional articulation: a fossil trilobite with many similar legs and its modern crab descendent with fewer legs adapted to specialized roles (from Simpson, 1967)

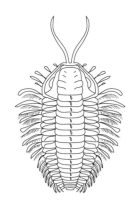

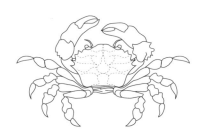

The Pantheon, Rome

Saint Peter's, Rome

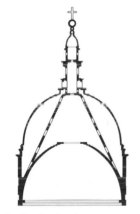

Saint Paul's, London

10.10
Functional articulation of domes

A tendency toward increasing functional articulation and specialization of parts may sometimes be observed in the evolution of organic forms, and biologists know this as evolution in accordance with "Williston's law" (Simpson, 1967). Figure 10.9, for example, compares a fossil trilobite with one of its modern crab descendents. The trilobite has many very similar legs, and within each leg the several segments are similar. The legs of the crab, on the other hand, are adapted in quite different ways for their various specialized roles in locomotion and grasping, and within each leg the forms of the segments vary according to their respective positions and roles.

Similar developments can also be observed in architecture. Consider, for example, the historically successive domes of the Pantheon in Rome, Saint Peter's in Rome and Saint Paul's in London (fig. 10.10). All three domes are at a vast scale and simultaneously perform the functions of enclosing an interior space, providing top-lighting to that space, and serving as a landmark in the heart of a great city. The dome of the Pantheon is a massive, unarticulated single masonry shell, with a simple oculus cut at the center to provide light. This shell performs all three of the functions. The dome of Saint Peter's is a good deal taller, and in this respect it is better adapted to the landmark function. It is also slightly more articulated; the lower part is a single, thick masonry shell as needed to resist the thrusts at the base, but the upper part is articulated into distinct inner and outer shells, which respectively enclose the interior space and give an appropriate exterior profile. Sir Christopher Wren took Saint Peter's as his model, but further articulated the dome of Saint Paul's into three distinct subsystems. Enclosure of the interior is accomplished by means of a relatively shallow masonry shell that carries just its own weight. The heavy stone lantern is supported by a separate brick shell, the elongated catenary shape of which is structurally advantageous for a concentrated load at the center, and which gives dramatic elevation to the lantern. The outer dome is a relatively light timber structure that achieves a greater ratio of height to span than would be possible in masonry without the introduction of buttresses or very heavy reinforcement.

In his famous "5 points d'une architecture nouvelle" (1927), Le Corbusier explicitly proposed a high level of functional articulation and optimal specialization of components as an aesthetic principle (figure 10.11). He wrote:

10.11
Le Corbusier's "five points"

1. Pilotis

2. Roof gardens

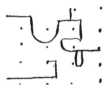

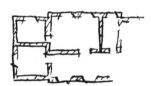

3. The free plan

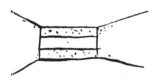

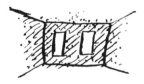

4. The elongated window

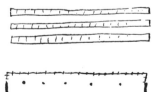

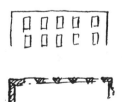

5. The free facade

THE LOGIC OF ARCHITECTURE

In order to solve a problem scientifically, you first have to identify the separate elements. In a building, therefore, you can immediately distinguish between the supporting and non-supporting members. Instead of the earlier kind of foundations, on which the building rested without calculating the stresses, we install individual pile foundations, and instead of walls, individual supports. The supports and their foundations are worked out exactly to meet the loads imposed on them. These supports are spaced out evenly and deliberately, without taking the individual arrangement of the house into account.

Of the new separation of structure from plan, he commented further:

The system of supports rise from the ground to the roof, carrying the floor slabs. The partition walls can be situated wherever they are needed, at will, since each storey is completely independent of all the others. There are no more bearing walls, only membranes of whatever thickness is required. What results from this is complete freedom to arrange the plan as you wish, freely deploying the means at your disposal.

Finally, of apertures in the facade, he noted:

By cantilevering the floor slab out over the supports like a balcony, all around the house, you move the whole facade away from the supporting structure. You take away the load-bearing nature of the facade and you are able to extend the windows as far as you like.

An architect, then, can choose either a highly articulated architectural vocabulary of functionally and formally specialized elements or a less articulated vocabulary of more broadly useful elements. An articulated vocabulary can be deployed to produce functionally expressive compositions, while a less articulated vocabulary invites an architectural rhetoric of ambiguity.

COMPOSITION PROBLEMS

Composition problems arise when an architect must choose, adapt, and arrange elements to satisfy specified formal and functional requirements. In bottom-up composition the architect begins with elements of known form and function. Grammatical rules specify various useful relationships of elements and subsystems—how to put them together in ways that establish functional connections. The task is to build up a system that, taken as a whole, functions in the required ways. The potential difficulty is in finding the right ways to build up high-level functions from lower-level ones. For example, an architect might want to compose given rooms into a plan, or given appliances into a kitchen layout, or given structural members into a frame, or given electrical components into an electrical system.

Recall that the half-hexagon table grammar which we considered in chapter 8 structures a bottom-up design process. If we now take account of the functions of tables, and the functional connections that we might want to establish between them, we can see how the rules specify useful ways to put tables together. Rule 1 provides for the formation of long work benches, rule 2 provides for the formation of large conference groupings, and rule 3 provides for the formation of small conference groupings (figure 10.12). Combinations of these rules result in various mixtures of these basic functions.

Although these functional ends might be achieved in many different ways, using differently shaped tables in different relationships, this language can be characterized by the very particular formal means that it provides for doing so. Rule 1 and rule 2 together provide for formation of straight lines of tables, meandering lines, and loops. Rule 3 allows tables to be doubled, where necessary. The spatial relationships of newly added tables to their predecessors are such that groupings with two-fold, three-fold, and six-fold dihedral symmetry frequently emerge. Rotational and frieze symmetries are also possible. Thus an architect working with this language produces solutions with characteristic formal qualities. A language of, say, square tables placed edge to edge would yield solutions with different rhythms and symmetries.

In top-down composition the architect begins with a concept of the form and function of the system as a whole and has to work out the details. Grammatical rules specify useful internal organizations for subsystems—how to meet interface requirements and conditions of functional adequacy that have been established at a higher level. The task is to refine the design to the point where the forms of the lowest-level elements are fully specified and their functional adequacy can be demonstrated. The potential difficulty is in finding realizable designs for functionally adequate lower-level elements, or in finding a way to detail a schematic design using available "target" lower-level elements. For example, an architect might begin with the footprint of a building and go on to work out detailed internal room arrangements. Or a structural engineer might begin with a single-line schematic layout of a structural frame and then work out member sizes and jointing details.

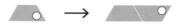 

Rule 1 yields long work benches

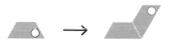 

Rule 2 yields large conference groupings

Rule 3 yields small conference groupings

10.12
Rules of the half-hexagon table
grammar specify useful ways to put
tables together

10.13
Structural roles of entablature, column, and pedestal

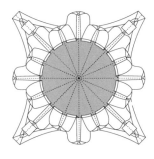

10.14
Capitals play the role of transition elements between rectangular entablature and circular column

The classical column grammar that we considered in chapter 8 structures this sort of design process. The basic concept of high-level functional organization, as established by the first rule, is that a horizontal structural member (the entablature) distributes loads to a vertical structural member (the column), which carries them down to a foundation resting on the ground (the pedestal). These actions are illustrated in figure 10.13. Each of the three subsystems must be detailed to satisfy conditions of functional adequacy in their roles, and rules of the grammar specify how to do this. A second rule, for example, specifies how a column may be articulated into an organization of base, shaft, and capital. The designer must shape the capital for the role of gathering the load from the rectangular entablature and concentrating it on the cylindrical shaft, size the shaft to carry the specified load, and shape the base to distribute the load from the shaft evenly onto the bearing surface of the pedestal. The rules suggest three basic ways to shape the capital so that it forms a graceful transition from a square top to a circular bottom: the Doric way, the Ionic way, and the Corinthian way (figure 10.14). Further rules suggest appropriate ways to shape the base, and so on.

When the Palladian villa language is functionally interpreted, we can see that its grammatical rules structure a top-down process of working out the details of room arrangement, circulation, and structural support (figure 10.15). First the designer must choose a gridded footprint that provides the right amount of floor area and satisfies requirements of site and budget. Next, this must be developed into a schematic room layout. The rules allow considerable freedom at this stage, so that villas can be individualized and precisely adapted to the needs of particular clients. Finally the rules specify how to develop the *poché* in a standard way to assure that the requirements of structural support, convenient circulation, ventilation, and natural light are satisfied. The rules also assure the formal property of bilateral symmetry (essential to this type) and allow for extensive variations on the theme of harmonic room proportioning (a way of distinguishing instances within the type).

In his "five points" Le Corbusier demonstrated how the introduction of functionally equivalent formal alternatives to the Palladian elements structured a different process of top-down plan refinement, leading to exploration of different formal themes (figure 10.16).[7] The footprint is punctuated by a grid of columns rather than subdivided by a grid of wall zones. Plan layout problems are solved by freely instantiating, translating, and rotating wall segments, rather than by concatenating grid cells. And there is no standard, symmetrical way to assure adequate circulation, lighting, and ventilation: The designer must work out these details in a way that forms appropriate connections between the features of the particular site and the spaces articulated in the plan. Just as Palladio explored the formal and functional possibilities of his language in a series of villa compositions, so Le Corbusier explored the potentials of *his* free-plan language in a sequence of compositions from the Domino House to the Villa Savoye.

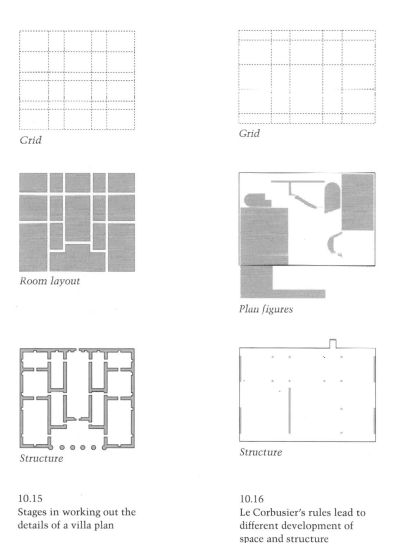

Grid

Grid

Room layout

Plan figures

Structure

Structure

10.15
Stages in working out the
details of a villa plan

10.16
Le Corbusier's rules lead to
different development of
space and structure

In general, if we approach architectural composition in bottom-up fashion, we rely on our knowledge of the formal and functional characteristics of given architectural vocabulary elements to suggest feasible and useful ways of putting them together in compositions. Conversely, if we approach design in top-down fashion, we rely on our knowledge of formal and functional characteristics to suggest appropriate choices and adaptations of elements to provide given functions in given contexts. In either case, our knowledge of how to select, shape, and put things together to serve architectural purposes can be expressed in the form of shape rules. We can understand the left sides of such rules as specifications of the architecturally interesting shapes in an evolving composition—those that the designer should look for and pay attention to. They are interesting because they can be developed further to accomplish potentially useful subgoals, and the right sides specify how to carry out this development. Thus the rules of an architectural grammar relate compositional means to formal and functional ends.

A given functional problem can usually be solved within several different architectural languages (as we saw from Schinkel's proposals for the Werdersche Kirche), though not necessarily with equivalent ease or with the same economy of means. The rules of a given language may allow many ways to satisfy a specified set of functional requirements, thus providing the architect with freedom to explore alternative solutions with varying formal and symbolic qualities. Or the rules may rigorously restrict formal directions, as in strict classical architecture or the late work of Mies van der Rohe.

The rules of an established language can be changed by introducing new elements to play established roles, as Le Corbusier did in his "five points," or by using old elements in new ways, as when Alberti combined the temple front with the triumphal arch to create a new language of Renaissance church facades. Figure 10.17 shows how Alberti deployed classical vocabulary elements inherited from antiquity. Rules 1, 2, and 3 reflect ancient usage in temples and triumphal arches, and rule 4 represents Alberti's extension of this usage to provide a solution to the problem of giving a classical facade to a church with a wide central nave and narrow flanking aisles. Figure 10.18 illustrates the motifs that develop from the rules of usage.

Alberti's innovation, here, was to use a triumphal arch *as* a church front. It fits into the context where a church front

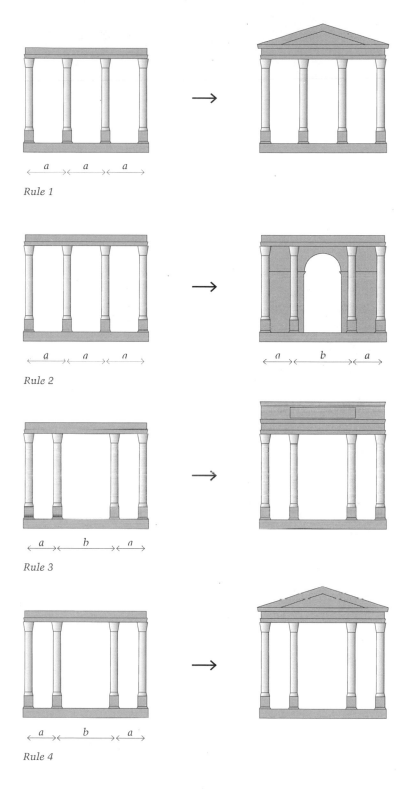

Rule 1

Rule 2

Rule 3

Rule 4

10.17
Rules of usage: rules 1 to 3 specify
traditional Roman usage, and rule 4
specifies Alberti's extension of it

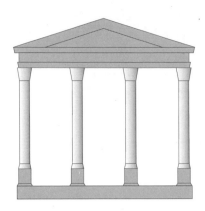

Temple front motif

Arch of Trajan motif

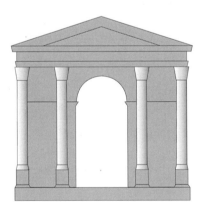

S. Andrea, Mantua, motif

10.18
Combinations allowed by Alberti's
rules of usage

would normally be and assumes the church front's functional connections. Similarly, a modernist might use a metal pipe *as* a handrail—fitting it into a context where a handrail would normally be, so that it assumes the handrail's functional connections (and detailing it to proclaim "this is not a pipe"). The success of such ploys depends, of course, on the element's functional adequacy in its new role and context. The triumphal arch succeeds for Alberti because it has the requisite tripartite subdivision and because it has the opening in the right place. The metal pipe succeeds for the modernist because it is long, graspable, and smooth. In effect, such successes modify the syntax of an architectural language by allowing a new alternative on the right side of a shape rule.

Thus architectural languages evolve, but not arbitrarily. The strict classical language, for example, does not create contexts in which the flying buttress serves a structural purpose, so there was no compelling reason to introduce that element into ancient classical architecture. But the gothic language creates contexts that demand something like a flying buttress to resist lateral thrusts: hence Choisy's famous remark that the flying buttress was not invented, but imposed itself. When Sir Christopher Wren designed Saint Paul's Cathedral within the classical language, but gave it a dome that produced lateral thrusts, he introduced flying buttresses to play the role of resisting them—thereby extending the strict classical language.

From a functional viewpoint, then, the rules of an architectural language are not just arbitrary restrictions on the application of shape operators. They are, more positively, expressions of knowledge about how to make available objects appropriately serve purposes in buildings. It is rarely the case, however, that requirements for formation of functional connections uniquely determine where an element must be located: a column might function properly if located at any one of several positions under a beam, and a window might function properly if located at any one of several positions in a wall. Under these circumstances, the rules of usage may allow arbitrary choice within the functionally defined limits, or (more commonly) they may specify location according to formal principles of centering, alignment, rhythm, symmetry, and so on.

A useful distinction can be drawn between "strong" and "weak" rules of usage according to the amount of functional knowledge that they express. In general, grammars consisting of strong rules have narrowly specialized application but allow confident, efficient solution of design problems, while grammars consisting of weak rules have wider application but promise less in the way of useful results.[8] The classical column grammar and the Palladian villa grammar (which were discussed in chapter 8) are examples of strong grammars: they tell precisely how to design specialized types of artifacts. At early stages in design processes, though, architects often use vocabularies of abstract shapes and weak rules for putting them together. A particular shape, for example, may indicate nothing more specific than "square-shaped thing." Since "square-shaped things" can be used for many different purposes in buildings, rules providing strong guidance about placement are not available: the architect must make arbitrary choices or fall back on general formal principles. Usually, as the design process progresses, shapes acquire more precise references in the construction world, contexts within the composition become more precisely and completely defined, and stronger systems of rules come into play.

Conventions of depiction and interpretation usually reflect the strength of the grammar that is being used. An early representation of an evolving design, such as a quick line sketch, typically specifies so few properties that little knowledge of conditions of functional adequacy is brought into play, and function consequently remains ambiguous. Thus a creative designer can legitimately see shapes as many different things, which evoke different expectations about behavior and possible functions and lead further development and critical discussion in different directions. This is not just an idle game. At this stage the designer is most interested in ranges the uses that are not inconsistent with a given shape and the shapes that are not inconsistent with a given use. The design is full of unbound variables and so serves as a framework for speculation about possibilities.

As the design develops, more variables are bound so that properties are specified more precisely and in more detail, with the result that functional interpretations become correspondingly better defined, and situations demand more specific responses. The designer's task becomes progressively less speculative and more one of responding correctly to the precise imperatives of role and context. Eventually, creative speculation about possibilities within the framework of a weak grammar evolves into technical problem-solving within the framework of a strong grammar.

In one sense this view of rules of usage is consistent with Julien Guadet's (1894) academic notion that to compose "is to make use of what is known." But Guadet placed his faith in universal first principles and in universal rules by means of which the new could be deduced from the known. Here I have suggested that design rules are much more contingent—that designers both apply and construct them, in much the same way that courts both apply and construct the law by engaging specific contexts of application.

CONCLUSION

At the beginning of this essay I considered architectural composition at the atomic level—the level at which geometric primitives and operators in a design world establish an algebra. Then, at a molecular level, I demonstrated how languages of architectural form can be embedded in such algebras. Finally, I have shown how an architectural grammar may be regarded as a summary of an architect's current knowledge of the elements available to create buildings (the vocabulary), and of how to make appropriate use of them for that purpose. Formally, design is execution of a computation in a shape algebra to produce required shape information, and the rules of a shape grammar specify how to carry out that computation.

These rules encode knowledge of form, function, and the relationship of the two. Essentially, a designer knows that, by virtue of their characteristic shape and material properties, certain types of objects can appropriately by used for certain purposes by being placed in certain contexts. What an object can be used *as* determines the type of thing it *is*: its architectural essence is its function together with the the context, shape, and material properties necessary for performance of that function. Contexts for its use (as specified by rules of usage) are established by the rules of usage of *other* types of elements with which it forms functional connections.

The left sides of shape rules define the recognizable situations for which the designer should watch out, to which attention should be paid, and to which response should be considered. Due to the discontinuous nature of design interpretations (resulting from the designer switching attention to different subshapes and seeing them as different things), these situations can emerge in highly unexpected, unpredictable ways. The right sides of shape rules specify responses worth considering. Other responses might also be worth considering, but the rules of the grammar specify the known ones. Choices among possible responses might be made mechanically, but this is not characteristic of skilled human designers. Critical reflection on the entailments of possible responses normally lies at the heart of architectural design processes. It is this reflective aspect of what would otherwise merely be instantiation of a formal type, the conscious and informed play of intention against a structure of givens to yield three-dimensional form, that gives a significant work of architecture its intellectual and emotional power.

An architect's knowledge of the shapes and materials of available elements and how to use them establishes a characteristic architectural language—a personal style.[9] This style may evolve as the architect becomes sensitive to new sorts of situations, learns to make use of new types of elements, and discovers new uses for known elements. Possession of a style is essential. Without this, an architect attempting to design is like the scholars Gulliver encountered at the Academy of Lagado, who tried to write books by randomly combining words. That way, one would never get to the end.

NOTES

1

The idea of a language of architectural form has frequently arisen, in various different guises, in architectural theory. Among recent works to make explicit use of it are Abel (1980), Alexander (1979), Alexander et al. (1975, 1977), Bonta (1979), Hesselgren (1969), Jencks (1977), Koenig (1964), Meunier (1980), Norberg-Schulz (1985), Portoghesi (1967), Prak (1968), Preziosi (1979), Summerson (1963), and Zevi (1978). On the other hand, Pettit (1975) and Scruton (1979) develop arguments against the idea.

1 BUILDING DESCRIPTIONS

1

See Gibson (1950, 1966) for detailed discussion of the idea of a perceptual field.

2

Segmentation, object perception, and related issues are discussed in depth by Ballard and Brown (1982), Horn (1986), Hurlbert and Poggio (1988), Jackendoff (1983), Marr (1982), Richards (1988), and Stillings et al. (1987). See also Quine (1987) on "Things."

3

See, for example, Wertheimer (1923), Kohler (1929), Koffka (1935), and Arnheim (1974).

4

See Fischler and Firschein (1987), Chapter 3, "Recognition and Labeling of Scene Objects," for a collection of key papers on this topic. Pinker (1985) provides a survey of competing theories.

5

Here we take the large step of beginning to relate language and perception. See Miller and Johnson-Laird (1976) for a detailed exploration of this topic from a psychological viewpoint.

6

Programmers will recognize that this can be done in different ways. In a procedural programming language, such as Pascal, the value *white* would be assigned to the variable **X**. In a declarative language, such as Prolog, the variable **X** would be instantiated to the value *white*.

7

The Cartesian product of n sets A, B, C, . . . is the set of all ordered n-tuples $\langle a, b, c, . . . \rangle$ that can be formed from their elements.

8

This is not always a defensible assumption, but it will serve our purposes for the moment.

9

Higher-order and modal logics have less attractive formal properties than classical first-order logic and in general they are less well understood. However, they have important uses in formalizing various kinds of sentences found in natural language. See Allwood, Andersson, and Dahl (1977) and Martin (1987) for discussions.

10

See Miller and Johnson-Laird (1976) for a detailed discussion of how such prepositions are used to express spatial relations.

11

Programming languages like Pascal make use of this. They provide for the construction of negations, conjunctions, and disjunctions of expressions containing variables. When values are assigned to the variables, the truth-values of the constituent expressions can be computed, and from these the truth-values of the compound expressions can be computed.

12

A constant denoting an individual in the universe of discourse can be thought of as a nullary relation—with no arguments.

13

For an example of a systematic attempt to provide an explicit conceptualization as a basis for describing a class of buildings, see Brunskill (1965–66).

2 ARCHITECTURAL FORM

1

Many programming languages allow use of functions as arguments of expressions in this way. This is a particularly important feature of Lisp. See Abelson and Sussman (1965) for a discussion.

2

This raises questions of ontology—of whether we want to be committed to the existence of such objects and of what it means to be. See Quine (1953) for a famous discussion of this point.

3

See Pollitt (1972, 1974) for detailed discussions of this term.

4

The *Canon* has not been preserved, but its contents can be reconstructed, to a certain extent, from references and quotations in extant ancient texts. See Pollitt (1972, 1974) and Leftwich (1988).

5

Other Pythagorean rules, such as those prohibiting eating beans or stepping over crowbars, seem to have held less sway over the architectural imagination.

6

See Scholfield (1958) and Wittkower (1962, 1978) for useful surveys of proportioning systems. Eco (1986) discusses medieval views on the subject.

7

See Summers (1981) for an extended discussion of this passage.

8

The modern group-theoretic concept of symmetry emerged during the nineteenth century and has been much elaborated during the twentieth century. See Weyl (1952) for a brief, classic introductory discussion. Shubnikov and Koptsik (1974) provide a more detailed treatment. March and Steadman (1974) give architectural illustrations of the plane symmetry groups. Baglivo and Graver (1983) extensively discuss the principles of architectural symmetry.

9

Emond (1964) gives an extensive survey.

10

For example, the order of a polygon is measured by a formula that takes into account degree of symmetry, a measure of "equilibrium," and various other factors. Complexity is defined by the number of distinct straight lines containing at least one side of the polygon. Eysenck (1968) has proposed that Birkhoff's formula should actually take the form $m = o \times c$. Stiny and Gips (1978) provide a useful discussion of these formulae.

11

See, for example, Moles (1958), Attneave (1959), Hiller and Isaacson (1959), Meyer (1959) and Arnheim (1971). Gombrich (1979) makes use of the idea in a less doctrinaire, more subtle and convincing way. Green and Courtis (1966) develop some criticisms.

12

The terminology is taken from the English translation by John James, published under the title *A Treatise on the Five Orders of Columns in Architecture* in 1708. Herrmann (1973) gives a detailed account of Perrault's theory.

13

Kant produced three great *Critiques: Critique of Pure Reason*, *Critique of Practical Reason*, and *Critique of Judgement*. The *Critique of Aesthetic Judgement* (the first part of the third *Critique*) is perhaps the most famous and important of all major philosophical works on aesthetics, and also one of the most difficult. See Osborne (1968) for a concise and readable introduction.

14

See, for example, Mead (1952).

---

3   DESIGN WORLDS

1

See Panofsky (1968) for a detailed discussion.

2

R. G. Collingwood, for one, would not have been at all comfortable with it. In his *The Principles of Art* (1938) he spoke of artifacts in tones closely reminiscent of Alberti: "The matter was there in the shape of raw material before the form was imposed upon it, and the form was there in the shape of a preconceived plan before being imposed upon the matter; and as the two coexist in the finished product we can see how the matter might have accepted a different form, or the form have been imposed upon a different matter." But he then went on to argue against "assimilating a work of art to an artifact, and the artist's work to the craftsman's": in a work of art, he claimed, "there is nothing in it of which we can say, 'this is a matter which might have taken on a different form,' or 'this is a form which might have been realized in a different matter.'"

3

Here I shall be concerned principally with designs that are "externally" modeled as drawings, etc. Descartes held that we "internally" represent the outside world by means of mental objects that stand for things outside. Craik (1943) discussed thought as the manipulation of mental models, and Johnson-Laird (1983) has presented a more recent view of mental models. In modern cognitive science the nature of "internal" representations is a crucial and controversial question.

4

See Shirari (1981) for details.

5

See Udupa (1983) for a discussion of applications in digital tomography.

6

See Rogers and Adams (1976), Newman and Sproull (1979), and Foley and Van Dam (1982) for details.

7

See Mortenson (1985) and Woodwark (1986) for details.

8

See Yessios (1987) for a detailed discussion of this point and an exploration of its implications for computer-aided design.

9

The problem to which stereotomy responded was the production of *traits*—precise layout drawings for use by masons in cutting component masonry blocks for complex architectural forms such as vaults. Philibert Delorme devoted a great deal of attention to the construction of *traits* in his *Première tome de l'architecture* (1567). Girard Desargues made major contributions to the theory of stereotomy, described in Abraham Bosse's *La Practique du trait* (1643). See Pérouse de Montclos (1982).

10

See Mortenson (1985), Mitchell (1986), Mantyla (1988), and Kalay (1989) for details.

11

Arnheim (1974) proposed that we should sidestep this issue by considering only "genuine" subshapes with good Gestalt properties. Stiny (1982, 1986, 1987, 1989) has shown how it can be handled formally, in a general way, within the framework of the calculus of individuals.

12

There have also been some studies of designers at work in which the sequence of states of the design world is recorded continuously on videotape. See, for example, Akin (1986).

---

4 CRITICAL LANGUAGES

1

See Tarski (1944, 1956, 1969) for discussions of the original idea by its inventor. Carnap's views are set out in Carnap (1942, 1947). Allwood, Andersson, and Dahl (1977) and Martin (1987) have provided clear and readable introductory textbooks on the topic. For further treatments, from various viewpoints, see Devitt and Sterelny (1987), Henkin (1967), Kalish (1967), Lyons (1977), and Quine (1970, 1987). Genesereth and Nilsson (1987) give a detailed example in which the world is a very simple one of square blocks. Stiny (1981, 1989) develops related ideas with particular reference to design.

2

Kirsch's (1963, 1964) notion of "picture language machines" introduced the possibility of using a computer to evaluate predicates of shapes. The idea of interpreting languages in microworlds of three-dimensional blocks was first explored in depth by Winograd (1972). Winograd's pioneering SHRDLU system has a more complex microworld than Tarski's World, and the interpretation is of a subset of English rather than first-order logic. Clark, Carpenter, and Just (1973) investigate from a psychological viewpoint the comparison of sentences against pictures.

3

We can think of it as highly abstracted, simplified English cast into a strictly uniform format. The role of nouns, verbs, and adjectives in denoting subject matter is played by predicate (i.e., object, function and relation) symbols. All the rest is done by variables, quantifiers, and connectives. It cannot express imperatives, questions, "mights," or "oughts." See Quine (1987) on "Predicate Logic" and McCarthy (1987, 1988) for discussion of the expressive power of first-order logic and related formalisms.

4

Goodman and Elgin (1988) have shown that depiction is not as simple and natural a matter as it might seem. Pictorial competence depends on knowledge of assumptions and conventions, and skill in applying that knowledge. Such competence must be learned by beginning designers.

5

There is an extensive literature on the history of use of these conventions in architectural drawing and on their role in structuring design exploration processes. See Bois (1981), Booker (1963), Edgerton (1975), Evans (1986), Lotz (1977), and Scolari (1984). Hagen (1986) discusses projections in representational painting and drawing. Goodman (1976) considers how drawings specify works of architecture.

6

This technique is of great antiquity—going back at least to the second millennium BC: there are ancient Egyptian architectural drawings made in parallel projection. Claudius Ptolemy discussed the underlying principles in his work on sundials, around 300 AD.

7

Maver (1988) has provided a useful survey of the use of analysis routines in integrated computer-aided design systems.

---

5   REASONING ABOUT DESIGNS

1

See McCarthy (1988) for a readable introductory discussion of the strengths and limitations of first-order logic for knowledge representation. See also Winston (1984).

2

The Prolog logic programming language (Kowalski, 1979) exploits this. It allows knowledge to be expressed as first-order logic facts and rules and employs the resolution principle to prove or disprove specified facts. It is straightforward to write simple criticism programs in Prolog.

3

This specializes the general point that cognition and artificial intelligence have an epistemological part (observation, representation, and inference rules) and a heuristic part (processing the available knowledge to produce useful results). See McCarthy and Hayes (1969).

4

See Genesereth and Nilsson (1987) for a more complete discussion of rules of inference and their uses.

5

See Clocksin and Mellish (1987) and Genesereth and Nilsson (1987) on clausal form.

6

The Prolog programming language, for example, allows the programmer to specify facts, rules, and goals to be proved, then automatically performs backward-chaining inference in an effort to prove goals.

7

Gero and Maher (1988) provide a useful survey of early attempts to develop knowledge-based computer-aided architectural design systems. See also Sharpe, Marksjö, and Thomson (1987).

8

The literature on possible worlds goes back at least to Leibnitz, who held that our world is the best of all possible worlds. The idea of possible worlds has played an important (and often controversial) role in modern semantic theory. Martin (1987) provides a useful exposition of it.

9

This is discussed in Kowalski (1979) and McCarthy (1988). Theoretical treatments of nonmonotonicity have been proposed by Doyle (1981), de Kleer (1986), McCarthy (1980, 1986), McDermott and Doyle (1980), Moore (1985), Rankin (1988), and Reiter (1980).

10

See Larkin and Simon (1987) for an exploration of this point.

6   TYPES AND VOCABULARIES

1

Mechanisms for handling inheritance are a cornerstone of object-oriented programming and of related programming languages such as Simula (Birtwistle, Dahl, Myhrhaug, and Nygaard,1973) and Smalltalk (Goldberg and Robson,1983). See Danforth and Tomlinson (1988) for a survey of this topic.

2

See also Quine (1987) on "Type versus Token." The concept of type has a very long and complex history, in which ideas drawn from several different fields become interwoven. In philosophy it may be traced back to Plato's "Ideas" and Aristotle's "Forms," and it has been continually under discussion since. Modern logicians and mathematicians have often found it necessary to draw careful distinctions between different types of abstract objects; Bertrand Russell's "theory of types" is a particularly famous example of this. A closely related development is the reliance of computer scientists on the idea of data types and the use of this idea in programming languages such as Pascal and Ada (Danforth and Tomlinson, 1988). Biologists, social scientists, and historians have frequently (sometimes with misgivings) relied on the notion of an "ideal type." Archaeologists have been concerned with establishing typologies of artifacts. Linguists have made much of the distinction between "types" and "tokens." In architectural theory, Quatremère de Quincy (1832) established a particularly influential concept of type, and an updated version of this has been revived by Argan (1963, 1965). Colquhoun's (1967) essay "Typology and Design Method" has been a major recent influence, and Colquhoun (1981) has followed this up with several further essays on the topic. Rossi's (1982) ideas on typology have received a great deal of recent attention. Moneo (1978), Bandini (1984), and Oechslin (1986) have provided useful summaries and comparisons of different views on the subject in architectural theory and criticism. Hawkes (1976) has explored the relationship of typology and architectural research.

3

This is the most traditional way to characterize types, and is appropriate for our immediate purposes here. It is adopted by Argan (1963, 1965) in his pioneering discussion of architectural type. Argan suggests that architectural types are formed by identification of the commonalities in a collection of architectural works. But other ways can be suggested, for example, characterization in terms of "family resemblances," along lines proposed by Wittgenstein (1953) and Rosch and Mervis (1975).

4

This will serve for our purposes here, but it is an over-simplification and ignores some of the subtleties that are involved. See Stebbing (1952) for an exceptionally clear development of the point in more detail. See also Copi (1954).

5

See Herrmann (1962) for a detailed discussion of Laugier's theory. Rykwert (1972) sets it within a broader context of ideas.

6

See Russell (1916) and Steadman (1979) for more detailed discussions. Woodger (1945) developed a rigorous treatment of the idea of organism *bauplans*.

7

Controversy rages over the issue of how, in general, the meanings of common nouns are established—particularly those, such as "gold" and "tiger," that refer to natural kinds (see Schwartz, 1977). However, I am less concerned here with the general philosophical question than with the narrower and more technical question of how to interpret critical languages in design worlds.

8

This idea has received a lot of recent attention in the field of knowledge-based systems, but it goes all the way back to the Aristotelian notions of *genus* and *differentiae*. See *Metaphysics*, V.

9

This example is adapted from Stillings et al. (1987). See Barr and Feigenbaum (1981) for further examples and for a concise introduction to the theory of frames.

10

For further discussion, from various viewpoints, see Berlin and Kay (1969), Minsky (1977), Putnam (1975), Schank and Abelson (1977), Smoke (1932), and Wittgenstein (1953).

11

This problem appears to have been first noted and discussed by Evans (1964) in his well-known paper on geometric-analogy problems.

12

The computational issues have been discussed, and recognition algorithms proposed, by Krishnamurti (1980, 1981), Krishnamurti and Giraud (1986), Kurlander and Bier (1988), and Chase (1989).

13

This discussion is closely based on the work of Clowes (1971) and Huffman (1971). See also Winston (1984).

14

Hanrahan (1982) and Markowsky and Wesley (1980) discuss algorithms for interpretation of wire frames as three-dimensional solids.

15

This figure, and the mechanisms of its interpretation, are discussed by Hoffman and Richards (1985).

16

Wittgenstein makes some penetrating remarks about this sort of situation (and uses the rabbit/duck figure as an example) in *Philosopical Investigations* (1953).

---

7 DESIGN OPERATIONS

1

This has become known as the frame problem. See Raphael (1971), Hayes (1973), and Dennett (1984). Eastman (1978, 1985, 1987), Gross, Ervin, Anderson, and Fleischer (1987), and Leler (1988) discuss aspects of how to trace the logical consequences of design operations.

2

In the computer-aided design world, construction of designs in this way is known as primitive instancing: see Voelcker and Requicha (1977) and Kemper and Wallrath (1987).

3

Various mechanisms for filling in the missing information are used in computer graphics and computer-aided design systems. For example, essential properties might be expressed in the code of a procedure which produces a fully detailed drawing of an instance when parameter values specifying the instance are passed in (Mitchell, Liggett, and Kvan, 1987). Alternatively, type descriptions might be stored in a catalogue database and instance parameter values in a project database: fully detailed drawings are produced through combination of data from the two sources (Mitchell, 1977). Object-oriented programming of such systems uses class hierarchies and inheritance mechanisms to accomplish much the same thing.

4

See Gould (1971) for a discussion of D'Arcy Thompson's ideas.

5

Hégron (1988) details algorithms for performing these operations.

6

See Mortenson (1985), Mantyla (1988), and Woodwark (1986).

7

See Stiny (1982, 1986, 1987, 1989) on the algebra of line shapes.

8

Regularized set operators may be introduced to remedy this deficiency. See Requicha (1980).

8   LANGUAGES OF ARCHITECTURAL FORM

1

Here the forward arrow is pronounced "is replaced by" rather than "if... then." But use of the same symbol is no accident: recall that, in *modus ponens*, we replace the left-hand side by the right-hand side (see Gips and Stiny, 1980).

2

The use of production systems in this way is grounded on pioneering work by Post (1943) and Markov (1954). Chomsky (1957) led the way in application to specification of spoken languages. Numerous texts, for example Hopcroft and Ullman (1969) and Harrison (1978), discuss applications to specification of computer programming languages.

3

Clocksin and Mellish (1987) discuss simple Prolog programs for this purpose. Gonzalez and Thomason (1978) discuss applications in pattern recognition.

4

For discussions of Durand's method, see Banham (1960), Hernandez (1969), Szambien (1984), de Sola-Morales (1987), and Villari (1987).

5

For an earlier version, see Stiny and Gips (1972).

6

For additional examples see Flemming (1981, 1986, 1987), Knight (1981, 1986), Koning and Eizenberg (1981), Stiny (1977, 1980), and Stiny and Mitchell (1981).

7

Modification to produce biaxial plans, if desired, is straightforward: see Stiny and Mitchell (1978a).

8

Similar arguments are developed by March and Stiny (1985) and Earl (1986).

9

See Newell and Simon (1972) for a detailed discussion of such trial-and-error search processes in human problem-solving. Search in artificial intelligence is thoroughly treated by Nilsson (1971) and Pearl (1984). The older literature on blind search is surveyed by Campbell (1960). Additional theoretical perspectives are given by Hofstadter (1982), Reitman (1965), and Simon (1967, 1972). Mitchell (1977) surveys early applications of systematic search techniques in architecture.

9   FUNCTION

1

In English, "function" has both a mathematical and logical sense, which I employed in earlier chapters, and an everyday sense which I employ here. The older traditions of architectural thought concerning function are summarized by De Zurko (1957). The pathbreaking paper of Rosenblueth, Wiener, and Bigelow (1943) stimulated the development of an extensive philosophical literature concerned with the interrelated topics of purposeful behavior, teleology, and the status of functional descriptions and explanations in biology and the social sciences. Two classic contributions, upon which I rely heavily in the following discussions, are Hempel (1965) and Nagel (1979). Additional perspectives are offered by Ayala (1970), Beckner (1968), Bock and von Wahlert (1965), Braithwaite (1946, 1953), Canfield (1964, 1966), Cohen (1951), Cummins (1975), Ducasse (1925), Frankfurt and Poole (1966), Fritz and Plog (1979), Gruner (1966), Guthrie (1924), Hempel and Oppenheim (1948), Hofstader (1941), Kauffman (1971), Lehman (1965), Mayr (1974), Nagel (1951, 1953, 1954, 1956, 1979), Nissen (1971), Noble (1967), Rignano (1931), Rosenblueth and Wiener (1959), Ruse (1971), Scheffler (1959), Sorabji (1964), C. Taylor (1964, 1967), R. Taylor (1950a, 1950b), Wimsatt (1972), Woodfield (1976), and Wright (1968, 1972, 1973, 1976).

2

The idea of affordance has been developed and explored by J. J. Gibson (1977, 1979). More recently, it has been taken up and used (in a rather different way) by Donald A. Norman in *The Psychology of Everyday Things* (1988).

3

The treatment developed here is based upon the classic definition given by Hall and Fagen (1956). There is a vast recent literature on systems. A good introduction to this literature is provided by the collection of readings edited by Buckley (1968). The collection edited by Emery (1969) also contains some useful discussions.

4

See Simon (1981) on "The Architecture of Complexity," Alexander (1967), Pattee (1973), Weiss (1971), and Whyte, Wilson, and Wilson (1969) for discussions of this point.

5

This kind of description is sometimes referred to as a systematic explanation. See Haugeland (1978).

6

Christopher Alexander pointed this out in the article "A City is not a Tree" (1972), and his pattern language (1977) explicitly deals with this issue.

7

See Firth (1956) for an overview.

8

Egbert (1980) gives a complete list of Grand Prix programs.

9

See Jencks and Baird (1969) and Broadbent, Bunt, and Jencks (1980).

10

Note the distance of this position from that of the formalist critics considered in chapter 1.

11

See also Elgin (1983).

12

Goodman (1985).

13

Several versions of this story are recounted in Ashton (1972).

14

The approach taken here is based upon analyses by Ross (1930), Hare (1952), and Beardsley (1981). See also Foot (1961), Katz (1964), Rawls (1971), and von Wright (1963).

15

Lodoli left no writings, but his views were recorded and discussed by various contemporaries, notably Andrea Memmo, Francesco Algarotti, and Francesco Milizia. See Kaufman (1955) for an excellent summary.

---

10   FUNCTIONALLY MOTIVATED DESIGN

1

There are other important cases of functional inference. Biologists try to infer the functions of organs, archaeologists try to infer the functions of artifacts from vanished cultures, and military engineers reverse-engineer captured weapons to find out how they work. The papers in Bobrow (1985) discuss the issue from an artifical intelligence perpective.

2

Translated by May (1968). For an excellent historical account of attempts by biologists to analyze relations between form and function, see Russell (1916).

3

This analysis closely follows Hempel (1965).

4

A good survey of optimization applications and methods in architectural design is given by Radford and Gero (1988).

5

This excerpt is from the essay "American Architecture." Greenough's major essays are reprinted in the collection *Form and Function* (1947).

6

The concept of Pareto-optimality comes from economics, where much attention has been given to problems of rational choice in relation to multiple objectives. Radford and Gero (1988) discuss its application to design problems.

7

See Rowe (1976) for a classic analysis of the similarities and differences between Palladio's and Le Corbusier's villa languages.

8

This relates to Newell's (1973) well-known distinction between strong and weak problem-solving methods in general. Strong results imply strong information demands and weak demands can yield only weak results.

9

Many historians and critics have alluded to the connection between the concepts of language and style. Focillon (1948), for example, wrote:

What, then, constitutes a style? First, its formal elements, which have a certain index value, and which make up its repertory, its vocabulary and occasionally, the very instruments with which it wields its power. Second, although less obviously, its system of relationship, its syntax.

And another well-known definition of style, given by Ackerman (1962), echoed this:

Conventions of form and symbolism yield the richest traits by which to distinguish style. I mean by conventions an accepted vocabulary of elements—a scale of color, an architectural order, an attribute of a god or a saint—and a syntax by which those elements are composed into a still life, a temple, or a frieze.

See Ackerman (1962), Gombrich (1968), and Schapiro (1953) for classic introductory discussions of style. A more recent symposium volume, edited by Lang (1979), contains some valuable critical analyses and a useful bibliography on the topic. Knight (1986) has treated stylistic change in terms of the shape grammar formalism.

BIBLIOGRAPHY

Abel, Chris. 1980. "The Language Analogy in Architectural Theory and Criticism." *Architectural Association Quarterly* 12, no. 3:39–47.

Abelson, Harold, and Gerald Jay Sussman. 1985. *Structure and Interpretation of Computer Programs*. Cambridge, Mass.: MIT Press.

Abelson, Robert P., and John B. Black. 1986. "Introduction to Knowledge Structures." In *Knowledge Structures*. Ed. James A. Galambos, Robert P. Abelson, and John B. Black. Hillsdale, N. J.: L. Erlbaum Associates.

Ackerman, James S. 1962. "A Theory of Style." *Journal of Aesthetics and Art Criticism* 20, no. 3:227–37.

Akın, Ömer. 1986. *Psychology of Architectural Design*. London: Pion.

Alberti, Leon Battista. [1452]. 1955. *Ten Books on Architecture*. Trans. J. Leoni. Ed. Joseph Rykwert. London: Tiranti.

Alberti, Leon Battista. [1452]. 1988. *On the Art of Building*. Trans. Joseph Rykwert, Neil Leach, and Robert Tavernor. Cambridge, Mass.: MIT Press.

Alexander, Christopher. 1967. *Notes on the Synthesis of Form*. Cambridge, Mass.. Harvard University Press.

Alexander, Christopher. 1972. "A City is not a Tree." Reprinted in *Human Identity in the Built Environment*. Eds. Gwen Bell and Jaqueline Tyrwhitt. London: Butler and Tanner.

Alexander, Christopher. 1979. *The Timeless Way of Building*. New York: Oxford University Press.

Alexander, Christopher, M. Silverstein, S. Angel, S. Ishikawa, and D. Abrams. 1975. *The Oregon Experiment*. New York: Oxford University Press.

Alexander, Christopher, S. Ishikawa, and M. Silverstein. 1977. *A Pattern Language*. New York: Oxford University Press.

Allwood, Jens, Lars-Gunnar Andersson, and Östen Dahl. 1977. *Logic in Linguistics*. Cambridge: Cambridge University Press.

Aquinas, Thomas. 1912–36. *The Summa Theologica*. London. Partially reprinted in *Basic Writings of Saint Thomas Aquinas*. Ed. Anton C. Pegis. New York: Random House, 1945.

Argan, Giulio Carlo. 1963. "On the Typology of Architecture." *Architectural Design* 33, no. 12: 564–65.

Argan, Giulio Carlo. 1965. *Progetto e Destino*. Milan: Casa editrice Il Saggiatore.

Aristotle. 1933. *The Metaphysics*. Books I–IX. Loeb Classical Library. Cambridge, Mass.: Harvard University Press.

Aristotle. 1957. *De Anima*. Loeb Classical Library. Cambridge, Mass.: Harvard University Press.

Aristotle. 1957. *The Physics*. Loeb Classical Library. Cambridge, Mass.: Harvard University Press.

Aristotle. 1961. *Parts of Animals*. Loeb Classical Library. Cambridge, Mass.: Harvard University Press.

Aristotle. 1962. *Nichomachean Ethics*. Loeb Classical Library. Cambridge, Mass.: Harvard University Press.

Arnheim, Rudolf. 1971. *Entropy and Art*. Berkeley: University of California Press.

Arnheim, Rudolf. [1954]. 1974. *Art and Visual Perception*. Rev. ed. Berkeley: University of California Press.

Ashton, Dore (ed.). 1972. *Picasso on Art*. New York: Da Capo.

Attneave, Fred. 1959a. *Applications of Information Theory to Psychology*. New York: Holt.

Attneave, Fred. 1959b. "Stochastic Composition Processes." *Journal of Aesthetics and Art Criticism* 17:503–10.

Augustine. 1983. *De Vera Religione*. Stuttgart: Phillip Reclam.

Ayala, Francisco J. 1970. "Teleological Explanations in Evolutionary Biology." *Philosophy of Science* 37, no. 1:1–15.

Baglivo, Jenny A., and Jack E. Graver. 1983. *Incidence and Symmetry in Design and Architecture*. Cambridge: Cambridge University Press.

Ballard, Dana H., and Christopher M. Brown. 1982. *Computer Vision*. Englewood Cliffs: Prentice-Hall.

Bandini, Micha. 1984. "Typology as a Form of Convention." *AA Files* 6:73–82.

Banham, Reyner. 1960. *Theory and Design in the First Machine Age*. New York: Praeger.

Barwise, John, and John Etchemendy. 1987. *Tarski's World*. Santa Barbara: Kinko's Academic Courseware Exchange.

Barr, Avron, and Edward A. Feigenbaum. 1981. *The Handbook of Artificial Intelligence*. Los Altos, Calif.: Morgan Kaufmann.

Bartlett, Frederic C. [1932]. 1967. *Remembering*. Cambridge: Cambridge University Press.

Beardsley, Monroe C. 1958. *Aesthetics: Problems in the Philosophy of Criticism*. New York: Harcourt, Brace and World, Inc.

Beardsley, Monroe. 1966. *Aesthetics from Classical Greece to the Present*. New York: Macmillan.

Beckner, Morton. 1968. *The Biological Way of Thought*. Berkeley: University of California Press.

Bell, Clive. 1914. *Art*. London: Chatto and Windus.

Bell, Clive. 1922. *Since Cézanne*. London: Chatto and Windus.

Bemis, Albert Farwell. 1936. *The Evolving House*. Cambridge, Mass.: MIT Press.

Berlin, Brent, and Paul Kay. 1969. *Basic Color Terms: Their Universality and Evolution*. Berkeley: University of California Press.

Birkhoff, George D. 1933. *Aesthetic Measure*. Cambridge, Mass.: Harvard University Press.

Birtwistle, G. M., O.-J. Dahl, B. Myhrhaug, and K. Nygaard. 1973. *Simula BEGIN*. Lund, Sweden: Studentlitteratur.

Blondel, Jacques-François. 1771–77. *Cours d'architecture*. 9 vols. Paris.

Bobrow, Daniel G. (ed.). 1985. *Qualitative Reasoning About Physical Systems*. Cambridge, Mass.: MIT Press.

Bobrow, Daniel G., and Terry Winograd. 1977. "An Overview of KRL: A Knowledge Representation Language." *Cognitive Science* 1:3–46.

Bock, Walter J., and Gerd von Wahlert. 1965. "Adaptation and the Form-Function Complex." *Evolution* 19, no. 3:269–99.

Bois, Yves-Alain. 1981. "Metamorphosis of Axonometry." *Daidalos* 1:40–58.

Bonta, Juan Pablo. 1979. *Architecture and Its Interpretation*. New York: Rizzoli.

Booker, Peter Jeffrey. 1963. *A History of Engineering Drawing*. London: Chatto and Windus.

Bosse, Abraham. 1643. *La Practique du Trait*. Paris.

Braithwaite, Richard Bevan. 1953. *Scientific Explanation*. Cambridge: Cambridge University Press.

Bratko, Ivan. 1986. *Prolog Programming for Artificial Intelligence*. Wokingham, England: Addison Wesley.

Breton, André. 1927. *La Surréalisme et la Peinture*. Translated as "Surrealism in Painting" in Patrick Waldberg, *Surrealism*. New York: Oxford University Press.

Broadbent, Geoffrey, Richard Bunt, and Charles Jencks. 1980. *Signs, Symbols, and Architecture*. Chichester, England: John Wiley.

Brunskill, R. W. 1965–66. "A Systematic Procedure for Recording English Vernacular Architecture." *Transactions of the Ancient Monuments Society* 13.

Buckley, Walter (ed.). 1968. *General Systems Research for the Behavioral Scientist: A Sourcebook*. Chicago: Aldine.

Burke, Edmund. [1757]. 1958. *A Philosophical Enquiry into the Origins of our Ideas of the Sublime and Beautiful*. Notre Dame: University of Notre Dame Press.

Campbell, Donald T. 1960. "Blind Variation and Selective Retention in Creative Thought as in Other Knowledge Processes." *Psychological Review* 67, no. 6:380–400.

Canfield, John. 1964. "Teleological Explanation in Biology." *British Journal for the Philosophy of Science* 14, no. 56:285–95.

Canfield, John (ed.). 1966. *Purpose in Nature*. Englewood Cliffs: Prentice-Hall.

Carelman, J. 1971. *Catalog of Fantastic Things*. New York: Ballantine.

Carnap, Rudolf. 1942. *Introduction to Semantics*. Cambridge, Mass. Harvard University Press.

Carnap, Rudolf. 1947. *Meaning and Necessity*. Chicago: University of Chicago Press.

Carpenter, Rhys. 1959. *The Esthetic Basis of Greek Art*. Bloomington: Indiana University Press.

Chase, Scot C. 1989. "Shapes and Shape Grammars: From Mathematical Model to Computer Implementation." *Planning and Design* 16, no. 2 : 215–42.

Chen, Peter P. 1976. "The Entity-Relationship Model—Towards a Unified View of Data." *ACM Transactions on Database Systems* 1:9–36.

Chitham, Robert. 1985. *The Classical Orders of Architecture*. New York: Rizzoli.

Choisy, Auguste. [1899]. 1964. *Histoire de l'architecture*. 2 vols. Paris: Editions Vincent, Fréal et Cie.

Chomsky, Noam. 1957. *Syntactic Structures*. The Hague: Mouton.

Cicero. 1971. Vol. V, *Brutus, Orator*. Loeb Classical Library. Cambridge, Mass.: Harvard University Press.

Clark, Herbert H., Patricia A. Carpenter, and Marcel Adam Just. 1973. "On the Meeting of Semantics and Perception." In *Visual Information Processing*. Ed. William G. Chase. New York: Academic Press.

Clocksin, William F., and A. R. Mellish. 1987. *Programming in Prolog*. 3d ed. Berlin: Springer-Verlag.

Clowes, M. 1971. "On Seeing Things." *Artificial Intelligence* 2:79–116.

Codd, E. F. 1970. "A Relational Model of Data for Large Shared Data Banks." *Communications of the ACM* 13:377–87.

Cohen, Jonathan. 1951. "Teleological Explanation." *Proceedings of the Aristotelian Society*.

Collingwood, Robin George. 1938. *The Principles of Art*. London: Oxford University Press.

Colquhoun, Alan. 1967. "Typology and Design Method." *Arena* 83:11–14. Reprinted in Colquhoun, 1981.

Colquhoun, Alan. 1981. *Essays in Architectural Criticism.* Cambridge, Mass.: MIT Press.

Conklin, Harold C. 1962. "Lexicographical Treatment of Folk Taxonomies." *International Journal of American Linguistics* 28, no. 2, part 4:119–41.

Conrads, Ulrich. 1970. *Programs and Manifestoes on 20th-Century Architecture.* Cambridge, Mass.: MIT Press.

Copi, Irving M. 1954. "Essence and Accident." *The Journal of Philosophy* 51:706–19.

Cowan, Henry J. 1977. *An Historical Outline of Architectural Science.* 2d ed. New York: Elsevier.

Coyne, Richard D., M. A. Rosenman, A. D. Radford, M. Balachandran, and J. S. Gero. 1989. *Knowledge-Based Design Systems.* Reading, Mass.: Addison-Wesley.

Craik, Kenneth J. 1943. *The Nature of Explanation.* Cambridge: Cambridge University Press

Cummins, Robert. 1975. "Functional Analysis." *Journal of Philosophy* 72, no. 20:741–65.

Cuvier, Georges. 1800. *Leçons d'anatomie comparée.* Paris.

Daley, Janet. 1982. "Design Creativity and the Understanding of Objects." *Design Studies* 3, no. 3:133–37.

Danforth, Scott, and Chris Tomlinson. 1988. "Type Theories and Object-Oriented Programming." *Computing Surveys* 20, no. 1:29–72.

Davis, R., and J. King. 1977. "An Overview of Production Systems." In *Machine Intelligence.* Vol. 8. Eds. E. W. Elcock and D. Michie. New York: John Wiley.

Dee, John. [1570]. 1975. *The Mathematicall Praeface to the Elements of Geometrie of Euclid of Megara.* Intro. by Allen G. Debus. New York: Science History Publications.

de Kleer, J. 1986. "An Assumption-Based Truth Maintenance System." *Artificial Intelligence* 28:127–62.

Delorme, Philibert. 1567. *Premier Tome de l'Architecture.* Paris. Reprinted in *L'Architecture de Philibert De l'Orme.* Ed. Pierre Mardaga. Brussels, 1981.

Dennett, Daniel. 1984. "Cognitive Wheels: The Frame Problem in AI." In *Minds, Machines and Evolution.* Ed. Christopher Hookway. Cambridge: Cambridge University Press.

Dennett, Daniel. 1987. *The Intentional Stance.* Cambridge, Mass.: MIT Press.

de Sola-Morales, Ignasi. 1987. "The Origins of Modern Eclecticism: The Theories of Architecture in Early Nineteenth-Century France." *Perspecta 23*: 120–33.

Devitt, Michael, and Kim Sterelny. 1987. *Language and Reality*. Cambridge, Mass.: MIT Press.

Dewey, John. 1938. *Logic: The Theory of Inquiry*. New York: Holt.

Dowty, David R., Robert E. Wall, and Stanley Peters. 1981. *Introduction to Montague Semantics*. Dordrecht: D. Reidel.

Doyle, J. 1981. "A Truth Maintenance System." In *Readings in Artificial Intelligence*. Eds. B. L. Webber and N. J. Nilsson. Palo Alto: Tioga.

Ducasse, Curt J. 1925. "Explanation, Mechanism and Teleology." *Journal of Philosophy* 22, no. 6:150–55.

Duncker, Karl. 1945. "On Problem-Solving." *Psychological Monographs* 58, no. 270.

Durand, Jean-Nicolas-Louis. 1802. *Précis des leçons d'architecture*. Paris: Ecole Polytechnique.

Durand, Jean-Nicolas-Louis. 1821. *Partie graphique des cours d'architecture*. Paris: Ecole Polytechnique.

Dürer, Albrecht. [1528]. 1970. *Vier Bücher von menschlicher Proportion*. (Four Books of Human Proportion). London: G. M. Wagner.

Durkheim, Emile. 1933. *The Division of Labor in Society*. Trans. George Simpson. New York: Free Press.

Dym, Clive L. (ed.). 1985. *Applications of Knowledge-Based Systems to Engineering Analysis and Design*. New York: American Society of Mechanical Engineers.

Earl, Christopher F. 1986. "Creating Design Worlds." *Planning and Design* 13, no. 2:177–88.

Eastman, Charles M. 1978. "The Representation of Design Problems and Maintenance of Their Structure." In Jean-Claude Latombe (ed.) *Artificial Intelligence and Pattern-Recognition in Computer-Aided Design*. Amsterdam: North Holland.

Eastman, Charles M. 1985. "A Conceptual Approach for Structuring Interaction with Interactive CAD Systems." *Computers and Graphics* 9, no. 2:97–105.

Eastman, Charles M. 1987. "Fundamental Problems in the Development of Computer-Based Architectural Design Models." In *Computability of Design*. Ed. Yehuda E. Kalay. New York: John Wiley.

Eco, Umberto. 1986. *Art and Beauty in the Middle Ages*. New Haven: Yale University Press.

Edgerton, Samuel Y. 1975. *The Renaissance Rediscovery of Linear Perspective*. New York: Harper and Row.

Egbert, Donald Drew. 1980. *The Beaux-Arts Tradition in French Architecture*. Princeton: Princeton University Press.

Eisenman, Peter. 1982. *House X*. New York: Rizzoli.

Elgin, Catherine Z. 1983. *With Reference to Reference*. Indianapolis: Hackett.

Emery, Frederick E. (ed.). 1969. *Systems Thinking*. Harmondsworth: Penguin.

Emond, T. 1964. *On Art and Unity*. Lund, Sweden: Gleerups.

Enderton, Herbert B. 1972. *A Mathematical Introduction to Logic*. New York: Academic Press.

Euclid. 1956. *The Thirteen Books of Euclid's Elements*. Trans. Thomas L. Heath. New York: Dover.

Evans, Robin. 1986. "Translations from Drawing to Building." *AA Files*. London: Architectural Association School of Architecture, 12:3–18.

Evans, T. G. 1964. "A Heuristic Program to Solve Geometric-Analogy Problems." *Proceedings of the Spring Joint Computer Conference*. American Federation of Information Processing Societies. Reprinted in Fischler and Firschein, 1987.

Eysenck, Hans J. 1968. "An Experimental Study of Aesthetic Preference for Polygonal Figures." *Journal of General Psychology* 79.

Firth, Raymond. 1956. "Functionalism." In *Yearbook of Anthropology*. Ed. William L. Thomas. Chicago: University of Chicago Press.

Fischier, Martin A., and Oscar Firschein (eds.). 1987. *Readings in Computer Vision*. Los Altos, Calif.: Morgan Kaufmann.

Flemming, Ulrich. 1981. "The Secret of Casa Giuliani Frigerio." *Environment and Planning B* 8:87–96.

Flemming, Ulrich. 1986. "More Than the Sum of Parts: The Grammar of Queen Anne Houses." *Planning and Design* 14, no. 3:323–50.

Flemming, Ulrich. 1987. "The Role of Shape Grammars in the Analysis and Creation of Designs." In *Computability of Design*. Ed. Yehuda E. Kalay. New York: John Wiley.

Fletcher, Banister. [1896]. 1987. *A History of Architecture on the Comparative Method*. 19th ed. Ed. John Musgrove. London: Butterworths.

Focillon, Henri. 1948. *The Life of Forms in Art*. New York: Wittenborn Schultz.

Foley, James D., and Andries Van Dam. 1982. *Fundamentals of Interactive Computer Graphics*. Reading, Mass.: Addison-Wesley.

Foot, Philippa. 1961. "Goodness and Choice." *Proceedings of the Aristotelian Society*, supplementary volume 35. Reprinted in *The Is–Ought Question*. Ed. W. D. Hudson. London: Macmillan, 1969.

Frake, Charles O. 1962. "The Ethnographic Study of Cognitive Systems." In *Anthropology and Human Behavior*. Eds. T. Gladwin and W. C. Sturtevant. Washington, D.C.: Anthropological Society of Washington.

Frankfurt, Harry G., and Brian Poole. 1966. "Functional Analyses in Biology." *British Journal for the Philosophy of Science* 17, no. 1:69–72.

Frankl, Paul. 1945. "The Secrets of the Medieval Masons." *Art Bulletin* 27, no. 1:46–60.

Freeman, Peter, and Allen Newell. 1971. "A Model for Functional Reasoning in Design." *International Joint Conference on Artificial Intelligence* (IJCAI) 2:621–40.

Fritz, John M., and Fred T. Plog. 1970. "The Nature of Archaeological Explanation." *American Antiquity* 35, no. 4:405–12.

Fry, Roger. 1926. *Transformations*. London: Chatto and Windus.

Fry, Roger. 1937. *Vision and Design*. Harmondsworth: Penguin.

Fry, Roger. 1939. *Last Lectures*. Cambridge: Cambridge University Press.

Galen. 1968. *On the Usefulness of the Parts of the Body*. Trans. M. T. May. Ithaca: Cornell University Press.

Galileo. [1632]. 1952. *Dialogues Concerning Two New Sciences*. Trans. Henry Crew and Alfonso de Salvio. New York: Dover.

Genesereth, Michael R., and Nils J. Nilsson. 1987. *Logical Foundations of Artificial Intelligence*. Los Altos, Calif.: Morgan Kaufmann.

Gero, John S. (ed.). 1985. *Knowledge Engineering in Computer-Aided Design*. Amsterdam: North Holland.

Gero, John S. (ed.). 1987. *Expert Systems in Computer-Aided Design*. Amsterdam: North Holland.

Gero, John S. (ed.). 1988. *Artificial Intelligence in Engineering: Design*. Amsterdam: Elsevier/CMP.

Gero, John S., and Mary Lou Maher. 1988. "Future Roles of Knowledge-Based Systems in the Design Process." In *CAAD Futures 87*. Eds. Tom Maver and Harry Wagter. Amsterdam: Elsevier.

Gero, John S., and T. Oksala (eds.). 1989. *Knowledge-Based Systems in Architecture*. Helsinki: Acta Scandinavica.

Gibbs, James. 1728. *A Book of Architecture*. London.

Gibson, James J. 1950. *The Perception of the Visual World*. Boston: Houghton Mifflin.

Gibson, James J. 1966. *The Senses Considered as Perceptual Systems*. Boston: Houghton Mifflin.

Gibson, James J. 1977. "The Theory of Affordances." In *Perceiving, Acting, and Knowing*. Eds. R. E. Shaw and J. Bransford. Hillsdale, N. J.: Erlbaum Associates.

Gibson, James J. 1979. *The Ecological Approach to Visual Perception*. Boston: Houghton Mifflin.

Gips, James, and George Stiny. 1980. "Production Systems and Grammars: A Uniform Characterization." *Environment and Planning B* 7:399–408.

Goethe, Johann Wolfgang von. 1795. *Erster Entwurf einer allgemainen Einleitung in die vergleichende Anatomie*. Trans. as *First Draft of a General Introduction to Comparative Anatomy*.

Goldberg, Adele, and D. Robson. 1983. *Smalltalk 80: The Language and Its Implementation*. New York: Addison-Wesley.

Gombrich, Ernst H. 1960. *Art and Illusion*. New York: Pantheon.

Gombrich, Ernst H. 1968. "Style." In *International Encyclopaedia of the Social Sciences*. Ed. David L. Sills. New York: Macmillan.

Gombrich, Ernst H. 1979. *The Sense of Order*. Oxford: Phaidon.

Gonzalez, Rafael C., and Michael G. Thomason. 1978. *Syntactic Pattern Recognition*. Reading, Mass.: Addison-Wesley.

Goodman, Nelson. 1976. *Languages of Art*. 2d ed. Indianapolis: Hackett.

Goodman, Nelson. 1984. "Routes of Reference." In *Of Mind and Other Matters*. Cambridge, Mass.: Harvard University Press.

Goodman, Nelson. 1985. "How Buildings Mean." *Critical Inquiry* 11: 642–53.

Goodman, Nelson, and Catherine Z. Elgin. 1988. *Reconceptions in Philosophy and Other Arts and Sciences*. Indianapolis: Hackett.

Gottschaldt, K. 1926. "Uber den Einfluss der Erfahrung auf die Wahrnehmung von Figuren." *Psychologische Forschung* 8:261–317.

Gould, Stephen J. 1971. "D'Arcy Thompson and the Science of Form." *New Literary History* 2:229–58.

Grayer, A. R. 1977. "The Automatic Production of Machined Components Starting from a Stored Geometric Description." In *Advances in Computer-Aided Manufacture*. Ed. D. McPherson. Amsterdam: North Holland.

Green, R., and M. Courtis. 1966. "Information Theory and Visual Perception: The Metaphor that Failed." *Acta Psychologica* 25.

Greenough, Horatio. 1947. *Form and Function.* Berkeley: University of California Press.

Gross, Mark, Steven Ervin, James Anderson, and Aaron Fleisher. 1987. "Designing with Constraints." In *Computability of Design.* Ed. Yehuda E. Kalay. New York: John Wiley.

Gruner, Rolf. 1966. "Teleological and Functional Explanations." *Mind.* 2d ser., 75, no. 300:516–26.

Guadet, Julien. 1894. *Eléments et théories de l'architecture.* Paris: Librairie de la Construction Moderne.

Guarini, Guarino. [1737]. 1964. *Architettura Civile.* Farnsborough: Gregg International.

Guthrie, E. R. 1924. "Purpose and Mechanism in Psychology." *Journal of Philosophy* 21, no. 25:673–81.

___

Hagen, Margaret A. 1986. *Varieties of Realism: Geometries of Representational Art.* Cambridge: Cambridge University Press.

Hall, A. D., and R. E. Fagen. 1956. "Definition of System." *General Systems* 1. Also published in Buckley, 1968.

Hanrahan, P. 1982. "Creating Volume Models from Edge-Vertex Graphs." *Computer Graphics* 16, no. 3:77–84.

Hanslick, Eduard. 1854. *Vom Musikalisch-Schönen.* Trans. Geoffrey Payzant as *On the Musically Beautiful.* Indianapolis: Hackett, 1986.

Hare, Richard M. 1952. *The Language of Morals.* Oxford: Clarendon Press.

Harrison, Michael A. 1978. *Introduction to Formal Language Theory.* Reading, Mass.: Addison-Wesley.

Haugeland, John. 1978. "The Nature and Plausibility of Cognitivism." *The Behavioral and Brain Sciences* 2:215–60. Reprinted in Haugeland 1981.

Haugeland, John (ed.). 1981. *Mind Design.* Cambridge, Mass.: MIT Press.

Hawkes, Dean. 1976. "Types, Norms and Habit in Environmental Design." In *The Architecture of Form.* Ed. Lionel March. Cambridge: Cambridge University Press.

Hayes, P. J. 1973. "The Frame Problem and Related Problems in Artificial Intelligence." In *Artificial and Human Thinking.* Eds. A. Elithorn and D. Jones. San Francisco: Jossey-Bass.

Hégron, Gérard. 1988. *Image Synthesis: Elementary Algorithms.* Cambridge, Mass.: MIT Press.

Hempel, Carl. 1965. "The Logic of Functional Analysis." In *Aspects of Scientific Explanation.* New York: Free Press.

Hempel, Carl, and Paul Oppenheim. 1948. "Studies in the Logic of Explanation." *Philosophy of Science* 15, no. 2:135–75.

Henkin, Leon. 1967. "Systems, Formal, and Models of Formal Systems." In *The Encyclopedia of Philosophy*. Ed. Paul Edwards. New York: Macmillan.

Hernández, A. 1969. "J. N. L. Durand's Architectural Theory." *Perspecta 12*: 153–64.

Herrmann, Wolfgang. 1962. *Laugier and Eighteenth Century French Theory*. London: Zwemmer.

Herrmann, Wolfgang. 1973. *The Theory of Claude Perrault*. London: Zwemmer.

Hesselgren, Sven. 1969. *The Language of Architecture*. Kristianstad, Sweden: Studentlitteratur.

Hiller, Lejaren A., and Leonard M. Isaacson. 1959. *Experimental Music*. New York: McGraw-Hill.

Hitchcock, Henry-Russell. 1963. *Architecture: Nineteenth and Twentieth Centuries*. 2d ed. Harmondsworth: Penguin.

Hoffman, D. D., and W. Richards. 1985. "Parts of Recognition." *Cognition* 18:65–96. Reprinted in Fischler and Firschein, 1987.

Hofstader, Albert. 1941. "Objective Teleology." *Journal of Philosophy* 38, no. 2:29–39.

Hofstadter, Douglas R. 1982. "Variations on a Theme as the Essence of Imagination." *Scientific American* (October).

Hogarth, William. [1753]. 1955. *The Analysis of Beauty*. Ed. Joseph Burke. Oxford: Clarendon Press.

Hogger, Christopher John. 1984. *Introduction to Logic Programming*. London: Academic Press.

Home, Henry. [1761]. 1846. *Elements of Criticism*. New York: Huntington and Savage.

Hopcroft, John E., and Jeffrey D. Ullman. 1969. *Formal Languages and Their Relation to Automata*. Reading, Mass.: Addison-Wesley.

Horn, Berthold K. P. 1986. *Robot Vision*. Cambridge, Mass.: MIT Press.

Huffman, D. A. 1971. "Impossible Objects as Nonsense Sentences." In *Machine Intelligence 6*. Eds. B. Meltzer and D. Michie. Edinburgh: Edinburgh University Press.

Hurlbert, Anya, and Tomaso Poggio. 1988. "Making Machines (and Artificial Intelligence) See." In *The Artificial Intelligence Debate*. Ed. Stephen R. Graubard. Cambridge, Mass.: MIT Press.

Hutcheson, Francis. 1969. *An Inquiry into the Origin of Our Ideas of Beauty and Virtue*. Farnborough: Gregg International.

Jackendoff, Ray. 1983. *Semantics and Cognition*. Cambridge, Mass.: MIT Press.

Jeanneret-Gris, Charles Edouard, and Amedée Ozenfant. 1920. "Purism." *L'Esprit Nouveau* 4.

Jencks, Charles A. [1977]. 1987. *The Language of Post-Modern Architecture*. 5th rev. enl. ed. London: Academy Editions.

Jencks, Charles, and George Baird (eds.). 1969. *Meaning in Architecture*. London: Barrie and Rockliffe.

Johnson-Laird, Philip N. 1983. *Mental Models*. Cambridge, Mass.: Harvard University Press.

Johnson-Laird, Philip N. 1988. *The Computer and the Mind*. Cambridge, Mass.: Harvard University Press.

Jones, Owen. [1856]. 1982. *The Grammar of Ornament*. New York: Van Nostrand Reinhold.

Kalay, Yehudla E. 1989. *Modeling Objects and Environments*. New York: John Wiley.

Kalish, Donald. 1967. "Semantics." In *The Encyclopedia of Philosophy*. Ed. Paul Edwards. New York: Macmillan.

Kant, Immanuel. [1781]. 1973. *Critique of Pure Reason*. Trans. Norman Kemp Smith. London: Macmillan.

Kant, Immanuel. [1790]. 1952. *The Critique of Judgement*. Trans. J. C. Meredith. Oxford: Clarendon Press.

Katz, Jerrold J. 1964. "Semantic Theory and the Meaning of 'Good'." *Journal of Philosophy* 61:739–66.

Kauffman, Stuart A. 1971. "Articulation of Parts Explanations in Biology and the Rational Search for Them." In *Boston Studies in the Philosophy of Science* 8. Eds. Roger C. Buck and Robert S. Cohen. Dordrecht: D. Reidel.

Kaufmann, Emil. 1955. *Architecture in the Age of Reason*. Cambridge, Mass.: Harvard University Press.

Kemper, Alfons, and Mechtild Wallrath. 1987. "An Analysis of Geometric Modeling in Database Systems." *Computing Surveys* 19, no. 1:47–91.

Kirsch, Russell A. 1963. "Symposium on Automated Processing of Illustrated Text." National Bureau of Standards Report 8144.

Kirsch, Russell A. 1964. "Computer Interpretation of English Text and Picture Patterns." *IEEE Transactions on Electronic Computers* EC-13, no. 4:170–210.

Knight, Terry Weissman. 1981. "The Forty-One Steps." *Environment and Planning B* 8:97–114.

Knight, Terry Weissman. 1986. "Transformations of Languages of Designs." Ph.D. dissertation, Graduate School of Architecture and Urban Planning, University of California, Los Angeles.

Koenig, Giovanni K. 1964. *Analisi del Linguaggio Architettonico.* Florence: Libreria editrice Fiorentina.

Koenig, Giovanni K. 1970. *Architettura e Communicazione.* Florence: Libreria editrice Fiorentina.

Koffka, Kurt. 1935. *Principles of Gestalt Psychology.* New York: Harcourt Brace.

Kohler, Wolfgang. 1929. *Gestalt Psychology.* New York: Liveright.

Kolmogorov, Andrei N. 1968. "Logical Basis for Information Theory and Probability Theory." *IEEE Transactions on Information Theory* IT-14, no. 5:662–64.

Koning H., and J. Eizenberg. 1981. "The Language of the Prairie: Frank Lloyd Wright's Prairie Houses." *Environment and Planning B* 8:295–323.

Kowalski, Robert A. 1979. *Logic for Problem Solving.* Amsterdam: North Holland

Krauss, R. 1952. *A Hole is to Dig.* New York: Harper and Row.

Krishnamurti, R. 1980. "The Arithmetic of Shapes." *Environment and Planning B. Planning and Design* 7:463–84.

Krishnamurti, R. 1981. "The Construction of Shapes." *Environment and Planning B: Planning and Design* 8:5–40.

Krishnamurti, R., and C. Giraud. 1986. "Towards a Shape Editor: The Implementation of a Shape Generation System." *Planning and Design* 13, no. 4:391–404.

Kurlander, David, and Eric A. Bier. 1988. "Graphical Search and Replace." *Computer Graphics* 22, no. 4:113–20.

Labov, William. 1973. "The Boundaries of Words and Their Meanings." In *New Ways of Analyzing Variation in English.* Eds. C.-J. N. Bailey and R. W. Shuy. Washington, D.C.: Georgetown University Press.

Lakoff, George. 1972. "Hedges: A Study of Meaning Criteria and the Logic of Fuzzy Concepts." *Papers from the Eighth Regional Meeting of the Chicago Linguistic Society.* Chicago: Chicago Linguistic Society.

Lang, Beryl (ed.). 1979. *The Concept of Style.* Philadelphia: University of Pennsylvania Press.

Larkin, Jill, and Herbert A. Simon. 1987. "Why a Diagram is (Sometimes) Worth Ten Thousand Words." *Cognitive Science* 11:65–99.

Laugier, Marc-Antoine. [1753]. 1977. *An Essay on Architecture.* Trans. W. Herrmann and A. Herrmann. Los Angeles: Hennessey and Ingalls.

Le Corbusier. [1923]. 1946. *Towards a New Architecture*. Trans. Frederick Etchells. London: The Architectural Press.

Le Corbusier and Pierre Jeanneret. [1927]. 1975. "Five Points of a New Architecture." In *Form and Function*. Eds. T. Benton, C. Benton, and D. Sharp. London: Crosby Lockwood Staples. Also in Conrads, 1970.

Leftwich, Gregory. 1988. "The Canon of Polykleitos: Tradition and Context." *Canon* 3 : 37–80.

Lehman, Hugh. 1965. "Functional Explanations in Biology." *Philosophy of Science* 32, no. 1:1–20.

Leler, William. 1988. *Constraint Programming Languages*. Reading, Mass.: Addison-Wesley.

Levine, Neil. 1982. "The Competition for the Grand Prix in 1824." In *The Beaux-Arts and Nineteenth-Century French Architecture*. Ed. Robin Middleton. Cambridge, Mass.: MIT Press.

Lewis, Clarence I. 1946. *An Analysis of Knowledge and Valuation*. La Salle, Ill.: Open Court.

Locke, John. [1690]. 1979. *An Essay Concerning Human Understanding*. Ed. Peter H. Nidditch. Oxford: Clarendon Press.

Lotz, Wolfgang. 1977. "The Rendering of the Interior in Architectural Drawings of the Renaissance." In *Studies in Italian Renaissance Architecture*. Cambridge, Mass.: MIT Press.

Loudon, John Claudius. 1846. *Encyclopaedia of Cottage, Farm and Villa Architecture*. London: Longman.

Lyons, John. 1963. *Structural Semantics: An Analysis of Part of the Vocabulary of Plato*. Oxford: Blackwell.

Lyons, John. 1977. "Logical Semantics." In *Semantics*. Cambridge: Cambridge University Press.

MacCormac, Richard C. 1974. "Froebel's Kindergarten Gifts and the Early Work of Frank Lloyd Wright." *Environment and Planning B* 1, no. 1:29–50.

Malinowski, Bronislaw. 1936. "Anthropology." In *Encyclopaedia Britannica*. Supplementary vol. 1. New York.

Mäntylä, Martti. 1988. *An Introduction to Solid Modeling*. Rockville, Md.: Computer Science Press.

March, Lionel, and Phillip Steadman. 1974. *The Geometry of Environment*. Cambridge, Mass.: MIT Press.

March, Lionel, and George Stiny. 1985. "Spatial Systems in Architecture and Design: Some History and Logic." *Planning and Design* 12, no. 1:31–53.

Markov, Andrei A. [1954]. 1971. *Theory of Algorithms*. Trans. Jacques J. Schorr-Kon. Jerusalem: Israel Program for Scientific Translations.

Markowsky, G., and M. A. Wesley. 1980. "Fleshing Out Wire Frames." *IBM Journal of Research and Development* 24, no. 5:582–97.

Marr, David. 1979. "Visual Information Processing: The Structure and Creation of Visual Representations." *International Joint Conference on Artificial Intelligence* (IJCAI) 6:1108–26.

Marr, David. 1982. *Vision*. San Francisco: W.H. Freeman.

Martin, John N. 1987. *Elements of Formal Semantics*. Orlando: Academic Press.

Maver, Thomas W. 1988. "Software Tools for the Technical Evaluation of Design Alternatives." In *CAAD Futures 87*. Eds. T. Maver and H. Wagter. Amsterdam: Elsevier.

Mayr, Ernst. 1974. "Teleological and Telenomic, a New Analysis." In *Methodological and Historical Essays in the Natural and Social Sciences*. Eds. Robert S. Cohen and Marx W. Wartofsky. Dordrecht: D. Reidel.

McCarthy, John. 1956. "The Inversion of Functions Defined by Turing Machines." In *Automata Studies, Annals of Mathematics Studies* 34. Eds. C. E. Shannon and J. McCarthy. Princeton: Princeton University Press.

McCarthy, John. 1980. "Circumscription—A Form of Non-Monotonic Reasoning." *Artificial Intelligence* 13:27–39.

McCarthy, John. 1986. "Applications of Circumscription to Formalizing Common Sense Knowledge." *Artificial Intelligence* 28:89–116.

McCarthy, John. 1987. "Generality in Artificial Intelligence." *Communications of the ACM* 30, no. 12:1030–35.

McCarthy, John. 1988. "Mathematical Logic in Artificial Intelligence." In *The Artificial Intelligence Debate*. Ed. Stephen R. Graubard. Cambridge, Mass.: MIT Press.

McCarthy, John, and P. J. Hayes. 1969. "Some Philosophical Problems from the Standpoint of Artificial Intelligence." In *Machine Intelligence* 4. Eds. D. Michie and B. Meltzer. Edinburgh: Edinburgh University Press.

McDermott, Drew, and Jon Doyle. 1980. "Non-Monotonic Logic 1." *Artificial Intelligence* 13:41–72.

Mead, Hunter. 1952. *An Introduction to Aesthetics*. New York: Ronald Press.

Mendelson, Elliott. 1987. *Introduction to Mathematical Logic*. 3d ed. New York: Van Nostrand Reinhold.

Meunier, John (ed.). 1980. "Language in Architecture." *Proceedings of the ACSA 68th Annual Meeting*, Association of Collegiate Schools of Architecture, Washington D.C.

Meyer, Hannes. 1928. "Building." *Bauhaus*, Year 2, no. 4. Translated in Conrads, 1970.

Meyer, Leonard B. 1959. "Some Remarks on Value and Greatness in Music." *Journal of Aesthetics and Art Criticism* 17, no. 4:486–500.

Milizia, Francesco. [1832]. 1972. *Principj di Architettura Civile*. Milan: Gabrielle Mazzotta.

Miller, George A. 1977. "Practical and Lexical Knowledge." In *Thinking: Readings in Cognitive Science*. Eds. P. N. Johnson-Laird and P. C. Wason. Cambridge: Cambridge University Press.

Miller, George A. and Philip N. Johnson-Laird. 1976. *Language and Perception*. Cambridge, Mass.: The Belknap Press of Harvard University Press.

Minsky, Marvin L. 1975. "A Framework for Representing Knowledge." In *The Psychology of Computer Vision*. Ed. P. M. Winston. New York: McGraw-Hill. Reprinted in Haugeland, 1981.

Minsky, Marvin L. 1977. "Frame-System Theory." In *Thinking: Readings in Cognitive Science*. Eds. P. N. Johnson-Laird and P. C. Wason. Cambridge: Cambridge University Press.

Mitchell, William J. 1977. *Computer-Aided Architectural Design*. New York: Van Nostrand Reinhold.

Mitchell, William J. 1986. "Solid Modeling and Volumetric Composition in Architecture." *Design Computing* 1, no. 2:123–35.

Mitchell, William J., Robin S. Liggett, and Thomas Kvan. 1987. *The Art of Computer Graphics Programming*. New York: Van Nostrand Reinhold.

Moles, Abraham. 1968. *Information Theory and Esthetic Perception*. Urbana: University of Illinois Press.

Moneo, Rafael. 1978. "On Typology." *Oppositions* 13:22–45.

Moore, R. C. 1985. "Semantical Considerations in Nonmonotonic Logic." *Artificial Intelligence* 25:75–94.

Mortenson, Michael E. 1985. *Geometric Modeling*. New York: John Wiley.

Mumford, Lewis (ed.). 1952. *Roots of Contemporary American Architecture*. New York: Grove Press.

Nagel, Ernest. 1951. "Mechanistic Explanation and Organismic Biology." *Philosophy and Phenomenological Research* 11, no. 3:327–38.

Nagel, Ernest. 1953. "Teleological Explanation and Teleological Systems." In *Readings in the Philosophy of Science*. Eds. Herbert Feigl and May Brodbeck. New York: Appleton-Century-Crofts.

Nagel, Ernest. 1954. "Concept and Theory Formation in the Social Sciences." In *Contemporary Philosophy*. Eds. J. L. Jarret and S. M. McMurrin. New York: Henry Holt.

Nagel, Ernest. 1956. "A Formalization of Functionalism." In *Logic Without Metaphysics*. Glencoe, Ill.: Free Press.

Nagel, Ernest. 1979a. *Teleology Revisited*. New York: Columbia University Press.

Nagel, Ernest. 1979b. *The Structure of Science*. 2d ed. Indianapolis: Hackett.

Nelson, Katherine. 1973. "Some Evidence for the Cognitive Primacy of Categorization and Its Functional Basis." *Merrill-Palmer Quarterly of Behaviour and Development* 19:21–39. Reprinted in *Thinking*. Eds. P N. Johnson-Laird and P. C. Wason. Cambridge: Cambridge University Press, 1977.

Nervi, Pier Luigi. 1956. *Structures*. Trans. Giuseppina and Mario Salvadori. New York: F. W. Dodge.

Newell, Allen. 1973. "Artificial Intelligence and the Concept of Mind." In *Computer Models of Thought and Language*. Eds. R. C. Schank and K. M.Colby. San Francisco: W. H. Freeman.

Newell, Allen, and Herbert A. Simon. 1972. *Human Problem Solving*. Englewood Cliffs: Prentice-Hall.

Newman, William M., and Robert R. Sproull. 1979. *Principles of Interactive Computer Graphics*. 2d ed. New York: McGraw-Hill,

Nilsson, Nils J. 1971. *Problem-Solving Methods in Artificial Intelligence*. New York: McGraw-Hill.

Nilsson, Nils J. 1980. *Principles of Artificial Intelligence*. Palo Alto: Tioga.

Nissen, Lowell. 1971. "Neutral Functional Statements Schemata." *Philosophy of Science* 38, no. 2:251–57.

Noble, Denis. 1967. "Charles Taylor or Teleological Explanation." *Analysis* 27, no. 3:96–103.

Norberg-Schulz, Christian. 1985. *The Concept of Dwelling*. New York: Rizzoli.

Norman, Donald A. 1988. *The Psychology of Everyday Things*. New York: Basic Books.

Oechslin, Werner. 1986. "Premises for a Resumption of the Discussion of Typology." *Assemblage* 1:37–54.

Osborne, Harold. 1968. *Aesthetics and Art Theory*. New York: E. P. Dutton.

Osherson, Daniel N., and E. E. Smith. 1981. "On the Adequacy of Prototype Theory as a Theory of Concepts." *Cognition* 9, no. 1:35–58.

Owen, Richard. 1848. *On the Archetype and Homologies of theVertebrate Skeleton*. London.

Palladio, Andrea. [1570]. 1965. *The Four Books of Architecture*. Trans. Isaac Ware. New York: Dover.

Panofsky, Erwin. 1968. *Idea: A Concept in Art Theory*. New York: Harper and Rowe.

Park, Robert E., Ernest W. Burgess, and Roderick D. MacKenzie (eds.). 1925. *The City*. Chicago: University of Chicago Press. Reprinted 1967.

Pattee, Howard W. (ed.). 1973. *Hierarchy Theory*. New York: Braziller.

Pearl, Judea. 1984. *Heuristics*. Reading, Mass.: Addison-Wesley.

Peirce, Charles Sanders. 1931–35. *Collected Papers of Charles Sanders Peirce*. Eds. C. Harteshorne and P. Weiss. Cambridge, Mass.: Harvard University Press.

Pérouse de Montclos, Jean-Marie. 1982. *L'architecture à la française*. Paris: Picard.

Perrault, Claude. 1673. *Les dix livres d'architecture*. Paris: Coignard.

Perrault, Claude. [1683]. 1708. *A Treatise of The Five Orders of Columns in Architecture*. Trans. John James. London.

Pettit, Philip. 1975. *The Concept of Structuralism*. Berkeley: University of California Press.

Pevsner, Nikolaus. 1976. *A History of Building Types*. Princeton: Princeton University Press.

Pinker, Steven (ed.). 1985. *Visual Cognition*. Cambridge, Mass.: MIT Press.

Plato. 1959. *Timaeus*. Ed. O. Piest. Trans. F. M. Cornford. Indianapolis: Bobbs-Merrill.

Plato. 1971. *Meno*. Trans. W. K. C. Guthrie, with essays edited by Malcolm Brown. Indianapolis: Bobbs-Merrill.

Plato. 1973. *The Republic and Other Works*. Trans. B. Jowett. Garden City, N.Y.: Anchor.

Plotinus. 1962. *The Enneads*. Trans. Stephen MacKenna. 3d ed. revised by B. S. Page. London: Faber and Faber.

Pollitt, Jerome J. 1972. *Art and Experience in Classical Greece*. Cambridge: Cambridge University Press.

Pollitt, Jerome J. 1974. *The Ancient View of Greek Art*. New Haven: Yale University Press.

Portoghesi, Paolo. 1967. *Borromini: Architetture come Linguaggio*. Milan: Electa.

Pospesel, Howard. 1976. *Introduction to Logic: Predicate Logic*. Englewood Cliffs: Prentice-Hall.

Post, Emil L. 1943. "Formal Reductions of the General Combinatorial Decision Problem." *American Journal of Mathematics* 65:197–268.

Prak, Niels Luning. 1968. *The Language of Architecture*. The Hague: Mouton.

Preziosi, Donald. 1979a. *Architecture, Language, and Meaning*. The Hague: Mouton.

Preziosi, Donald. 1979b. *The Semiotics of the Built Environment*. Bloomington: Indiana University Press.

Pugin, Augustus Welby. 1841. *The True Principles of Pointed or Christian Architecture*. London: John Weale.

Putnam, Hillary. 1975. "The Meaning of 'Meaning'." In *Language, Mind and Knowledge*. Ed. Keith Gunderson. Minneapolis: University of Minnesota Press.

Quatremère de Quincy, Antoine-Chrysostome. 1832. "Type." In *Dictionnaire historique d'architecture*. Paris: Librairie d'Adrien le Clere et cie.

Quine, Willard Van Orman. 1961. *From a Logical Point of View*. Cambridge, Mass.: Harvard University Press.

Quine, Willard Van Orman. 1970. *Philosophy of Logic*. Englewood Cliffs: Prentice-Hall.

Quine, Willard Van Orman. 1987. *Quiddities: An Intermittently Philosophical Dictionary*. Cambridge, Mass.: The Belknap Press of Harvard University Press.

Radcliffe-Brown, Alfred R. 1952. *Structure and Function in Primitive Society*. Glencoe, Ill.: Free Press.

Radford, Antony D., and John S. Gero. 1988. *Design by Optimization in Architecture, Building, and Construction*. New York: Van Nostrand Reinhold.

Rankin, Terry L. "When is Reasoning Nonmonotonic?" In *Aspects of Artificial Intelligence*. Ed. James H. Fetzer. Dordrecht: Kluwer.

Raphael, Bertram. 1971. "The Frame Problem in Problem Solving Systems." In *Artificial Intelligence and Heuristic Programming*. Eds. N. Findler and B. Meltzer. New York: American Elsevier.

Rawls, John. 1971. *A Theory of Justice*. Cambridge, Mass.: The Belknap Press of Harvard University Press.

Reiter, Raymond A. 1980. "A Logic for Default Reasoning." *Artificial Intelligence* 13:81–132.

Reitman, Walter R. 1965. *Cognition and Thought*. New York: John Wiley.

Requicha, Aristides A. G. 1980. "Representations for Rigid Solids: Theory, Methods and Systems." *Computing Surveys* 12, no. 4:437–64.

Rescher, Nicholas. 1975. *A Theory of Possibility*. Pittsburgh: University of Pittsburgh Press.

Reynolds, Joshua. [1771]. 1961. *Discourses on Art.* New York: Collier.

Richards, Whitman. 1988. *Natural Computation.* Cambridge, Mass.: MIT Press.

Rignano, Eugenio. 1931. "The Concept of Purpose in Biology." *Mind* 40, no. 159:335–40.

Robinson, John A. 1965. "A Machine-Oriented Logic Based on the Resolution Principle." *Journal of the Association for Computing Machinery* 12:23–41.

Rogers, David F., and J. Alan Adams. 1976. *Mathematical Elements for Computer Graphics.* New York: McGraw-Hill.

Rosch, Eleanor. 1973. "On the Internal Structure of Perceptual and Semantic Categories." In *Cognitive Development and the Acquisition of Language.* Ed. T. M. Moore. New York: Academic Press.

Rosch, Eleanor, and C. B. Mervis. 1975. "Family Resemblances: Studies in the Internal Structure of Categories." *Cognitive Psychology* 7:573–605.

Rosenblueth, Arturo, Norbert Wiener, and Julian Bigelow. 1943. "Behavior, Purpose and Teleology." *Philosophy of Science* 10, no. 1:18–24.

Rosenblueth, Arturo, and Norbert Wiener. 1950. "Purposeful and Non-Purposeful Behavior." *Philosophy of Science* 17, no. 4:318–26.

Rosenman, Michael A., Richard D. Coyne, and John S. Gero. 1987. "Expert Systems for Design Applications." In *Applications of Expert Systems.* Ed. J. R. Quinlan. Sydney: Addison-Wesley.

Ross, William David. [1930]. 1988. *The Right and the Good.* Indianapolis: Hackett.

Rossi, Aldo. 1982. *The Architecture of the City.* Cambridge, Mass.: MIT Press.

Rowe, Colin. 1976. *The Mathematics of the Ideal Villa and Other Essays.* Cambridge, Mass.: MIT Press.

Ruse, Michael E. 1971. "Functional Statements in Biology." *Philosophy of Science* 38, no. 1:87–95.

Russell, Edward S. [1916]. 1982. *Form and Function.* Introduction by George V. Lander. Chicago: University of Chicago Press.

Rychener, M. D. 1985. "Expert Systems for Engineering Design." *Expert Systems* 2, no. 1:30–44.

Rychener, M. D. (ed.). 1988. *Expert Systems for Engineering Design.* New York: Academic Press.

Rykwert, Joseph. 1972. *On Adam's House in Paradise.* New York: Museum of Modern Art.

Schank, Roger C., and Robert P. Abelson. 1977. *Scripts, Plans, Goals and Understanding*. Hillsdale, N. J.: L. Erlbaum Associates.

Schapiro, Meyer. 1953. "Style." In *Anthropology Today*. Ed. A. L. Kroeber. Chicago: University of Chicago Press. Reprinted in *Aesthetics Today*. Rev. ed. Eds. Morris Philipson and Paul J. Gudel. New York: Meridian, 1980.

Scheffler, Israel. 1959. "Thoughts on Teleology." *British Journal for the Philosophy of Science* 9, no. 36:265–84.

Scholfield, P. H. 1979. *The Theory of Proportion in Architecture*. Princeton: Princeton University Press.

Schwartz, Stephen P. 1977. *Naming, Necessity and Natural Kinds*. Ithaca: Cornell University Press.

Scruton, Roger. 1979. *The Aesthetics of Architecture*. Princeton: Princeton University Press.

Serlio, Sebastiano. [1545]. 1982. *The Five Books of Architecture*. New York: Dover.

Shannon, Claude E., and W. Weaver. 1949. *The Mathematical Theory of Communication*. Urbana: University of Illinois Press.

Sharpe, Ronald, B. S. Marksjö, and J. V. Thomson. 1987. "Special Issue on Expert Systems in Planning and Design." *Planning and Design* 14, no. 3:237–322.

Sheppard, Anne. 1987. *Aesthetics: An Introduction to the Philosophy of Art*. Oxford: Oxford University Press.

Shirari, S. N. 1981. "Representation of Three Dimensional Digital Images." *Computing Surveys* 13, no. 4:399–423.

Shubnikov, Aleksei V., and V. A. Koptsik. 1974. *Symmetry in Science and Art*. New York: Plenum.

Simon, Herbert A. 1967. "The Logic of Decision and Action." In *The Logic of Decision and Action*. Ed. N. Rescher. Pittsburgh: University of Pittsburgh Press.

Simon, Herbert A. 1972. "The Theory of Problem Solving." *Information Processing 71*. Amsterdam: North Holland.

Simon, Herbert A. 1973. "The Structure of Ill-Structured Problems." *Artificial Intelligence* 4:181–200.

Simon, Herbert A. 1975. "Style in Design." In *Spatial Synthesis in Computer Aided Building Design*. Ed. Charles M. Eastman. New York: John Wiley.

Simon, Herbert A. 1978. "On the Forms of Mental Representation." In *Perception and Cognition: Issues in the Foundations of Psychology*. Ed. C. W. Savage. Minnesota Studies in the Philosophy of Science, vol. IX. Minneapolis: University of Minnesota Press.

Simon, Herbert A. 1981. *The Sciences of the Artificial*. 2d ed. Cambridge, Mass.: MIT Press.

Simpson, George Gaylord. 1967. *The Meaning of Evolution*. Rev. ed. New Haven: Yale University Press.

Smoke, K. L. 1932. "An Objective Study of Concept Formation." *Psychological Monographs* 42, no. 191.

Smullyan, Raymond M. 1968. *First-Order Logic*. New York: Springer-Verlag.

Sorabji, Richard. 1964. "Function." *Philosophical Quarterly* 14, no. 57:289–302.

Sriram, D., and R. Adey (eds.). 1987. *Knowledge-Based Expert Systems in Engineering: Planning and Design*. Southampton, England: Computational Mechanics Publications.

Steadman, J. Philip. 1979. *The Evolution of Designs*. Cambridge: Cambridge University Press.

Stebbing, L. Susan. 1952. *A Modern Elementary Logic*. 5th ed. London: Methuen.

Stillings, Neil A., Mark M. Feinstein, Jay L. Garfield, Edwina L. Rissland, David A. Rosenbaum, Steven E. Weisler, and Lynne Baker-Ward. 1987. *Cognitive Science: An Introduction*. Cambridge, Mass.: MIT Press.

Stiny, George. 1977. "Ice-Ray: A Note on the Generation of Chinese Lattice Designs." *Environment and Planning B* 4:89–98.

Stiny, George. 1980a. "Introduction to Shape and Shape Grammars." *Environment and Planning B* 7:343–51.

Stiny, George. 1980b. "Kindergarten Grammars: Designing with Froebel's Building Gifts." *Environment and Planning B* 7, no. 4:409–62.

Stiny, George. 1981. "A Note on the Description of Designs." *Environment and Planning B* 8, no. 3:257–67.

Stiny, George. 1982. "Shapes are Individuals." *Environment and Planning B* 9:359–67.

Stiny, George. 1986. "A New Line on Drafting Systems." *Design Computing* 1:5–19.

Stiny, George. 1987. "Composition Counts: A + E = AE." *Planning and Design* 14, no. 2:167–82.

Stiny, George. 1989. "What Designers Do That Computers Should." In *Proceedings of the CAAD Futures 89 Conference*. (Pre-Publication Edition.) Ed. Malcolm McCullough, William J. Mitchell, and Patrick Purcell. Cambridge, Mass.: Harvard Graduate School of Design.

Stiny, George, and James Gips. 1972. "Shape Grammars and the Generative Specification of Painting and Sculpture." In *Information Processing 71*. Ed. C. V. Freiman. Amsterdam: North Holland, 1460–65.

Stiny, George, and James Gips. 1978. *Algorithmic Aesthetics*. Berkeley: University of California Press.

Stiny, George, and William J. Mitchell. 1978a. "The Palladian Grammar." *Environment and Planning B* 5, no. 1:5–18.

Stiny, George, and William J. Mitchell. 1978b. "Counting Palladian Plans." *Environment and Planning B* 5, no. 2:189–98.

Stiny, George, and William J. Mitchell. 1981. "The Grammar of Paradise." *Environment and Planning B* 7, no. 2:209–26.

Stravinsky, Igor. 1942. *Poetics of Music*. Cambridge, Mass.: Harvard University Press.

Sullivan, Louis. [1918]. 1947. *Kindergarten Chats*. Rev. ed. New York: Wittenborn Schultz.

Summers, David. 1981. *Michelangelo and the Language of Art*. Princeton: Princeton University Press.

Summerson, John. 1957. "The Case for a Theory of Modern Architecture." *Royal Institute of British Architects Journal* 64:307–10.

Summerson, John. 1963. *The Classical Language of Architecture*. Cambridge, Mass.: MIT Press.

Summerson, John. 1963. *Heavenly Mansions and Other Essays on Architecture*. New York: W. W. Norton.

Suppes, Patrick. 1957. *Introduction to Logic*. Princeton: Van Nostrand.

Sussman, Gerald Jay, and Guy Lewis Steele, Jr. 1980. "Constraints—A Language for Expressing Almost-Hierarchical Descriptions." *Artificial Intelligence* 14:1–39.

Swan, Abraham. [1758]. 1967. *The British Architect*. New York: Da Capo.

Szambien, Werner. 1984. *Jean-Nicolas-Louis Durand: de l'imitation à la norme*. Paris: Picard.

Tarski, Alfred. 1944. "The Semantic Conception of Truth." *Philosophy and Phenomenological Research* 4:341–75.

Tarski, Alfred. 1956. "The Concept of Truth in Formalized Languages." In *Logic, Semantics, Metamathematics*. London: Oxford University Press.

Tarski, Alfred. 1965. *Introduction to Logic and to the Methodology of Deductive Sciences*. Trans. Olaf Helmer. New York: Oxford University Press.

Tarski, Alfred. 1969. "Truth and Proof." *Scientific American* 194:63–77.

Taylor, Charles. 1964. *The Explanation of Behaviour*. London: Routledge and Kegan Paul.

Taylor, Charles. 1967. "Teleological Explanation—A Reply to Denis Noble." *Analysis* 27, no. 4:141–43.

Taylor, Richard. 1950a. "Comments on a Mechanistic Conception of Purposefulness." *Philosophy of Science* 17, no. 4:310–17.

Taylor, Richard. 1950b. "Purposeful and Non-Purposeful Behavior: A Rejoinder." *Philosophy of Science* 17, no. 4:327–32.

Thiis-Evensen, Thomas. 1988. *Archetypes in Architecture*. Oslo: Norwegian University Press.

Thompson, D'Arcy W. [1942]. 1961. *On Growth and Form*. Cambridge: Cambridge University Press.

Thompson, J. A., and Patrick Geddes. 1931. *Life: Outlines of General Biology*. London: Williams and Norgate.

Udupa, J. J. 1983. "Display of 3D Information in Discrete 3D Scenes Produced by Computerized Tomography." *Proceedings of the IEEE* 71, no. 3:420–33.

Veblen, Thorstein. [1899]. 1912. *The Theory of the Leisure Class*. London: Macmillan.

Vignola. [1562]. 1984. *Regola delli cinque ordini d'architettura*. Bolgna: Cooperativa libraria universitaria editrice Bologna.

Villari, Sergio. 1987. *J. N. L. Durand: arte e scienza dell'architettura*. Rome: Officinia.

Vitruvius, Pollio. 1960. *The Ten Books on Architecture*. Trans. Morris Hicky Morgan. New York: Dover.

Voelcker, H. B., and A. A. G. Requicha. 1977. "Geometric Modeling of Mechanical Parts and Processes." *Computer* 19:48–57.

von Wright, Georg Henrik. 1963. *The Varieties of Goodness*. New York: Humanities Press.

Warrington, E. K., and A. M. Taylor. 1973. "The Contribution of the Right Parietal Lobe to Object Recognition." *Cortex* 9:152–64.

Weiss, Paul A. (ed.). 1971. *Hierarchically Organized Systems in Theory and Practice*. New York: Hafner.

Wertheimer, Max. 1923. "Untersuchungen zur leher von der Gestalt." *Psychologische Forschung* 4:301–50. Translated in *Readings in Perception*. Eds. D. C. Beardslee and M. Wertheimer. Princeton: Van Nostrand.

Weyl, Hermann. 1952. *Symmetry*. Princeton: Princeton University Press.

Whyte, Lancelot Law, A. G. Wilson , and D. Wilson (eds.). 1969. *Hierarchical Structures*. New York: American Elsevier.

Wilenski, Reginald Howard. 1927. *The Modern Movement in Art*. London: Faber and Faber.

Wimsatt, William. 1972. "Different Senses of 'Function' and the Concept of Teleology." *Studies in History and Philosophy of Science* 3, no. 1:1–80.

Winograd, Terry. 1972. *Understanding Natural Language.* New York: Academic Press.

Winston, Patrick Henry. 1984. *Artificial Intelligence.* 2d ed. Reading, Mass.: Addison-Wesley.

Wittgenstein, Ludwig. 1953. *Philosophical Investigations.* Trans. G. E. M. Anscombe. New York: Macmillan.

Wittkower, Rudolf. 1962. *Architectural Principles in the Age of Humanism.* 2d ed. London: Tiranti.

Wittkower, Rudolf. 1978. "The Changing Concept of Proportion." In *Idea and Image: Studies in the Italian Renaissance.* London: Thames and Hudson.

Woodfield, A. 1976. *Teleology.* Cambridge: Cambridge University Press.

Woodger, Joseph H. 1945. "On Biological Transformations." In *Essays on Growth and Form Presented to D. Arcy Wentworth Thompson.* Eds. W. E. Le Gros Clark and P. B. Medawar. Oxford: Clarendon Press.

Woodwark, John. 1986. *Computing Shape.* London: Butterworth.

Wotton, Henry. [1624]. 1969. *The Elements of Architecture.* Farnborough: Gregg International.

Wren, Christopher. [1750]. 1965. *Parentalia.* Farnborough: Gregg International.

Wright, Larry. 1968. "The Case Against Teleological Reductionism." *British Journal for the Philosophy of Science* 19, no. 3:211–23.

Wright, Larry. 1972. "Explanation and Teleology." *Philosophy of Science* 37, no. 2:204–18.

Wright, Larry. 1973. "Functions." *Philosophical Review* 82, no. 2:139–68.

Wright, Larry. 1976. *Teleological Explanations.* Berkeley: University of California Press.

Xenophon. 1965. *Recollections of Socrates and Socrates' Defense Before the Jury.* Trans. Anna S. Benjamin. Indianapolis: Bobbs-Merrill.

Yessios, Chris I. 1987. "The Computability of Void Architectural Modeling." In *Computability of Design.* Ed. Yehuda E. Kalay. New York: John Wiley.

Zevi, Bruno. 1978. *The Modern Language of Architecture.* Seattle: University of Washington Press.

De Zurko, Edward Robert. 1957. *Origins of Functionalist Theory.* New York: Columbia University Press.

INDEX

Form-function relation, vii, 212, 214–15
  and architectural language, 217
  and composition problems, 228, 230–33
  and constraints, 218
  and definition or classification, 218–20
  and element design, 221–25
  and element selection, 220–21
  and form variables, 215–17
  and functional adequacy, 210, 212–13, 216–17
  and functional articulation, **226**, 226–28
  and functional equivalence, 210–11, **211**
  and functional interpretation, 209–10
  and meanings, 201–3
  and multifunctionality, 225–26
  and rules of usage, 234–37
Forward-chaining inference, 77
Fractals, 42, **42**
Frake, Charles O., 12
"Frame problem," 74
Freeman, Peter, 188
Freeman and Newell notation, 188, **189**, 190, **191**
Froebel blocks, 49, **50**
Fry, Roger, 36
Function (logical), 10, **10**, 11, 22
  action as, 183–84
  of shape, 52–53
"Function" (architectural), vii
Functional adequacy, 210
  conditions of, 212–13, 216–17
  and constraints, 218
  and definition or classification, 219, **219**
  and shape rule novelties, 236
  in top-down design, 232
Functional articulation, **226**, 226–28
Functional basis set, 22
Functional connections, 186–87, 187–88, **187–88**
Functional descriptions, 183
  actions in, 183–84
  and architectural programs, 196–200

  and connections, 186–87, 187–88, **187–88**
  and context, 184–85
  and goal-directedness, 185–86, 204
  meanings in, 200–3
  and physical systems, 187–**92**
  and social systems, 193–96
  typology from, 203–4
Functional equivalence, 210–11, **211**
Functional essences, 220, 224, 237–38
Functional expression, 218
Functional interpretation, 209–10
Functionalist criticism, 204–7
Functional typology, 203–4
Function-form relation. *See* Form-function relation
Function mapping, 16, **16**

Galen, 212–13
Galileo
  on bone proportion, 114, **115**
  on calculating beam strength, 71
Gaudi, Antonio, 121
Generate-and test process, 179, **180**, 181
Genesereth, Michael R., 23
Geometric symmetry, 30
Geometric transformations, 30, 121, **121**
Geometry, and line worlds, 42, 43, **43**
Gestalt laws, 4, 6, **6**
Gibbs, James, **93**, **134**, 135, **135**
Gips, James, 33
Goals, and functional descriptions, 185–86, 204. *See also* Ends of architecture; Value
Goethe, 90, **90**, 91
Good continuation, law of, 6, **6**
Goodman, Nelson, 8, 200, 201, 202
Gottschaldt, K., 102, **104**
Grammar(s), 138, **138**, 141, 237
  of classical column, 131–33, 232, 237

Urpflanze, **90**
Usage, rules of, 234–37

Valuation, rules of, 78–79
Value
  aesthetic, 31–33, 34–36, 204
  associational, 35
  formal, 31–33, **34**
  and social function, 194
Value (logical)
  of function, 10, **10**, 11, 13, 22
  of predicate, 9
  storage of, 13–14
  for variable, 12–13
Van Doesburg, Theo, **55**
Van Eesteren, Cornelis, **55**
Van Eyck, Aldo, **55**
Variables, 12–13
  form, 215–17
  and relationships, 20
Veblen, Thorstein, 225
Vertices, **45**, **47**
Vignola, **93**, **142**, **201**
Vila Angarano, 167, **172**
Villa Badoer, 167, **172**
Villa Emo, 167, **172**
Villa Hollywood, **179**
Villa Malcontenta, 153, **153**, 154,
  158, **160**, **166**, 167, **168**, **170**,
  172, 176
Villa plans, grammar for, 152–79
Villa Pisani, 167, **172**
Villa Poiana, 167, **172**
Villa Ragona, 167, **172**
Villa Sarraceno, **172**, 176
Villa Snellman, 4, **4**, 6
Villa Vine, **179**
Villa Zeno, 167, **172**
Viollet-le-Duc, Eugène-
  Emmanuel, 221

Visual field, 2, **2**, **3**
Vitruvius, Pollio, 27
  architectural program by,
    196–98
  functional classification by, 194
  and grammar of columns, 131
  and orders of classical
    architecture, 92, **93**
  and prescriptive rules, 134
  on symbolism, 200–2
Vocabularies, architectural, 98,
  99, 100, **101**, 179, 220–21
  and computer databases, 70
  of critical language, 83
  and design algebras, 128, 138
Voids, 49, **49**. *See also* Shape(s);
  Space
Volumetric worlds, 49–51
Voxels, 40, **40**, 41

Wallrath, Mechtild, 126
Warrington, E. K., 183
Weaver, W., 33
Werdersche Kirche, Berlin, 211,
  211
Wholes, and parts, 14–16
Wilenski, R. H., 25
Williston's law, **226**, 227
Windows, classical vocabulary of,
  99
Wire-frame modeling systems,
  43, **43**, **44**
  as ambiguous, 106, **107**
Wittkower, Rudolf, **128**, 131
Wotton, Sir Henry, 207
Wren, Sir Christopher, 34, 35,
  227, 236
Wright, Frank Lloyd, 49, **50**, 116,
  120, 122